Contents

Abbreviations used in this book

BB	Blackboard
CA	Contrastive Analysis
CILT	Centre for Information on Language Teaching
Dip TEO	Diploma in the Teaching of English Overseas
EA	Error Analysis
EAP	English for Academic Purposes
EFL	English as a Foreign Language
ELT	English Language Teaching
ELTJ	English Language Teaching Journal
ESL	English as a Second Language
ESP	English for Specific Purposes
FL	Foreign Language
IRAL	International Review of Applied Linguistics
L	Listening
LTM	Long-Term Memory
MT	Mother Tongue
P	Pupil
PP	Pupils
R	Reading
RP	Received Pronunciation
S	Speaking
STM	Short-Term Memory
T	Teacher
TB	Text-Book
TENOR	Teaching English for No Obvious Reason
TESOL	Teaching English to Speakers of Other Languages
TG	Transformational-Generative
W	Writing
*	Erroneous form follows

Pronunciation symbols used in this book

The symbols used are those of GIMSON, A. *An introduction to the pronunciation of English.* Arnold, third edition, 1980, with two exceptions:

(i) We have omitted the length mark (:) which can occur after the vowels /ɑ,i,ɔ,u,ɜ/.

(ii) The symbol = is used in this book to mark an unaspirated consonant, as in /p=/.

Where an English key-word is given, the symbol represents the sound usually or always occurring in the RP pronunciation of the word.

a	vowel in French *patte*	m	consonant in *me*
aɪ	diphthong in *fine*	n	consonant in *no*
ɑ	vowel in *car*	ŋ	final consonant in *sing*
aʊ	diphthong in *cow*	o	vowel in French *eau*
æ	vowel in *cat*	ɔ	vowel in *saw*
b	consonant in *bee*	ɔɪ	diphthong in *boy*
β	2nd consonant in Spanish *cabeza* (voiced bilabial fricative)	ɒ	vowel in *dog*
		pʰ	consonant in *pea* (aspirated)
ç	consonant in German *ich* (voiceless palatal fricative)	p	consonants in *pip* (used for the English phoneme which includes both aspirated and unaspirated p)
d	consonant in *die*		
dʒ	consonants in *judge*		
ð	consonant in *other*	p=	consonant in *up* (unaspirated)
θ	consonant in *oath*	r	consonant in *ray*
e	vowel in *bed*	ʁ	consonant in French *heure* (voiced uvular fricative or frictionless continuant)
eɪ	diphthong in *say*		
ɛə	diphthong in *there*		
ə	vowel in *the*	s	consonant in *see*
əʊ	diphthong in *so*	ʃ	consonant in *she*
ɜ	vowel in *bird*	t	consonant in *tea*
f	consonant in *four*	tʃ	consonant in *chair*
g	consonant in *eager*	u	vowel in *do*
h	consonant in *how*	ʊ	vowel in *put*
i	vowel in *see*	ʊə	diphthong in *poor*
ɪ	vowel in *sit*	ʌ	vowel in *cup*
ɪə	diphthong in *ear*	v	consonant in *ever*
j	semi-vowel in *you*	w	semi-vowel in *we*
k	consonant in *car*	x	final consonant in Scottish *loch*
l	consonant in *lay* ('clear l') (also used for the English phoneme which includes both 'clear l' and 'dark l')	z	consonant in *ease*
		ʒ	medial consonant in *measure*
		ʔ	consonant which may occur before *out* in *go out* (glottal stop – used by many RP speakers as a syllable boundary marker when the initial sound of the next syllable is a vowel)
ɫ	consonant in *ill* ('dark l')		
l̩	final consonant in *table* ('syllabic l')		

Introduction: Who knows best?

by Gerry Abbott and Peter Wingard

This is a book for teachers and student teachers, both those who are native speakers of English and those who are not. It was planned and written by a group of colleagues at Manchester University, who co-operated in deciding what the book would deal with and what the main content of each chapter would be. Each chapter is the responsibility of its own author, however. We may not agree in every detail, but we think we have a broad approach in common. We have tried to produce a book which, while not neglecting theory, has a strong practical bias. As far as space has allowed, we have tried to include applications of all ideas discussed. Nearly every chapter begins with two practical illustrations, which we call 'Examples'.

Our title refers to 'English as an international language'. We intend this term to cover both English as a foreign language (EFL) and English as a second language (ESL). EFL and ESL are 'blanket' terms, each covering part of a very wide spectrum. In an extreme EFL situation, English may be so foreign to the learners that it is merely a subject on the school timetable which they study for three or four lessons a week, never using it otherwise. In an extreme ESL situation, on the other hand, English may play a large part in the daily life of the learners, in that all or most of their teachers use English for teaching, whatever the subject, and they may often hear, speak, read or write English outside school hours. When they leave school they may often use English in communication with people of their own country whose mother tongue (MT) is different from their own. The expression 'English as an international language' should remind us that we are not just concerned with communication between native speakers and non-native speakers, but even more with communication among non-native speakers all over the world, both as individuals and as members of multi-national bodies.

No single method could encompass the extreme EFL and the extreme ESL position. So much must depend on the country, the level, the age-group, the working conditions, the student, the teacher. But we believe there is a basis of principle which does apply to the whole range of situations. Chapter 1 of this book attempts to outline such a basis.

After this partly theoretical beginning, we deal with topics which seem to us to be of practical interest to all EFL and ESL teachers, whatever their situation. In Chapters 2 to 6 we get down to the classroom practising of listening, speaking, reading and writing. We then deal, in Chapters 7 to 9, with other practical matters facing every teacher: how to assess students' work, how to judge the significance of errors and how to plan remedial work. In Chapters 10 and 11 we come to more general topics: the planning of lessons and the management of classes. Finally Chapter 12 tries to put things into perspective.

While this book was being prepared, our attention was drawn to an article in the *London Times* (9 June 1980) about some research done by Dr Scott Armstrong of the University of Pennsylvania. Dr Armstrong measured the readability of journals in his field (Management) and found that the higher the prestige of a journal, the more difficult it was to read. Was this simply because less readable journals dealt with more difficult ideas? No. Dr Armstrong took passages from some of the journals and rewrote them in simpler English, making sure in each case that the simpler version had essentially the same meaning as the original one. Here is an example:

Original	Simpler version
This paper concludes that to increase the probability of keeping a customer in queue the server should attempt to influence the customer's initial subjective estimate of the mean service time to give him the impression that it is small.	You are more likely to ensure that a customer waits in a queue if you can get the person to think that he will not have long to wait.

Using sometimes the original and sometimes the simpler version, Dr Armstrong then asked his Faculty colleagues to judge the quality of the research that was being reported. For each passage, the rating given to the original version was higher!

Perhaps people (including us teachers) do not trust simple language. Perhaps we think, 'If I find it easy to understand, it can't be very important.' Nevertheless, we have decided to take a risk in this book, and have made an effort to express ourselves as straightforwardly as the subject permits.

There is another assumption often made in the educational world which seems curious to us – that the more removed from the schoolroom you are, the more right you have to tell the schoolteachers what to do. Over the past quarter of a century, psychologists, linguists, psycholinguists, sociolinguists and applied linguists have all pressed their views upon language teachers. Indeed, EFL and ESL teachers may be forgiven for believing that it is their duty to take notice of what is said by anyone who professes to know anything about teaching – except another teacher! Someone at some stage even coined the term 'classroom teacher', presumably in order to distinguish the real thing from such pseudo-teachers. Even teacher-trainers such as ourselves may – as this book shows – be guilty of thinking that we know best. In our own case, we can only plead that we have taught English in schools in various parts of the world; that we see a lot of school-teaching going on all the time; and that we still do a little teaching as well as training others to do so.

The pressure exerted by the pseudo-teachers would not be a serious matter if the conscientious teacher were in the habit of rejecting out of hand any piece of advice that flew in the face of common sense. Unfortunately, however, such is the love-hate relationship between teacher and pseudo-teacher that, although the teacher may scorn the ivory-tower academic, he somehow feels bound to take note of the advice offered. He has been brain-washed into the assumption that academics *must* know more about the business than mere teachers. Many teachers consequently get guilt complexes and even speak disparagingly of their own teaching methods. It used to be 'Well, I'm afraid I translate some of the difficult words'; nowadays it is 'Well, I still teach structurally, I'm afraid'.

Why should a teacher apologise to a pseudo-teacher?

In this spirit, the authors of this book look with a certain suspicion on the novelties of fashion, and have a high regard for what actually seems to work in a specific situation with specific objectives. To quote Henry Sweet (1845–1912), the original of Professor Higgins in Bernard Shaw's 'Pygmalion':

> 'Nothing will ever make the learning of languages easy. Until everyone recognises that there is no royal road to languages, the public will continue to run after one new method after another, only to return disappointed to the old routine.'

What works well in one situation, or for one teacher, may not work well for another. The many sample exercises in this book are not necessarily meant to be used as they stand, or as exact models, but rather as ideas to be adapted by you for your own classes. If any of the techniques we suggest strikes you as worth trying, give it a fair trial. If you find that it does not work as well as some other technique, by all means drop it. But try to analyse what makes your technique preferable to ours. By so doing you may continue to grow in your thinking and practice, rather than just 'return disappointed to the old routine'.

We hope this book will be useful on pre-service and in-service training courses, and that individual teachers will turn to it for stimulus when faced with a specific problem. It is a book to have at hand rather than just a book to read and put away.

Finally, we would be happy to hear from you. If you want to

comment, complain, suggest changes, or challenge something we say, please write to

Gerry Abbott and Peter Wingard
Department of Education
University of Manchester
Manchester M13 9PL
England

We value your response, and will do our best to reply to any letters received.

Chapter 1: Approaches to English teaching

by Gerry Abbott

EXAMPLE 1

> A dozen young men and women in their late teens and twenties are sitting at desks placed in a semicircle. We can see (and hear by their accents) that they come from various countries. . . . Miss Taylor – her students call her Liz – is explaining something. . . . Now they are listening to a cassette recording and writing on their handouts. . . . The class ends. The students put on their warm coats and, chatting to each other in English, go out into the High Street. Above the door it says 'Oxbridge School of English'.

EXAMPLE 2

> The room is full of cheerful young boys, row upon row, sitting four to a bench. There are a dozen benches, all bolted to the floor. These 11-year olds are listening respectfully to their teacher, whom we cannot understand because he is explaining something in their mother tongue. One or two children per bench have a grubby textbook, and they all have a grubby exercise-book. . . . The class ends. The boys stand up while the teacher leaves, then rush shouting out of the stuffy room into a hot, sandy compound. In all the noise, not a word of English is heard.

Part 1: The setting

Education is an abstract noun, but it takes place in concrete circumstances. In that part of education which takes place in the classroom, these circumstances impose certain restrictions on what can usefully be done just as surely as, in my second example above, the bolts prevent any rearrangement of the benches. The examples do not typify the teaching of English as a foreign or second language, but simply show two rather contrasting sets of circumstances. Let us therefore look at half a dozen factors which, in any EFL teaching situation, will play a large part in determining what does and does not happen in the classroom. You will see that each factor is labelled in crude 'A versus B' terms although all sorts of 'in-between' cases are possible; and that under each heading I attempt not to be exhaustive but simply to illustrate.

11

A   Class: children or adults?

Adults learning EFL anywhere are usually doing so because they need to or want to; as in my first example above, they may even be paying substantial fees and may consequently be prepared to demand what they want. They are usually very well-motivated, and as their teacher you would seldom need to use your authority.

However, the majority of the world's learners of EFL are school children who are not well-motivated at all. If you were to ask one of these young learners why he was studying English, he would probably say: 'I don't know'. A slightly older one might say: 'Because it's compulsory'. And an older one still: 'Because we have to pass in English in order to get our secondary school leaving certificate'. This is the sort of situation for which I created the label TENOR: the Teaching of English for No Obvious Reason – that is, for no reason obvious to the learner. Unmotivated children may (deliberately or unwittingly) make your job difficult, and you will have to build motivation into your lessons and observe at least some of the rules of class management. (See Chapter 11.)

B   Class: large or small?

'Large' and 'small' are relative terms, of course, and I leave you to decide what they mean to you. In a class of (say) 50, everyone can read simultaneously; everyone can write simultaneously; and everyone can listen to the teacher simultaneously. But they cannot all speak to the teacher simultaneously unless they have all been carefully trained to utter the same sentence in chorus. In this case there is the double disadvantage of the combined noise, which (i) masks the speech of any one student and (ii) can disturb one's colleagues in neighbouring rooms. On the other hand, you cannot give individual practice to all 50: each would receive less than one minute of your attention even if you did this for the whole of a 50-minute lesson.

This sort of problem either does not arise or is far less serious when small classes are taught.

C   Class: monolingual or multilingual?

If a class has a language in common, its members will understand, and perhaps even demand, translations and mother-tongue (MT) explanations. They will tend to revert to using MT in oral practice when you are not within earshot, especially if they are not highly motivated. Furthermore, they will probably be subject to 'Abbott's Paradox', which states that the more you try to motivate them by giving them stimulating oral tasks, the more eager they will be to communicate and therefore to use the natural vehicle of communication, their MT.

The techniques of translating and giving MT explanations are not normally practicable in multilingual classes, of course, though they are feasible in bilingual education. One advantage of the multilingual class is that its members do attempt to communicate in English. One disadvantage, however, is that the 'Paradox' still operates, in that the students tend to lapse into a kind of 'pidgin'. They may for example have been practising *When does the London train/bus leave?* but, when excited, lapse into **Bus of London – when leave?* (An asterisk (*) is placed before any form that is erroneous.)

D   Teacher: local or expatriate?

As we have seen, translations and MT explanations may be demanded by a monolingual class. Local teachers can, if they choose, supply these. Many expatriate teachers on the other hand have to demonstrate meanings by means of pictures or gestures, or give explanations in simple English that the learner can understand, because they cannot speak the students' MT. This can be a time-consuming business.

Again many local teachers are unsure about their own command of English and may therefore avoid certain activities, whereas the native speaker of English has no such doubts.

E   School: well-equipped or poorly-equipped?

Most learners expect to have their own textbook and exercise book. Most teachers expect to have a blackboard and a supply of chalk. To expect more than this is still, in many parts of the world, unrealistic. The teacher who has access to a duplicator or an overhead projector is, in global perspective, lucky indeed, and is free to supplement the textbook with visual aids, alternative passages and exercises and so on. The rest have to base almost all their work on the textbook.

F   School: in Britain or in home country?

(For 'Britain' read 'any English-speaking territory'.) Students in Britain, e.g. in language schools, are in a position to hear and use English from morning till night. They therefore have strong practical reasons for learning English and their exposure to English can be as high as they wish; indeed, they would not be in Britain in the first place if they did not have a good reason. On the other hand, the student in his home country may have no reason to learn English; but even if he has, he may be unable to hear or use it at all outside his English lessons at school.

These are some of the more important variables in EFL teaching-situations. Before continuing, you might glance back at the two examples at the beginning of this chapter to see how many of them are illustrated.

I have dwelt on these variable circumstances for two reasons:
(i) because people who recommend certain teaching methods often fail

to take such factors sufficiently into account; and
(ii) because such variety suggests very strongly that no single 'method' could possibly be equally suitable in all settings.

It would be foolish unthinkingly to transfer to another setting any method that has been found suitable in one's own; what works in the Oxbridge School of English may fail miserably in, say, an Asian lower secondary school.

Our teaching, then, is partly shaped by such environmental circumstances. But only partly, for there is a much more powerful influence at work; everything we do when we are teaching is coloured by our own (often unconscious) assumptions about how our students learn. We must therefore turn to the heart of the matter: the nature of the language learning process. We now step from the known into the unknown.

Part 2: The learner

Learning is something that people normally do all through their lives – there does not have to be a teacher. But no-one has ever seen it happening; as an activity it is invisible. Teaching, on the other hand, is an observable activity. Perhaps that is why we teachers are usually much more happy to talk about teaching-techniques than about learning-processes. We recognise that a good teaching-technique is one that 'works'; but we tend to forget that, if it does work, it must be because in some way it harmonises with the students' learning-techniques. But what are these learning-techniques? How do people learn?

We cannot insult the human race by assuming the mind is like a pot or a sheet of blotting paper, a mere receptacle. We may think that it can receive information as a pot receives water, or record images as blotting-paper does; we talk about information going 'in one ear and out of the other', viewing the mind as a pot that may leak while being filled; and we speak of memories that 'fade', just as ink-marks do. But these metaphors are misleading: if the mind merely stored information, no-one would ever think anything new. Nor can we simply liken humans to parrots or mynah-birds; although these have the ability to imitate sentences that they repeatedly hear, they have never said anything new – that is, they cannot produce sentences which they have not heard before. Such creative acts can be achieved reliably only by the use of rules for the formation of sentences; and an ability to form and apply rules consistently implies thinking. Receiving and storing information; imitation and repetition; thinking and creation; it is agreed that all these play a part in the learning of a language, although the process is by no means fully understood.

If we do not know how this invisible process works, we can at least express our guesses. One way of doing this is to devise a 'model'. This sort of model is not a small-scale reproduction of something – like a model aeroplane, for instance. Far from it. Rather, it is a convenient visual way of responding to the question 'How does it work?' when we know in advance that our knowledge of the subject is deficient. For example, if I asked you 'How do people learn?' you might say, 'I don't know. But I'm sure that successful learning involves at least three things: being able to understand something, being able to remember it and being able to make use of it. But of course, we are not always successful at all three'. Using that reply as a basis, let us build up our own model of foreign language learning.

We will call the 'something' that is to be learned INPUT (see Fig. 1): the right-hand box represents the learner and the left-hand box his environment.

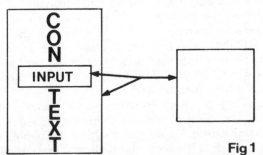

Fig 1

The input is a verbal experience, visual or auditory, which may consist of language in use, as when listening to someone during a conversation; or of deliberately selected usage, as when reading the examples preceding an exercise; or of metalanguage – that is, remarks *about* some aspect of the foreign language. Whatever it is, it has first to be noticed and given some attention if it is going to be understood at all. The amount of attention given will depend largely on the learner's MOTIV-ATION. (The arrows are intended to show that the learner is paying attention to the input and that features of the non-linguistic CON-TEXT, or 'situation', must also be attended to.) Before adding to our model then, we must consider motivation.

A secondary school boy in the Wadi Hadhramaut (P.D.R. Yemen) once told me through an interpreter that he did not want to learn English because it was 'the language of Jews and imperialists'. This victim of inaccurate propaganda did not want to understand English and so he had learned none, although it was a compulsory subject. Such anti-motivation may not be common, but lack of motivation certainly is. People's attitudes to learning a foreign language can very roughly be divided into the 'instrumental' and the 'sentimental' (or 'integrative'). If a man studies English because it is vital for his job, he is definitely *instrumentally* motivated; if on the other hand he studies it because the English-speaking cultures seem in some way admirable to him, then he is definitely *sentimentally* (or integratively) motivated; of course, he may

15

be positively motivated, or neutral or negatively motivated in both ways:

Motivation	Neg	Neut	Pos
Instrumental	−1	0	+1
Sentimental	−1	0	+1

If your learners score less than + 1 by this rough-and-ready measurement you will have to create motivation by providing interest, fun and a sense of achievement. But even among the highly motivated, a little fun is invaluable for counteracting fatigue, and all learners need to have their attention focused on the task in hand to have an appropriate mental 'set' before the task is begun. The class with a good 'set' for a listening or reading exercise is alert, quiet and on the look-out for something; the ideal 'set' for conversation work is the feeling of confidence that comes from thorough practice and the knowledge that any mistakes will be received with good humour. Without attention, understanding will not be achieved.

In answer to my question 'How do people learn?', the ability to understand and the ability to remember were mentioned as if they were acquired in that sequence. But no-one would be able to hold any input in his head long enough to begin the comprehension process if it were not for his memory. Very little is known for certain about the operation of memory in language-learning. It is obvious that remembering is necessary if we are to learn, but not so obvious that forgetting is also necessary: just imagine what might happen to our minds if we remembered every detail of all our unhappy and painful experiences, or what the learner's English would be like if he remembered all his mistakes! The problem, of course, is how to get the learner to remember all the right things. In considering this problem, we will have to distinguish between two operations which are called the short-term memory (STM) and the long-term memory (LTM).

Imagine a friend talking to you in your own language. The stream of speech going into your ear enters a system (the STM) designed to turn these external sound-waves into internal meanings. In order to do this, your STM continuously 'holds' (or 'freezes') stretches of speech while it operates on them – possibly decoding stretches of sound into sound units, recognising and using intonations as boundaries, and so on. Probably the amount of attention devoted to these stretches varies from very high to very low, since the occurrence of certain features in one stretch increases the likelihood of certain other features occurring in a following stretch. You are therefore able to make predictions about what you are going to hear, often with a high degree of accuracy. (This will be taken up in Chapter 3.) Whatever the exact operation, STRATEGIES FOR UNDERSTANDING in your STM (see Fig. 2) turn stretches of speech into meaningful phrases which can in turn be passed on for storage in the LTM, where they are given an appropriate place in an existing network of meaning. Meanings are stored in such a way that although you may forget exactly how your friend expressed himself, you will nevertheless remember his message – for a short time, at least.

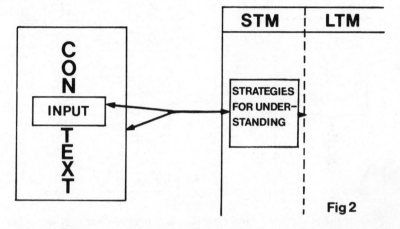

Fig 2

But what if the hearer is one of your students and the message is coded in EFL? At least two difficulties may arise. Firstly, the STM may simply find the rate of input too fast, so that it has insufficient time to process the incoming signals; and secondly, even if the speed of the signals is not too fast, parts of the code may be unknown. When the signals are visual (i.e. when we are reading), we have plenty of time to re-scan a message and to reflect upon it. When we are listening, time is an enemy: the STM (as its name tells us) has a very limited capacity, and a too-rapid stream of sound may therefore not be fully decoded, let alone fully understood. Incoming signals will either push out any earlier ones that have not been sufficiently processed, or will themselves drop out while the STM is still struggling to deal with the earlier input. Any input lost in any way at this stage disappears, becoming DROPOUT. (See Fig. 3.)

Learners who will soon need to deal with English spoken at normal speeds (e.g. in the lecture-room or in social interaction) therefore need to be carefully trained to increase their listening speed, thus reducing 'dropout'; the less practice they have had, the more pressed for time they will be. Speakers will seem to be talking too fast, so the listeners will probably resort to one or both of the following strategies (and perhaps others).

(i) They may turn for help to the non-linguistic context. Trying to look intelligent and attentive, they will note the speaker's facial expressions, gestures, places pointed to and so on, while the linguistic message races past like a non-stop train.

(ii) They may simply scan the other person's speech in order to be able to pick out a known word or two here and there and hope that they will get the right message.

The next two chapters of this book will develop these aspects of listening.

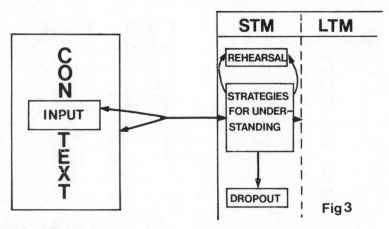

Fig 3

Even if the STM holds and decodes the input perfectly, some of the input will 'drop out' rapidly if there is no opportunity for RE-HEARSAL. Rehearsal is simply a rapid, private repetition of new information, whether overtly ('out loud') or covertly ('to oneself'), as attempts are made to understand it. In language-learning it is the form of a message that is rehearsed, while its meaning is being extracted. Rehearsal appears to be acoustic in nature: that is, even visual linguistic input is transformed into 'internal sound', if not actually muttered to oneself. No matter how well your students perceive and understand a new item that you have presented, they will not be ready to use it until they have had a few seconds to rehearse – an appropriate term in language-learning, since it suggests preparation for a performance. We are sometimes, I think, in too much of a hurry to get a performance out of a student – for example, an oral imitation of a presented sentence.

But when the learner is rehearsing, what strategies for understanding does he employ? I assume that the experience of meeting a new item of language is dealt with in ways very similar to those that we employ for all new experiences. The young child who has learnt what a dog looks like will, on seeing a horse for the first time, tend to associate this new phenomenon with the familiar one. It is almost as if the child's policy in coping with the new experience is to ask, 'What do I know already that is like this . . . Not-human, four-legged living-thing . . .?' The strategies employed seem to be:

(i) to refer to previous experiences;

(ii) to find among them an experience similar to the new one; and

(iii) to associate the two similar experiences.

The similarities (not-human, four-legged, etc.) often cause the horse and the dog to be understood as members of the same group, labelled 'goggy' (doggie) by many small British children.

It seems to me that in learning a new item of a foreign language we do much the same. The main difference is that we have experiences of two kinds to refer back to:

(i) all our previous experience involving use of the mother tongue (MT EXPERIENCE); and

(ii) any previous experience involving use of the foreign language (FL EXPERIENCE).

Calling the new item of language NEW FL EXPERIENCE 'X', let us see how the STRATEGIES FOR UNDERSTANDING box might be elaborated:

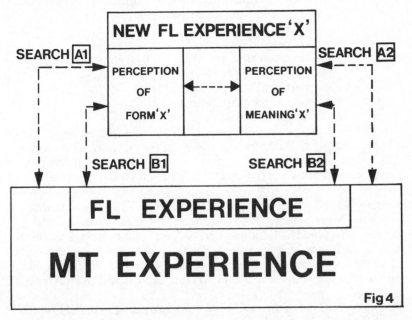

Fig 4

According to this model, a learner may undertake any or all of four 'searches' into his experience (I have used the word 'experience' in order to suggest that the learner scans his memory not only for linguistic but also for associated non-linguistic information) whenever he is attempting to cope with a new foreign language experience. Let me illustrate by telling you about something I can remember when I was a beginner studying Spanish. (When you make a fool of yourself, you do not forget the matter very easily!) My worksheet contained the new word *caramelos*. As far as I could explain my 'strategies' afterwards, this is what happened – all within a matter of seconds, of course:

19

Searches	What I found	My conclusions
A 1	A similar form in English: the noun *caramels* – a sort of toffee.	Perhaps *caramelos* means '*toffees*', '*sweets*'.
B 1	Some grammatical structures that I had recently been practising, e.g. dámelos – (give-me-them) enséñamelos – (show-me-them)	Perhaps *caramelos* is *three* words, meaning ' ? – *me – them*'
B 2	The context of the word was simply: – Qué quería, señorita? (What would you like Miss?) – Caramelos, por favor.	The context does not help me much, but . . .
A 2	. . . a customer is not likely just to refer to 'THEM' . . but perhaps this customer is *pointing* at what she wants (my experience told me).	I give up. I'll ask the teacher.

The teacher said, 'But there's no accent on the first part of the word – didn't you notice?' I had not noticed. And I had been right first time: *caramelos* meant *sweets*. (Sometimes you can be too cautious!)

These 'searches' can be regarded as STM activities that attempt to satisfy the desire to understand. Beginners will always turn immediately to their MT (Search A1 and/or A2) for forms and meanings similar to those in their new FL experiences; after all, they have as yet little or no FL experience to turn to. But even when they have progressed quite a long way, there is still a tendency to compare FL and MT forms and meanings.

Sometimes this can prove to be helpful, providing FACILITATION as in the case of *caramelos→caramels*. But as we all know, it is often unhelpful, and causes EXTERNAL INTERFERENCE. To the English child learning French, *Il a assisté à la conférence* (He was present at the lecture) might be understood as *He helped at the conference*; and beginners reading the German sentence *Sie bekam einen Hund* (She got a dog) are likely to think it means *She became a dog*.

Although, like the child meeting the horse, we fasten on to similarities where we find them, we do not really expect a word in a FL to be like its equivalent in our MT. Nevertheless, we do expect the two words to have similar ranges of meaning. Where these ranges are not co-extensive, interference can be very strong, and learning can be correspondingly difficult. Consider, for example, the English child's difficulties in learning to express in Spanish the meanings illustrated on the left:

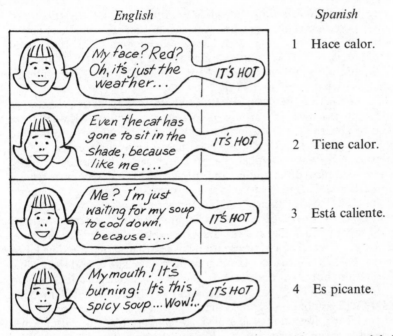

English		*Spanish*
	1	Hace calor.
	2	Tiene calor.
	3	Está caliente.
	4	Es picante.

Before we go any further, perhaps we should add to our model the LTM, which until how has only been mentioned. Or rather, it has been

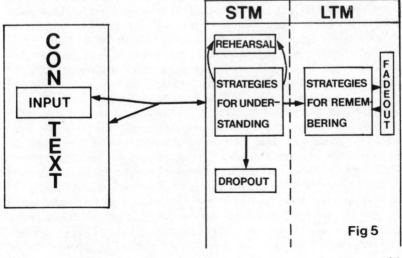

Fig 5

21

taken for granted. I have said, for example, that the learner refers to his previous experiences: where else would these be represented than in his long-term memory store? The STM must, in other words, have access to the LTM.

The broken line dividing the two is an admission that it is difficult to know where one begins and the other ends. Indeed, some authorities doubt whether the memory really has two such components. It may well be that it is the STM that operates the STRATEGIES FOR RE-MEMBERING, and that the LTM is simply a store of remembered items. But what is 'remembering'?

The distinction between RECOGNITION and RECALL is as important in language learning as in other human activities. If I am asked to give the name of one particular former student of mine who played the guitar, I may not be able to; that is, I may not recall it. But if I am asked 'Do you remember Steve?' I may say, 'Of course, he's that student who played the guitar'. In other words, I may recognise what I cannot recall. (This is as true of one's performance in foreign languages as in one's MT performance, and is an important factor, for example, in handling texts for receptive work; Chapter 4 takes this point further.) On the other hand, I may answer 'Steve? . . . No. Who's he?' In this case, the powers of recall and of recognition have both deserted me. The LTM can be thought of as containing both recognisable and recallable information; but if left undisturbed, the recognisable has a tendency to slip into FADEOUT and join the ranks of the forgotten. I imagine FADEOUT as containing both the forgotten (i.e. the unrecognisable) and the nearly-forgotten (the almost unrecognisable), the latter being retrievable through prompting – hence the two-way arrow – and the former being irretrievable.

Just as rehearsal is a means of holding input in the STM, so one of the purposes of PRACTICE is to ensure that information is retained in the LTM. This will help us to 'know what to say'. But knowing what to say in a foreign language is one thing; being able to say it fluently and accurately is another. In language-learning, practice is also a matter of training in the sensorimotor skills, e.g. the ability to hear accurately, the ability to imitate a sound accurately, and the ability to write neatly and with sufficient speed. Whereas a comprehension difficulty may be overcome in a flash of insight, a pronunciation difficulty may be overcome only by means of practice. Efficient recognition of new sounds requires ear-training, and efficient production necessitates pronunci- ation practice – the often frustrating task of changing one's oral habits. Reading and writing may demand drastic changes of visual and manual skills: it is extremely difficult for an Arab or Iranian student of English to reverse his literacy skills and achieve a reasonable reading speed and a reasonable fluency in his handwriting, for example. Even where the writing system of the learner's MT is similar to that of English, spelling and reading difficulties slow down the student's productive and receptive performance considerably. Practice is the only way of overcoming such difficulties.

Every normal person has sufficient cognitive ('thinking') and sensori-motor ability to learn a FL; but simple observation of language-learners shows that there are INDIVIDUAL DIFFERENCES. Some have 'a good ear' and are good mimics, some are not. Some are happy to rely upon the evidence of their ears, while some demand written confirmation. Some are good at (and therefore enjoy) creating rules by induction, while others prefer to be given a rule or an explanation. The best policy, surely, is to make everyone listen intently; to require everyone to attempt an oral imitation; to give everyone written confirmation as soon as possible; to ask everyone to try to find rules, but to provide them in the event of failure or if this will save wasting a lot of time; and to ensure that, whatever else is done, most of the students' time is spent practising and using the language appropriately.

When storing information in the LTM, it is much better for the learner to store RULES than to remember all the examples he has practised, both because rules take up less storage space and because rules can be applied to new experiences. Just as most children will mentally translate new words whether you want them to or not, so most learners look for rules whether you are in the habit of providing them or not. The question is whether learners should discover rules for themselves, as we all do in our MT, or whether you should provide them. Learners are far more likely, I think, to remember something that they have contributed to by making an effort than something that they are simply told; I therefore favour inductive learning.

For example, assuming that you do not know it already, find out by induction from these examples the unusual but simple rule for using *try and*. I am sure you will never forget it. *Try and* means the same as *try to*, but . . .

	. . . Whereas you can say this, . . .	. . . you cannot say this.
1	Try and do your homework, please.	*I am trying and doing it, but I'm not succeeding.
2	Does she ever try and do her homework?	*Well, she tries and does it, but she doesn't always succeed.
3	Is he going to try and do it?	*He's already tried and done it, but he hasn't succeeded.
4	Didn't you even try and do it?	*Well, I tried and did it, but I didn't succeed.

23

Of course, if no-one in a class can identify a rule inductively, there is no harm in your providing one. Rather this, than leave a learner attempting to memorise material in which he sees no rule at all. (The word 'rule', by the way, is ambiguous. In terms of language, a rule is a regularity; in terms of language-learning, 'knowing a rule' means being able to conform to a regularity; and in terms of language-description 'knowing a rule' means being able to state a regularity. There is no harm in being able to express a rule; but this in itself will not lead to the ability to conform to the rule when *using* the language.)

One aspect of the search for similarities (described earlier in this section) is the search for regularities – or rules. Very often, the learner's perception of regularities is successful and provides FACILITATION: that is, it leads to success in dealing with further input. But not always. Just as Searches A1 and A2 scan the MT and may either be helpful or give rise to EXTERNAL INTERFERENCE, so Searches B1 and B2 scan what is already known of – and about – the FL, and may either help or give rise to INTERNAL INTERFERENCE. They may, for example, lead to successful or unsuccessful ANALOGISING. Given a set of items in which we observe a regular feature, we expect the regularity to continue in further items that we consider to be members of a similar set. This seems to be a more deliberate 'strategy' than those that I have illustrated so far, being an often conscious thinking process well-known among teachers as a cause of indignant 'Why . . .?' questions when good analogising does not produce a correct form.

A few examples will suffice:

As A is to B is to C, . . .   so . . .   D is to E is to F.

1	A	Has he got many friends?	D	Has he got much money?
	B	He hasn't got many friends.	E	He hasn't got much money.
	C	He has got many friends.	*F	He has got much money.

2	A	It was sand.	D	It was a shock.
	B	It was a bit of sand.	E	It was a bit of a shock.
	C	It was a lot of sand.	*F	It was a lot of a shock.

3	A	All of the students left.	D	All the students left.
	B	Some of the students left.	*E	Some the students left.
	C	None of the students left.	*F	None the students left.

It is likely that expectations of FL regularity are influenced by MT regularities. For example, supposing that in his MT the words for *all, each* and *every* occur in the same grammatical patterns, a learner may expect the English words to behave in the same way, e.g.:

The students all received a gift The students each received a gift *The students every received a gift	All of them received a gift Each of them received a gift *Every of them received a gift

A somewhat different consequence of internal interference may occur when the STM attempts to retrieve information from the LTM, where experiences classed as 'similar' are presumably stored in close proximity – on the same shelf, as it were. We know from everyday experience that it is the very things we perceive as similar that we most frequently confuse. In British schools, for example, children often learn about stalagmites and stalactites in the same Geography lesson. The spellings and pronunciations of the two are alike and their meanings are similar, since the two phenomena differ only in direction of growth. The close association of the two leads to confusion. Many British children (and adults!) cannot remember which is which, and *stalagtite* is a common mis-spelling.

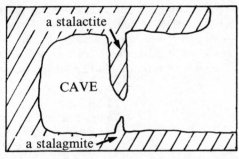

This aspect of internal interference is CROSS-ASSOCIATION. Two units of language that are sufficiently similar in form to invite comparison will be compared, especially if they are encountered in quick succession. If the two also have an element of *meaning* in common, the units will remain closely associated in the memory. When an attempt is made to recall one of them, either
(i) the wrong one is selected, e.g. *stalagmite* (for *stalactite*) or
(ii) elements of both are selected, e.g. *stalagtite* (for either of the two).
Cross-association operates at all levels of language from phonological to syntactic. One grammatical example in my recent mail was *With regards to your wife, . . .* The correspondent did not intend to send best wishes; he should have written one of two expressions, but produced a compound form of 1 and 2:

25

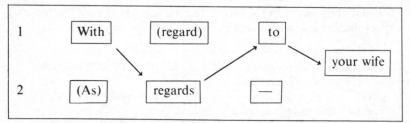

Cross-association, then, involves the transfer of some element of form and/or meaning from one member of a pair to the other, when the two members are considered to be similar. Stalactites and stalagmites may be considered similar in that they both occur in caves, are both formed by dripping water, and so on. This does not stop us from seeing them at the same time as opposites in that one points up and the other points down. Items seen as 'similar' to each other in meaning are not necessarily synonyms or near-synonyms. Whereas perceived similarity of form is easy to account for (*adapt-adopt*; *militate-mitigate*; *who's-whose*), it seems that perceived semantic similarity is less easy to define, and it may be best to speak of 'semantic connection' rather than 'semantic similarity': although very different from each other in form, *lend* and *borrow* have a semantic connection and are confused by many British children.

Before moving on to complete our model, I want to suggest that the value of MEMORY AIDS is underestimated. These are schemes devised in an attempt to remember something or remind someone of something: tying a knot in a handkerchief is a well-known everyday example. There are various types, including verbal ones such as:

> I before E
> except after C
> or when they say 'ay'
> as in *neighbour* and *weigh*

and visual ones such as:

which may help with problems of reading and spelling. Rhymes can be useful in countering a tendency to omit or insert words, for example; and the sort of visual aid that illustrates a grammatical rule can also be of use, even with adult learners. Here is one that is simple to make out of scrap cardboard and magazine pictures:

When the strip is moved across to the right, we see:

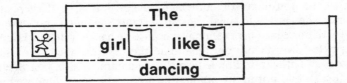

Another could be made to show that, after modals (such as *will*, *can*, etc.), verbs are not inflected:

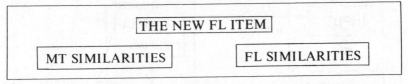

Devices such as these are certainly useful in remedial work.

Summarising what has been said so far, it seems to me that the learning process should be seen as a search for sense (i.e. meaning) and harmony (i.e. regularity, pattern); and that the learner's goal is to achieve sufficient predictability of form to enable him to concentrate on novelty of meaning. It may be, therefore, that we should regard all the 'strategies' that I have attempted to describe – and perhaps others of which I am not aware – as constituting one process of association:

THE NEW FL ITEM

MT SIMILARITIES   FL SIMILARITIES

It may be thought that, once something has been successfully stored away in the memory, it has been learnt. But just as the proof of the pudding is in the eating, so the proof of language-learning lies in the learner's ability to perform, to communicate in the foreign language. We come finally, then, to the STRATEGIES FOR COMMUNICATING, along with the monitor or CHECKOUT. (See Fig. 6.) Even if you have never had to communicate orally in a FL in which you were far from fluent, you will no doubt have observed that others put in this position seem to fall into two quite distinct groups: those who launch themselves into the task, happily oblivious of how they cripple the language, and those who are reluctant to speak at all for fear of making mistakes and 'sounding funny'. No doubt this phenomenon is partly explained by personality factors, but it is not simply that one group is made up of extroverts and the other of introverts. Whatever the truth is, some

27

learners seem to have a monitor so rigorous that it inhibits speech in a FL; and this phenomenon often sets in during puberty. It may well be that children at this stage of development (often at the age of 12 or 13) would benefit more from intensive listening-practice than from oral drilling.

We have seen that the listener trying to cope with too much input will either pick out a word or two here and there and hope for the best; or turn to the non-linguistic context for help. Similarly, if there is any urgency when he has to speak, he may just put together a known word or two (with no regard for grammar, because he has no rehearsal time); or his trickle of words may dry up and he may resort to facial expressions, gestures and other non-linguistic means of communicating. Strategies of this sort should not in my opinion be among those encountered in the EFL classroom, since what most learners want to do (if indeed they want to learn English at all) is not simply to communicate, but to communicate in good English. I shall pick up this theme in Chapter 5.

There is, of course, much more that could be said and argued about; but our model finally looks like this, with the STM taking note of the non-linguistic context, drawing upon the LTM store and allowing rehearsal of what is to be said:

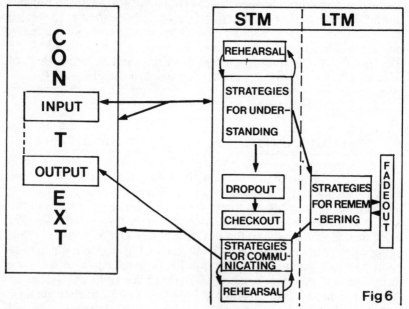

Fig 6

If all this is rather impressive or looks rather 'scientific' to you, remember that it is little more than guess-work. The point is simply this: if you believe that good teaching is teaching that is well-adjusted to the learning-strategies of the class, then (assuming you want to teach well) you will find a description of the learning process, however makeshift, very helpful in that it can:

(i) justify some of the things you do when you are teaching; and/or
(ii) show you that there is no good reason for some of the things you do when you are teaching; and/or
(iii) show how you fail to take some of the learning processes into account when you are teaching.

You may not be satisfied with the model suggested above. Neither am I. Almost all the evidence that we have on verbal learning comes from observations of learning *in* the MT; there is also a little psycholinguistic knowledge about the *acquisition* of the MT; but very little is known about the process of FL learning. The whole of this section on language-learning has therefore been an idiosyncratic attempt to describe the foreign language-learning process; if you do not like my model, just ignore it and make one that suits you better.

Part 3: The language

In deciding what sort of language to select for presentation to the EFL learner, we should first ask him the question 'Why are you studying it?' The answer might be 'For no reason that I know of'. In this TENOR situation it probably does not much matter what sort of texts he uses as long as his lessons provide him with a valuable educational experience in that, e.g.

(i) he may learn something new about the world (or indeed, other worlds) *through* English – many EFL lessons unfortunately have no content at all of this sort; or
(ii) he may learn something about language as a phenomenon – for instance, that different cultures are different ways of viewing the world and that their languages incorporate these varying perspectives; or
(iii) he may learn quite a lot about his own language as a result of mentally comparing it with English.

I do not believe that learning a FL is useless, even when it is studied for no predictable practical purpose.

A second learner might reply, 'Because the rest of my education is going to be done through the medium of English'. In this case there is every reason why a lot of his English lessons should be spent studying texts illustrating uses of language that he is likely to encounter – and indeed may already be encountering daily. As well as 'pedagogic English' taken from textbooks in such school subjects as Physics, Biology, History, Geography, etc., there could be spoken texts of the sort produced by teachers when giving laboratory instructions, explaining a geological process, describing the structure or function of an internal organ, setting out causes and effects in a historical episode, and so on.

A third learner might reply, 'Because I will have to keep up with developments in computer technology.' He is learning English for specific purposes (ESP) and here again, material directly relevant to his main tasks would be used – possibly texts from the journals he will have to read, but modified in some way for teaching purposes. But in all these and other cases, there is no need to be rigid in one's policy. Texts can be chosen for their fun-value in all cases, Literature in English can enliven classes in the English-medium situation, and in ESP situations we must remember that the learner is not only a 'nine-to-five' worker but also an off-duty socialised human being: a person with more than just professional interests.

I have mentioned 'texts' several times. Yet in dealing with beginners or near-beginners, especially those with little or no knowledge of the English orthography, it would be counter-productive to begin by using 'texts', in the usual sense of that word. Learning a FL is a difficult and time-consuming business, whatever some commercial organisations may say and some students think. Like any learning-material, the FL input has to be fed to the learner a little at a time if it is to be absorbed. The maker of the syllabus or scheme of work therefore has to have a policy for dividing up the learning material into units small enough for graded presentation to the learner. How should it be divided? What are these units?

For a long time, two rather different answers to this last question have existed side by side. One takes as its basic units paradigms and declensions such as:

1	I am; you are; he/she/it is; etc.
2	my, your, his/her/its, etc.
3	sing, sang, sung.

Grammatical lists such as these, together with rules (given in the MT) are intended as aids in learning the forms of the FL; explanations (in the MT) and translations deal with the meanings. Such GRAMMAR/ TRANSLATION approaches are widely used in many European universities, for example.

The younger school of thought identifies as the basic unit the sentence-pattern. Here are two patterns:

A	Have {you / they}	got	any {children? / brothers and sisters?}	B	Yes, {I / they} have.
	Has {he / she}		a {nice house? / car?}		{he / she} has.

Here, oral practice of the patterns themselves is intended as the main aid in learning the forms, while meanings are dealt with by means of demonstration (pictures, actions, etc.) and explanation in simpler English, use of the MT traditionally being avoided. Such STRUC-TURAL approaches are even more widely in evidence than grammar-translation ones. (I have talked about approaches in each case, because it is a mistake to think that actual practice has been an either/or business. More about this later.)

Recently, a third school of thought has suggested that the basic unit might be the function. The sentences in pattern A on p. 30 are grouped together because they are similar in form; the following sentences are grouped together because they are similar in purpose, or function:

> Why not forget all about it?
> I'd forget all about it if I were you.
> I think you should drop the whole thing.
> I would advise you to let the matter rest.

We could label this group, 'Advising someone to abandon a course of action' though, of course, the label itself is of no use to a learner unless he understands it. The four sentences are structurally very different but perform the same function; conversely, structurally similar sentences may perform very different functions. Imagine, for instance, four passengers in a railway carriage. Mrs A is talking to Mrs B, and Mr Y is talking to Mr Z.

Compare Mrs B's normal response . . .

Mrs A:	Have you got any children?
Mrs B:	Yes, two boys. One's just a baby, but the other's at school. Have *you*?

. . . with Mr Z's crazy reply. . . .

Mr Y:	Have you got any matches?
Mr Z:	Yes, two boxes. One's in my pocket, but the other one's at home. Have *you*?

(Mr Y's 'request for service' is interpreted as a 'request for information'

31

something which, in this case, not even a beginner in English would do if he were sane!) FUNCTIONAL approaches group together sentences similar in meaning rather than form.

Items of language can be grouped in at least three ways, then: by paradigm and declension; by sentence-pattern; or by function. Each kind of arrangement has its advantages and disadvantages, but it would be difficult to discuss these without touching on the methodology associated with each one. As the chapters that follow deal with methods of teaching, all that is needed here is a brief review of these three major types of approach (Grammar/translation, Structural and Functional) in the light of the learning-strategies suggested in Part Two.

A   Motivation

We have seen that some people learn English for practical purposes that are relatively easy to specify. In such cases, the use of these purposes or functions as a basis for teaching seems to have a great advantage over the use of paradigms or patterns as usually laid out in materials for 'general purpose English', in that it caters directly to the motivation of the learner.

Where there are no clear practical reasons for learning English, however – as with most school children learning EFL – there seems to be little point in using the function as a basis. Perhaps the basis is quite unimportant in such cases, provided that the lessons are inherently enjoyable and interesting. (We hope that the activities illustrated in the coming chapters will help you in this respect.)

B   External interference

Probably the first fact to come to terms with is that whatever approach is used translation will go on in every classroom – inside the learners' heads. Grammar/translation approaches not only accept this but also use translation as a rapid (but sometimes misleading) way of teaching meanings. This practice has been condemned; yet it seems to me far more sensible than to spend several minutes demonstrating a meaning, only to hear your students then say, 'Ah! You mean (MT equivalent)!' Just because expatriate teachers often have to do this, there is no need for local teachers to feel that they should do likewise, unless their classes are multilingual, of course.

On the other hand, it would be wrong to lead your class to think that you will always make things easy for them by spoonfeeding them with translations of new words and grammatical forms. (See Chapter 4 on this point, for example.) The important point is that, however its meaning has been taught, there should be adequate practice of the new item.

C Internal interference

We have to accept that this too will occur all the time, whatever approach is adopted. Grammar/translation coursebooks encourage it by exhorting the learner 'not to confuse X with Y', e.g.

Used to + ing	He is used to cooking for himself. (This is not to be confused with *used to* + inf, e.g. *He used to cook for himself.*)

If we had not noticed the similarity before, we certainly do now! One likely outcome is: *He is used to cook for himself.* Some structural approaches, too, encourage such cross-association through deliberately teaching by contrast or through carelessly juxtaposing two very confusable forms. Contrasting the Present Perfect and Past Simple tenses, for example, seldom achieves much, other than to confuse the learner even more; and the juxtaposition of, for instance,

| Biology is interesting | and | I am interested in Biology |

will often produce

| * I am interesting in Biology |

However, in structural courses it is possible to separate confusable forms so as not to draw the learner's attention to both at the same time.

The whole point of functional approaches, however, is to focus on meaning.

This means that the syllabus-maker and the textbook writer (and therefore the teacher and learner) are likely to juxtapose sentences similar in meaning. If these are also partly similar in form, the conditions for cross-association are perfect. The extract on pp. 33–4 shows just some of the forms from which a few could be selected for teaching. (Incidentally, I have heard British children confusing those marked (2) and (3) on the list, to produce, eg: *May you do this for me, please?*)

(1) O.K.? All right? Any objections?	(All accompanied by an appropriate gesture, e.g. lifting the telephone.)
(2) Can May Could Might	I use your telephone, (please)?
Could Might	I {possibly / perhaps} use your telephone?
(3) Please let me use your telephone? Will you let me use your telephone, if I pay for the call?	

B

(4) Is it all right to use your telephone?

If it's all right $\left\{\begin{array}{l}\text{with}\\\text{by}\end{array}\right\}$ you, I'll use your telephone?

(5) Am I allowed to use your telephone?

(6) Do you mind if I use your telephone?
Do you mind me using your telephone?
Would you mind if I used your telephone?
Would you mind me using your telephone?
Would you mind awfully if I used your telephone?
If you don't mind, I'll use your telephone.
You don't mind if I use your telephone, (do you?)
$\left.\begin{array}{l}\text{I'd like}\\\text{I want}\end{array}\right\}$ to use your telephone. $\left\{\begin{array}{l}\text{Would}\\\text{Do}\end{array}\right\}$ you mind?

(7)
Do you $\left\{\begin{array}{l}\text{object}\\\text{have any objection}\end{array}\right\}$ to me using your telephone?
If you have no objection, I'll use your telephone.
I wonder if you have any objection to me using your telephone.

(8) $\left.\begin{array}{l}\text{Will}\\\text{Would}\end{array}\right\}$ you $\left[\begin{array}{l}\text{permit}\\\text{allow}\end{array}\right\}$ me to use your telephone?

consent to me using your telephone?

give $\left\{\begin{array}{l}\text{your consent}\\\text{your permission}\end{array}\right\}$ $\left.\begin{array}{l}\text{for me to use}\\\text{your telephone?}\end{array}\right.$

(9) I (therefore) request that I be allowed to use your telephone.
(10)
Would you be so kind as to $\left\{\begin{array}{l}\text{let}\\\text{permit}\\\text{allow}\\\text{etc.}\end{array}\right\}$ me (to) use your telephone?

WILKINS, D.A. *Notional Syllabuses.* (Page 60.) Oxford University Press, 1976.

Perhaps the great disadvantage of functional approaches, then, may be their tendency to encourage cross-association. It might be suggested that just one form should be selected for teaching purposes as an exponent of a function; but this would be virtually a structural approach. Perhaps the safest policy would be to ensure that one simple exponent is practised for production; that two or three more are used for reception only; and that each is grammatically very different in form from the others. For example:

Productive use (simple)	Receptive use (more complex)	
Can I use your phone please?	Is it all right to	
	Do you mind if I	use your phone?
	I wonder if I might	

Even so, the variety of grammatical forms here presented to the learner may hinder his powers of analogising, whereas structural presentations can stimulate them.

D Practice

One criticism of grammar/translation approaches has been that they provide too little oral practice and give too much attention to the memorisation of rules. Accurate rehearsal of rules is not much use: being able to remember (say), '*some* for positive, *any* for negative and interrogative' is no guarantee of correct oral use of the rule in conversation. In any case, this rule is insufficient, failing among other things to account for offers and requests. (Would you like *some* more tea? Can I have *some* more cake?) So, as is often the case, it would probably take as long to memorise the corrected rule as it would to learn how to use it. On the other hand, there is a definite memory-jogging value in learning 'parts of speech', just as there is in learning multiplication tables. I still remember *fero, ferre, tuli, latum* from my Latin lessons thirty years ago; why not allow memorisation of *take, took, taken*?

Some structural approaches, on the other hand, may lead to too much oral practice and too little reinforcement by means of reading and written work. Structural oral practice has also been dismissed as merely 'language-like' behaviour which bears little resemblance to real communication. I regard this as one case where we must be careful not to expect that approaches which suit one situation will necessarily suit another. A functional approach aiming to achieve practices which are very similar to acts of real communication – this would be fitting (one might almost say inevitable!) in the Oxbridge School of English. But for as long as young people are required by law to attend school; made to sit in their dozens with one teacher in a school room; and compelled to study EFL for a few hours a week, year in, year out because it is a compulsory subject: for just so long will there be situations in which real communicating is done in the MT and anything resembling communication in English is play-acting in which the teacher is dependent on the goodwill and cooperation of the class, as indeed all teachers are.

People have for centuries learned languages from teachers following all sorts of approaches. There is no reason why we should feel obliged to adopt just one, and every reason why we should use the strengths of several. 'Either/or' attitudes seldom help; 'both/and' attitudes often do.

Further reading

If you feel in need of a basic book on the psychology of learning, the following (especially Chapters 3–10) should help, although there are literally thousands of suitable ones:

CHILD, D. *Psychology and the teacher.* Holt, Rinehart and Winston, 1973.

Also fairly easy to understand is:

GAGNÉ, R. *The conditions of learning.* Holt, Rinehart and Winston, third edition, 1977.

Of more obvious relevance to your everyday work is:

RIVERS, W. *Teaching foreign language skills.* University of Chicago Press, 1968.

And for some really thoughtful work on matters of fundamental importance, but less easy to read, try:

FREEDLE, R. and CARROLL, J. *Language comprehension and the acquisition of knowledge.* Winston and Sons, 1972.

As for further reading on ways of presenting language to the learner, you will find the main approaches described in:

WILKINS, D. *Notional syllabuses.* Oxford University Press, 1976.

Chapter 2: Pronunciation – perception and production

by John Greenwood

EXAMPLE 1

Situation: A Biology lesson in an English-medium school in East Africa; the teacher is African.

T: Now today, to begin with, we're going to have a chat about food-chains. You know about several food-chains already. Who can give me an example? . . .

(A few minutes later.)

P: Please.
T: Yes?
P: Please, where is the chart?
T: Chart? What chart?
P: The chart about food-chains. You said that we were going to have a chart . . .

EXAMPLE 2

Situation: A British teacher with Spanish-speaking learners in South America.

Blackboard:

1	2
/ b /	/ v /
berry	very

T: Listen to the words I say. Tell me if they are like 1 or 2. . . . /bɑ:n/ . . . Ana?
P: One.
T: Good . . . /bɔ:l/ . . . Carmen? . . .

(A few minutes later.)

T: You can all hear the difference now. Good. Now say the word after me . . . /best . . . best . . . best/ . . . José?
P: /best/
T: Good . . . /kʌbəd . . . kʌbəd/ . . . Miguel?
P: /kʌβəd/
T: Well, that sounds more like 'covered'. Put your lips together . . .

Note: The system of transcription used in Example 2 and throughout this chapter is given on p. 6. It is that used by Gimson (1980) – see Further Reading at the end of this chapter.

We have at some time all experienced, as language learners, difficulties with the sounds of a foreign language – both when listening and when speaking. It can be a traumatic experience, sometimes leading to panic or despondency. Trying to help students with their pronunciation difficulties can also be exasperating. Let us tackle this problem by considering first what the learner as listener has to deal with (i.e. the nature of spoken English), then how to help the learner to cope with the stream of sound as input, and finally how to help the learner to develop satisfactory pronunciation. Before continuing, however, we have to remember some of the factors mentioned in the previous chapter. Much will depend on whether you speak the MT of your class; on whether your class is multilingual; on whether English will be heard outside school and, if so, what sort of English it is or is likely to be; and on the equipment that you have at your disposal. Try to bear these factors in mind as you read on.

What kind of pronunciation?   The aim, of course, should be to speak English which is both intelligible and acceptable to the recipients, those who listen to the pronunciation. I think both criteria are important, especially when so much emphasis is given to communication nowadays. A speaker may be intelligible so that he communicates, but there may be such an accumulation of errors or deviations from any known standard that the listener finds it hard to accept the pronunciation. The learner should aim for a pronunciation that does not draw unfavourable attention to itself. This does not necessarily mean using the so-called Received Pronunciation (RP) of South-East England. In an ESL situation (for example, in Nigeria) some form of West African variety of English would be more appropriate perhaps than RP. As well as the local standard, there is the teacher's own accent, which will often be the most influential model for the learners. Where English is a foreign language, as in Europe, a decision has to be made whether we want the learners to aim at a British, American, or even Australian variety of English. Usually, there is no real choice, since the geographical position of the country often dictates the type. Still, the decision must be made, because it will determine the teaching material used, e.g. voices on a cassette: do you want British or American native-speakers?

We must, of course, bear in mind that while we need to have only one model for our learners to copy (and, as I said, this will often be the teacher's own pronunciation), we need to expose our learners to many different varieties of pronunciation for listening practice. This is particularly necessary if our learners are going to visit an English-speaking country.

Part 1: The nature of spoken English

When we speak, the listener hears a smooth continuity of combined sounds and not individual sounds in isolation. It is often this process of combination which the learner finds most difficult – both to understand and to produce. To a certain extent – and less than many teachers imagine – the flow of speech can be controlled by the teacher in the classroom; but speech heard outside is normally uncontrolled. Controlled or uncontrolled, there are many items to deal with, as the following example will indicate:

/teləmtəlɪvwɪðlez/

How do we as listeners interpret this utterance? We are helped, of course, by the context in which it occurs, but we still have to take note of the sounds themselves. Our knowledge of the context (i.e. our knowledge of who is speaking to whom and about what) and our recognition of the sounds will lead us to decide which of the following interpretations is most appropriate:

A   Tell him to live with Les.
B   Tell him to live with Liz.
C   Tell them to live with Les.
D   Tell them to live with Liz.
E   Tell him/them to leave with Les/Liz.
F   Tell him/them to live/leave with Les/Liz.
G   Tell him/them to live/leave with Les/Liz?
H   Tell him/them to live/leave with Les/Liz!

A and B differ according to whether we interpret a single vowel as /e/ or /ɪ/ (*Les* or *Liz*), just as E differs from the first four sentences when another vowel is heard as /iː/ or /ɪ/ (*leave* or *live*). The vowel difference causes a difference in meaning and can lead to misunderstanding and confusion, as we saw in **EXAMPLE 1**, where the African learner thought he heard *chart* and not *chat*. So individual sounds, known as vowels and consonants, have to be identified and distinguished one from the other. Is a speaker talking about a *coat*, or a *goat*, about a *pin* or a *bin*?

However, once vowels and consonants combine in the stream of speech, sounds seem to change. In the utterance, *tell* is spoken rather loudly (strong stress) and the following word rather softly (weak stress), so that a neutral vowel sound /ə/ may be used for either *him* or *them*. Furthermore, some kind of contraction or omission may take place; i.e.

Examples	*Strong form in isolation*	*Weak form in combination*
A and B	/hɪm/	/ɪm/ or /əm/
C and D	/ðem/	/əm/

Variation in the stress of different words in an utterance is another important feature of spoken English, since it determines the rhythm of the utterance and the quality of the vowel sounds. Does the listener interpret the utterance as a command (F) or as a request for confirmation (G) or a cry of disbelief (H)? It will depend on his ability to recognise the intonation pattern, i.e. the rise and fall of the voice.

I have drawn attention to three features of spoken English: vowels and consonants (technically known as segmental phonemes), stress, intonation. But consonants combine together to make difficult clusters; and special difficulties occur in linking consecutive words. Let us now look at these last two features.

A Consonant clusters

Learning difficulties may arise where the MT has a syllabic structure with single consonants and no clusters, so that the learner is inclined to insert a short vowel sound between adjacent consonants; e.g. *film* may be pronounced /fɪləm/. Or maybe the MT has an equivalent consonant cluster, but not in initial position, in which case a vowel is inserted initially; e.g. *sport* may be pronounced /espɔːt/ by a Spanish learner.

As to the selection and grading of consonant clusters, it would of course be possible to go through the dictionary and establish the number of words in which each of the different combinations occur in initial, medial and final position. But that would be only half the battle, because there are still the hundreds of combinations between words. Instead, the teacher may prefer a more pragmatic approach; viz.

(i) Concentrate on achieving satisfactory pronunciation of initial consonant clusters, rather than medial and final ones. The lexical selection in the textbook and the particular difficulties of the learners will determine which initial clusters to give special attention to.

(ii) However, certain final clusters are important, particularly those which involve grammatical inflections:

Consonant + /s/ ⎫	for the Simple	⎧ (he eats)
Consonant + /z/ ⎭	Present	⎩ (he digs)
Consonant + /s/ ⎫	for Noun plurals	⎧ (books, Pat's, cats')
Consonant + /z/ ⎭	and for 's and s'	⎩ (cards, Tom's, dogs')
Consonant + /t/ ⎫	for the Simple Past	⎧ (walked)
Consonant + /d/ ⎭	and Past Participle	⎩ (screamed)

All these are so basic to English, even from the early stages of learning, that adequate pronunciation is most desirable.

B Linkage between words

The term *liaison* is sometimes used to refer to this feature of continuous speech. A weakness in many learners' pronunciation is the jerky, staccato effect caused by not linking words together; e.g.

he | is | always | early instead of he's⌣always⌣early.

There is also a tendency with some learners to place a glottal stop before a word beginning with a vowel in a stressed syllable; e.g.

he always may be pronounced /hiʔɔːlweɪz/.

Here are a few examples of consonant clusters between words:

Final consonant(s)	+	*Initial consonant(s)*
1		1
take	/k/ + /m/	mine
1		2
keep	/p/ + /tr/	trying
2		1
first	/st/ + /l/	look
2		2
went	/nt/ + /kw/	quickly

And so on, sometimes to great complexity, at least potentially; e.g.

3		3
sixth	/ksθ/ + /str/	stranger

However, such linkage often results in
(i) omission of a consonant; e.g. *last week* may be pronounced /lɑːswiːk/;
(ii) assimilation, whereby a consonant changes to another by the influence of an adjacent consonant; e.g. *this year* may be pronounced /ðɪʃjɪə/. Omission and assimilation are not essential and not all native speakers consistently perform them, so we need not give them top priority in our pronunciation work. They would occur incidentally, we would hope, as our learners progress. Still, some assimilations are actually much easier for students to say than the non-assimilated forms. Most learners will find it simpler to pronounce *windbreak* as /wɪmbreɪk/, for instance.

C Intonation

This is the rise and fall of pitch in an utterance, that is, the tune. It may well entail a greater learning task than the individual consonants and vowels themselves, and an intonation error may be more detrimental to understanding the speaker than the occasional wrong vowel or consonant. A wrong intonation will not normally fail to convey any meaning at all, but will succeed in conveying a meaning different from that intended by the speaker. For instance, there is a world of difference in the wife's response to her husband's enquiry: Would you like that fur coat in the window?
– Yes. (with a high fall) – enthusiastic
– Yes. (with a low fall) – unenthusiastic

Even if the different tunes have different meanings, it is difficult to confine a particular meaning (often the attitude of the speaker) to a particular tune, or to list fully all the possible meanings to any one tune. In short, there is much overlap. For instance, the low-fall tune is sometimes characterised as definite, final, firm, sometimes rude or abrupt; while the low-rise tune is said to be friendly, polite, doubtful and encouraging. However, there are exceptions to these generalisations which the learner may not be aware of. With beginners, we could confine our attention to the two basic tunes I have just described. The other tunes (variations of these two) can be dealt with later.

D Stress and rhythm

Stress refers to the amount of energy with which a syllable is spoken, whereas rhythm is the combination of strong and weak stresses in a sentence and their timing. There are two types of stress: word-stress and sentence-stress.

1 Word-stress.　This is invariable and so the learner should always learn the stress pattern of a new word as well as its meaning. It is more important to get word-stress right than even intonation, because if it is wrong the listener may well fail to recognise the word altogether, even if the vowels and consonants are correctly pronounced. There are obviously many stress patterns because of the variation in the number of syllables in English words.

2 Sentence stress.　(i) English is often called a stress-timed language because, unlike French for example, it has strong stresses or beats at more or less regular intervals. The greater the number of weak-stressed syllables between two adjacent strong stresses, the quicker those weak-stressed syllables are uttered. For example:

Strong stress 1	*Weak stress(es)*	*Strong stress 2*
Go		home.
Go	to	John.
Go	to the	door.
Go-	-ing to the	game.

All the above would take roughly the same time to utter. Certain learners have great difficulty in copying the variation in rhythm which accompanies a succession of strong and weak syllables. Such learners tend to produce a uniform, syllable-timed pronunciation; e.g.

'Go 'a 'way 'from 'the 'door.

This sounds very odd to the native-listener.

(ii) Stressed words are usually the so-called content or lexical words (i.e. nouns, verbs, adjectives, adverbs and interrogatives), and it is these whose word-stress pattern should be especially learned, since these words will obviously stand out in the utterance. Unstressed words are usually the structure or function words (i.e. pronouns, determiners, auxiliary verbs, prepositions, conjunctions, relatives, etc). It is the rhythm of English speech which ensures that these unstressed words remain weak and that contractions (e.g. *I will* → *I'll*) occur.

In this first section I have dealt with some of the main features of spoken English. Now let us see how we can help our learners to cope with spoken English.

Part 2:   Ways of training the ear

At this point, a word of encouragement might be welcome: 'No one can hope to be a successful linguist unless he has a good ear. If his ear is insensitive by nature, it may be made more sensitive by training; and if his ear is good by nature, it can be made still better by training.' (Daniel Jones: *Outline of English Phonetics*.) For many a teacher, this may seem more like wishful thinking than the cold reality of the classroom situation, but I would like to take it as an act of faith that it is indeed possible to train our learners in aural perception.

We cannot expect our learners to speak English without first of all hearing English. The language heard acts as a model for the spoken language to follow. However, the relationship is not direct between the heard input and the spoken output. Given the spoken language input, what does the learner do? Until he is at a fairly advanced level, he finds difficulty in understanding everything bombarding his ears. He in fact hears, i.e. perceives, only a restricted number of items. A useful distinction is sometimes made between the terms 'input' and 'intake'. The first refers to the external data, the controlled or uncontrolled message, whereas 'intake' refers to what the learner perceives, what his mind is capable of absorbing. So obviously, given a certain input, the intake will vary according to the ability of the learner. To give an analogy: for many years on BBC television there has been a programme for children called 'Jackanory' in which somebody tells or reads a different story every day for about fifteen minutes. This has proved very popular with children of all ages. It is common to see five-year-olds watching with twelve-year-olds, all spellbound. All listening to the same story, but obviously the twelve-year-olds will perceive much more than the five-year-olds, i.e. the latter are able to take in, select, much less.

In **EXAMPLE 2** at the beginning of the chapter, Miguel is influenced by the phonological system of his MT, Spanish. /b/ in initial position is no problem either to perceive or to produce, because this consonant is roughly the same sound in both English and Spanish. However, in medial position (i.e. between vowels) Spanish uses a bilabial fricative /β/, rather than a bilabial plosive /b/. A bilabial consonant sound is one where the main obstacle to the air-stream is the two lips. For a plosive

43

they are closed and air is compressed behind them, then released when they are opened. For a fricative they are not quite closed, so the air passes between them with audible friction. Miguel therefore has a pronunciation problem. He may have 'heard' the English medial /b/ as /β/ and then produced /β/ himself; even if he has heard the /b/ sound correctly, he has found difficulty in producing it because of the strong MT influence.

Certain implications for ear-training arise from these observations.
(i) Since listening precedes and affects speaking we must aim at providing our learners with accurate and clear models.
(ii) Sufficient listening time should be given before we demand production from our learners. There is the temptation for the teacher to rush into the production stage, depriving the learner of adequate reception practice.
(iii) Awareness of the sound system of the MT of the learner will often help the teacher to provide appropriate practice.

I will now consider examples of ear-training practice for some of the features of Spoken English mentioned in Part I.

A Vowels and consonants

A lot of this practice entails discrimination between two items, the 'same-different' technique used for instance by Hill (see Further Reading). This contrastive method seems to be useful here for the receptive work of recognising an item of sound; but there is the obvious disadvantage of juxtaposing two or more items for speech practice, since the learner may be led through cross-association to commit errors in pronunciation, i.e. at the production stage.

Many learners have difficulty distinguishing between the vowel /ʌ/ as in 'cut' and the vowel /æ/ as in 'cat'. Thus, learners could be asked to indicate whether, in the following pairs of words, the sounds are the same or different:

cat	cat
cat	cut
hut	hat
lack	lack
luck	lack
etc.	etc.

Of course, this is only the first very limited stage in auditory discrimination. Your learners will rarely come across these words in such isolation, so you will need to use these words in phrases and sentences. Not only are phrases and sentences more authentic language, but the context will help the learner to discriminate accurately, e.g.

The hat/hut on the table.
The hat/hut on the hillside.

Although, as I have said, this contrastive work using minimal pairs can be useful for the learner, not all teachers or books are careful enough in their choice of examples, so that the learner is sometimes, if not actually confused, at least no nearer to overcoming his difficulty. For instance, here is a teacher dealing with the diphthong /eɪ/ which is a difficult sound for his learners:

T writes on the blackboard:

1	2
/e/	/eɪ/
met	mate

T: Listen to these words and tell me if they are like 1 or 2. /weɪt/. Well, Jo?

Jo: One.

T: No. Listen again. Listen for how long the sound is.

Now the learners probably tend to shorten the /eɪ/ diphthong and substitute the short /e/. The problem, then, is largely a question of vowel-length. So the teacher is not really helping his class to hear this length feature by using such words as: mate, wait, awake, tape, break. These words have a final voiceless plosive which tends to shorten the preceding /eɪ/ vowel, so that Jo perceives the shorter sound /e/ and therefore thinks the teacher said 'wet' and not 'wait'. Obviously, the learner will have to distinguish 'wet' from 'wait' eventually, but before he is asked to do so, he could be helped to perceive the length feature of /eɪ/ if the teacher chose words which emphasise the length. Thus to begin with:

say, pay, weigh, tray, play, etc., i.e. /eɪ/ in *final* position.

Then,

made, played, shame, etc., i.e. /eɪ/ + *voiced* consonant.

B Word-stress

You can help your learners by exploiting certain general rules. For example, with regard to two-syllable words,

(i) Nouns mostly have the strong stress on the first syllable,
e.g. TICKet, TAble, PENcil, CITy

(ii) Verbs have the strong stress on the first or second syllable.

e.g.	BOTHer	exPLAIN
	GATHer	deCIDE
	HAPpen	reFUSE
	FRIGHTen	proDUCE
	FINish	forGET
	POLish	acCEPT

In fact, two-syllable verbs can be further classified to reveal regularities,

e.g.	*Base+er*	*Base+en*	*Base+ish*
	bother	happen	finish
	gather	frighten	polish
	shudder	harden	perish
	mutter	brighten	furnish
	shiver	darken	tarnish

	ex+Base	*pro+Base*
	explain	produce
	expect	protect
	excite	propose
	exclude	provide

(iii) Noun-Verb distinction.

Noun	*Verb*
EXport	exPORT
SUSpect	susPECT
INcrease	inCREASE
INsult	inSULT
PROtest	proTEST
etc.	etc.

Such categories can give some indication of varying stress patterns. You could take one list and ask your learners to listen to the stress pattern. Tapping out the pattern with your hands or a pencil on a desk is a useful auditory help. You can easily represent the pattern visually on the blackboard, e.g.

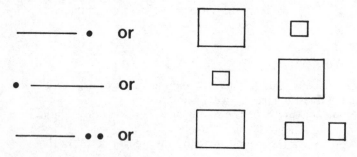

and so on.

C Intonation

The intonation patterns – the tunes of spoken language – vary from language to language. As I suggested in Part 1, you need to make sure your learners recognise the two basic patterns in English:

Tune 1: Falling Tune – the voice falls during the last stressed syllable and any following weak syllable(s),

e.g.　　We went to LONdon.

What TIME is it?

Tune 2: Rising Tune – the voice rises during the last stressed syllable and any following weak syllable(s),

e.g.　　Did you GO?

REALly?

To highlight the appropriate tune, you could sing or whistle the tune and move your arm up or down or show the curve of the tune on the blackboard. While doing this, of course, no language is uttered. Once the tune is established, then language is used. Furthermore, only after Tune 1 has been well established should you work on Tune 2. Then your class can attempt to distinguish between the two tunes, in the same way as was done for minimal pair work for vowels and consonants:

Blackboard:

　　　　1　　　　　　　　　　　　　2
I'll see you toMORrow.　　Did you go to YORK?

T: Listen to these sentences. Tell me if the tune is 1 or 2.
　　We ate a lot of potatoes.
　　Bill likes to go fishing.
　　Have you a match?
　　What time is it?
　　　　etc.

Part 3: Ways of teaching pronunciation

After perception, production. A common teaching method here is to use imitation or mimicry. The teacher gives the model and the learners copy. This happens in **EXAMPLE 2**. The trouble with mere imitation is that learners have to base their production primarily on auditory clues, though if they see the teacher's face there are usually visual clues as well (e.g. lip movements like rounding and closure). Often, of course, this is sufficient for the learner. However, not always. The learner sometimes wrongly perceives what is said, and this could lead him to produce the sound wrongly. The teacher too may wrongly perceive what he hears.

　　T: Say after me: *a pen.*

(The teacher, a native speaker of English, produces an aspirated /pʰ/ in word-initial position – that is, he produces the sound with a puff of air.)

　　P: A pen. /ə p⁼en/

(The pupil, an Indian, his perception and production influenced by his MT, uses a non-aspirated /p⁼/.)

> T: No, not *a ben; a pen.*

(The teacher, hearing an unaspirated sound, wrongly thinks the pupil is saying /b/, since that sound is normally unaspirated in English.)

> P: A pen. /ə p⁼en/.
> T: No, you are still saying *a ben.*

(And so on – mutual incomprehension may continue indefinitely!)

In this situation, to persist with mere imitation would be of no avail. Something more may be needed to help the learner. This is where an articulatory description would be appropriate so that the learner can feel where and how a sound is produced. A full description is usually not necessary. Drawing the learner's attention to a particular feature is often adequate (e.g. lip-rounding, tongue-position, voicing), together with a short directive. Here are a few well-known examples:

> Voiceless/Voiced sounds: Put your finger on your neck just below your chin – on your Adam's apple. Now say the pairs of sounds. In each pair the first is voiceless ('whispered') and your finger will feel no vibration. The second is voiced and you should feel the vibration: p/b; t/d; k/g; tʃ/dʒ; f/v; θ/ð; s/z; ʃ/ʒ.
> Initial /p, t, k/: Put a piece of paper in front of your mouth and make sure a puff of air moves the paper.
> /ɪ/: Say /i:/, then lower your tongue a little but keep your jaw and lips in the same position.

Such a short directive is used in **EXAMPLE 2**. A visual aid can occasionally be more effective than an oral description and most phonetics books have illustrations of the position of the organs of speech for the different vowels and consonants. A diagram of the curve of an intonation tune may also help:

> Do you go to London by train or bus?

I now want to consider the teaching of some specific sounds; my examples will include vowels, consonants and consonant clusters, liaison between words, and sentence stress. Each of these aspects of pronunciation is the subject of many separate practice books, so I do not intend to be comprehensive. I hope my remarks will help you to use such practice books more judiciously.

/ɪ/

This vowel is usually contrasted with /i:/ in minimal pair work (ship – sheep, etc). Most learners will have something similar to the English /i:/

in their MT, so that is not the problem. Rather, the learner tends to substitute his familiar long /i:/ for /ɪ/, as in the cliché example: I like feesh and cheeps. Though /ɪ/ is not just a short version of /i:/, length is probably the crucial feature here. We need to provide our learners with lots of practice of words where /ɪ/ is very short, e.g. bit, kit, fit, lip, tip, kick; i.e. followed by a voiceless plosive. Then only later do we practise a longer /ɪ/ as in bid, did, ill, sin, sing. All these examples will have to be practised first in isolation (i.e. in single words) and then in phrases.

/əʊ/

This is a difficult sound to produce for many learners, who tend to replace the diphthong with a monophthong /o/. This is normally due to MT interference and reinforced by the spelling (often the simple letter 'o' as in 'go'). The learner is therefore tempted to round his lips as for a back vowel and keep the lips and the tongue position constant. A back vowel is one for which the back of the tongue is raised towards the soft palate. The soft palate or velum is the soft fleshy part just behind the hard palate. The hard palate is the bony arch of the roof of the mouth.

Here is a suggested procedure for teaching:
(i) The teacher utters examples of the sound /əʊ/ in isolation and in words:
    oh, no, so.
(ii) The learners imitate the teacher.
(iii) If necessary, the teacher provides articulatory help, e.g. begin with the lips in neutral position to pronounce /ə/, then slight rounding and closing as for /ʊ/.
A blackboard diagram or hand-illustration might help.
(iv) Practice of /əʊ/ in words ending in voiced consonants like:
    bone, moan, showed, load.
(v) Only later (preferably in another lesson), practice of /əʊ/ in words ending in voiceless consonants which shorten the preceding /əʊ/; e.g.
    boat, float, bloke, stroke.
(vi) Only now will specific practice be given to words which have initial velar consonants like:
    go, goat, coal, coke.
In these consonants closure occurs between the velum (the soft palate) and the back of the tongue. Because of this, the velar position of the tongue will tend to be held on through the /əʊ/ and so a back vowel (/ɒ/ or /ɔ:/ or /ʊ/) may be produced rather than /əʊ/.

This procedure is of course a highly controlled one where the teaching aim is correct pronunciation of /əʊ/. I do not advocate avoidance of words like 'go' in the rest of the lessons where the input and the output of /əʊ/ are obviously uncontrolled.

/r/

To a large extent, how you tackle the consonant depends on the nature of the difficulty for the learner. For instance, a typical French learner of English will use his French uvular / ʁ / sound, so that you are asking for trouble if you try to practise the English /r/ sound with accompanying back vowels which will only reinforce the French learner's tendency to place his tongue towards the velar position. So to begin with, avoid words like:

/u:/ root, room
/ɔ:/ raw
/ɒ/ rot, rod, rock

For the same reason, avoid at first velar consonants /k/ and /g/ as in:

/k/ crew
/g/ great

Instead, practise /r/ with front vowels like:

/i:/ read
/ɪ/ rich
/e/ red
/æ/ rat

because the learner will be more likely to bring his tongue forward in anticipation of the following vowel.

As to the actual pronunciation of /r/, you ought to find at least one of these suggestions suitable for your learner:
(i) Say /æ/ as in 'pat', then slightly raise the tip of the tongue so that it comes near to, but does not actually touch, the alveolar ridge. /æ/ should change into a reasonable /r/.
(ii) Say /ɜ:/ as in bird and proceed as in (i).
(iii) Say 'ladder', then change the medial /d/ by not letting the tip of the tongue quite touch the alveolar ridge (the bony ridge, just behind the upper teeth), thus producing the American English flap sound. Then intend to say ladder again as /lærə/, but omit the first syllable so you say /rə/.

/s/ + consonant

This is a problem for speakers of Spanish, for example. An /e/ is placed before the /s/, as happens in Spanish. Hence the Spanish learner of English has great difficulty avoiding 'esport', 'eschool', etc. A possible procedure is:
(i) Begin by uttering a long /s/; i.e. sssssss . . .
(ii) Stop this /s/ by closing the lips in anticipation of the following /p/ or /m/, or by raising the tip of the tongue to the alveolar ridge in

anticipation of the following /t/ or /n/ or /l/, or by raising the back of the tongue to the velum in anticipation of /k/.

(iii) But continue to sound the /s/ until the closure, in order to avoid the intrusion of /ə/ as in /səp . . /. We do not want *sport* to be confused with *support*. Until our learners have had a chance to master this consonant cluster, we are definitely not helping them by using in our examples: *a school, a spot, a start, a stick*, etc., since the inclusion of the indefinite article is only reinforcing the MT habit. Instead, if we want to use these words, we can use them in the plural (*schools, sticks*, etc.) provided that the *final* clusters do not pose problems.

Omission of final consonant

Certain learners tend to omit the final consonant of an English word, because the structure of their MT is *consonant + vowel* largely or entirely, the (*consonant +*) *vowel + consonant* type of syllable being rare or absent. This omission can give rise to speech that causes comprehension problems; e.g.
– a word we hear as /laɪ/ could be *lie, like, light*, etc.
– a word we hear as /si:/ could be *see, seek, seed*, etc.
– a word we hear as /fɔ:/ could be *four, fork, ford*, etc.
A difficult MT habit to overcome, but we could help by providing practice of sentences where the words with final consonants are followed by words beginning with vowels; e.g.

He read‿a book‿at‿our table.
They sat‿on‿a chair.

The learner will very likely rearrange the syllable division to sound like:
/hɪ re də bʊ kæ taʊə teɪbl/ and /ðeɪ sæ tɒ nə tʃɛə/.

Of course, this is not ideal, but it will give practice in linking words together, so necessary to the flow of English speech.

Linkage between words

Learners can be told three simple rules for linking vowels and /r/ between words:
(i) Insert /j/ between a final /i:/ or /ɪ/ and an initial vowel,

e.g.	the answer	/ði:jɑ:nsə/
	he explained	/hɪjɪkspleɪnd/
	my aunt	/maɪjɑ:nt/
	they arrived	/ðeɪtjəraɪvd/

(ii) Insert /w/ between a final /u:/, /əʊ/ or /ʊ/ and an initial vowel,

e.g.	who else	/hu:wels/
	too early	/tu:wɜ:lɪ/
	so on	/səʊwɒn/
	go away	/gəʊwəweɪ/

(iii) If a written word ends in an 'r' or 're', pronounce /r/ before a following vowel,

e.g.	more and more	/mɔ:rənmɔ:/
	for instance	/fərɪnstəns/
	there is	/ðɛərɪz/
	father and I	/fɑðərəndaɪ/

Stress and rhythm

As I mentioned in Part 1, spoken English is made up of strong and weak stresses with the strong-stress syllables occurring at fairly regular time intervals. On the whole, it is not these strong-stress syllables which cause pronunciation difficulties, because they obviously stand out clearly, so they are easily recognised and usually pronounced satisfactorily. It is the weak-stress syllables which are the problem. Many learners find it difficult to refrain from overstressing them, and often fail to recognise and produce a required /ə/ vowel or contracted form.

Here are just a few suggestions for helping your learners, but you will find much more detailed help in some of the books mentioned in Further Reading:

1 Sentence-rhythm. Put a stress-pattern on the blackboard, either with or without an actual sentence. The important learning item here is to practise the beat, the rhythm. Distinguish between the two stresses by using such sounds as DA and DI.

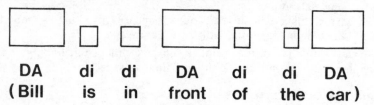

DA	di	di	DA	di	di	DA
(Bill	is	in	front	of	the	car)

You give the model rhythm and let the class join in. Provided a clear distinction is made between a loud and soft clap, you can clap your hands as another means of demonstration.

Then use a series of sentences for your learners to repeat after you,

e.g. 'Tom is in 'front of the 'door.
'Ann is a'way for the 'day.
'John is a 'boy with a 'car.
'Nice is a 'town near the 'sea.
'York is a 'town in the 'north.

You will ensure that there is a mixture of choral and individual production by your class, as well as avoiding too much practice at any one time. You must guard against excessive repetitive drilling.

Some teachers have found effective the technique of reverse build-up, whereby a fairly long sentence is divided into sections and instead of building up section by section from the beginning, you begin at the end,

e.g.   Sentence: The books were at the side of the radiator.

Sections: The books | were at the side | of the ¦ radiator.

T: Listen to this:

The books were at the side of the radiator.

Now say after me:

radiator.

Class: radiator.

T: of the radiator.

Class: of the radiator.

T: were at the side of the radiator.

Class: were at the side of the radiator.

T: The books were at the side of the radiator.

Class: The books were at the side of the radiator.

Artificial, yes; potentially too mechanical, yes. However, useful for learners having difficulty in maintaining continuity of the rhythm beyond a short phrase. Note that you maintain the overall intonation pattern, whereas if you start from the beginning, you practise an inappropriate series of falling tunes:

The books ↘

The books were at the side ↘

The books were at the side of the radiator ↘

Practice on sentence-stress or rhythm will expose your learners to plenty of practice on unstressed syllables, both in polysyllabic words and in one-syllable words which are normally unstressed in English. It is most important to pronounce correctly these very common one-syllable words which are estimated to make up about 25 per cent of the total words used in spoken English:

the /ðə/	to /tə/
a /ə/	in /ɪn/
and /ən/	he /(h)ɪ/
that /ðət/	for /fə/
of /əv/	from /frəm/

You should make sure your learners never say, for example, /ɒv/ instead of /əv/ in phrases like

the top of the hill

the front of the car.

2 Foreign accent.   Your learners may be helped by first listening to and then copying the way the English speak the learners' MT. As well as amusing your class, it could be a means of highlighting certain sounds or combinations of sounds they find difficult to pronounce. For instance, to highlight the different 'r' sounds in English and French, a class of French learners of English could be told to listen carefully to 'raison', 'très' and 'triste' in an Englishman's poor rendering of: 'J'ai raison. Jean est très triste'. Or Spanish learners could note how odd and 'typically English' it sounds when an English speaker uses in Spanish a series of low-rising intonations in an unfinished list; e.g.

Hay manzanas, plátanos, uvas, . . .

just as he would in saying in English:

We've got apples, bananas, grapes, . . .

What often marks somebody as British when speaking a foreign language is his tendency to use his English /əʊ/ rather than a pure /o/. A few examples by you of the stereotype Englishman using /əʊ/ instead of the MT /o/ will at least draw your learners' attention to the difference.

What to teach

Instead of attempting to deal comprehensively with all the English vowels and consonants and their combinations, and with all the English stress and intonation patterns, it would seem more realistic and desirable – because of lack of time and the particular difficulties of the learners – to concentrate on some carefully chosen pronunciation items. As a general rule learners should aim at pronouncing reasonably well the frequently occurring consonants and vowels, while not spending much time on infrequent ones. So, for instance, I would be concerned if my learners had problems pronouncing /l/ or /r/ but not so concerned if the relatively infrequent /ŋ/ were causing trouble. It is worth noting that /ð/ would be much less frequent a consonant if it were not for the word *the*, which accounts for about half the occurrences of /ð/. In initial position /ð/ occurs only in the words:

the, this, that, these, those, they, them, themselves, their, theirs, then, thence, there, thither, though, thus, than (plus derivatives of *there* like: thereafter, therefore).

As most of these are common function words likely to be used in many lessons, it is surely a good idea to ensure that the learners master this consonant.

However, this criterion of frequency, while useful, is not sufficient for our purposes because it obviously does not take into consideration the learner himself; that is, what his particular pronunciation difficulties are. It is accepted that MT influence will be a major factor. For example, whereas the voiceless dental fricative, /θ/, has low frequency in absolute terms, it may be a serious pronunciation difficulty for a learner, so that he will substitute either /s/ or /t/, thus creating such homophones as

/sɪŋ/ for *sing* and *thing* and
/tɔ:t/ for *thought* and *taught*.

Now this is not likely to cause a major breakdown in communication; after all, many Irish speakers of English substitute /t/ for /θ/. However, the cumulative effect of persistent substitution could cause occasional misunderstandings and irritation, so the teacher may wish to pay particular attention to /θ/.

There are many lists available – and some teachers make their own – of pronunciation difficulties of learners with different MTs. Here are just a few well-known examples:

MT	Consonants	Vowels
French	/θ, ð, h/	/ɪ, əʊ/
Spanish	/ʃ, ʒ/	/ɪ, ɔ:/
Japanese	/l, r/	
Yoruba		/ɜ:, ʌ/

Where the teacher has a group of learners homogeneous in terms of their MT background, he will easily identify the areas of difficulty and realise that quite often it is not a question of the sound as such but of its distribution. For instance, the German speaker has no difficulty with voiced plosives /b, d, g/ in initial or medial position, but only in final position,

e.g. *den* is no problem but *fed* becomes /fet/.

The Spaniard replaces /d/ with /ð/ in medial position but not in initial position,

e.g. *day* is all right but *ladder* becomes /læðə/.

The Japanese use /ç/ for /ʃ/ before /i:/, so they will tend to say /çi:/ for 'she', which may sound to the English ear like 'he'. And you will no doubt know many more examples yourself.

When to teach?

Of course, in a way we are teaching pronunciation indirectly all the time there is any oral work in the lesson because our learners will be listening to the pronunciation of the teacher or voices on the tape as a model for their own speaking. However, direct teaching has a place, since because of lack of time and opportunity we cannot solely rely on our learners automatically picking up an acceptable pronunciation. Explicit pronunciation teaching can take various forms. For example, the first five minutes of a lesson may be spent on a particular item as in **EXAMPLE 2**. Another approach is to use the 'blitz' technique whereby the teacher warns his learners that, say, for the next six lessons he will focus attention on an intonation tune, e.g. the falling tune for Wh – questions, and wants his learners to concentrate likewise on this item. This technique is particularly effective in the remedial situation where the learners' errors are a focus of attention.

Perhaps a final comment may reassure you. As happens with all languages, English has many varieties and dialects, so that there is much variation in its pronunciation. In spite of this, intelligibility is usually maintained. You should therefore not be too worried over sounds pronounced by your learners which, while not close to a native-speaker norm, nevertheless do not seriously interfere with communication.

Further reading

GIMSON, A. *An introduction to the pronunciation of English.* Arnold, third edition, 1980.

The most authoritative account of English pronunciation. For intonation the most useful work is probably:

O'CONNOR, J. AND ARNOLD, G. *The intonation of colloquial English.* Longman, second edition, 1973.

The above two are books for the teacher, though not books on teaching methods. A simpler work particularly useful where it is desirable for students to have a book on pronunciation is the following:

O'CONNOR, J. *Better English pronunciation.* Cambridge University Press, 1967.

Not a great deal is available on techniques of teaching pronunciation, but a simple book in this field is:

HAYCRAFT, B. *The teaching of pronunciation.* Longman, 1970.

A useful source-book for minimal pairs – that is, words differing in only one sound – is:

HILL, L. *Drills and tests in English sounds.* Longman, 1961.

A handy workbook for rhythm and stress patterns is:

HELIEL, M. and MCARTHUR, T. *Learning rhythm and stress* (Patterns of English series). Collins, 1974.

Finally, a series of five booklets, each dealing with a particular area of English pronunciation, with straightforward and clear presentation; a cassette is available to accompany each booklet:

MORTIMER, C. *Stress time, Link-up, Contractions, Clusters, Weak forms* (Elements of pronunciation series). Cambridge University Press, 1978.

Chapter 3: Comprehension and listening

by Douglas McKeating

EXAMPLE 1

Situation:	A medical school in a country where English is used in tertiary education but is not the medium of instruction at secondary level.
Student A:	I'm finding it very difficult to follow these lectures, aren't you? I wish we'd had some proper listening practice in our English lessons at school. All our teacher did was to read out a chapter from a book called 'Famous Men and Women of Medicine'. Then we had to answer questions. The texts were full of facts and figures and, by the time she'd finished, we'd forgotten just about everything.
Student B:	Well, *our* teacher said that listening was the easiest part of learning English, so he didn't bother about it at all. We spent most of our time reading and writing.

EXAMPLE 2

Situation:	Student C has just come home after her first visit to England. She has been learning English for six years in a European secondary school.
Student C:	. . . and it was really difficult, trying to understand what people were saying. English people talk so fast! And they have funny accents, too – even the characters on television and in the films. They didn't sound a bit like our teachers, who always speak slowly and clearly. I thought I was good at understanding English – I've always done well in the listening exercises at school – but, oh dear, . . .

Part 1: Listening – a neglected skill

Listening comprehension is a skill that tends to get neglected altogether, as in student B's classes, or is practised in inappropriate or inadequate ways. Student A's teacher saw the need for giving her students practice but failed to take account of several important things, such as the following:

(i) Texts written originally for *reading* are usually more difficult to understand when they can only be *heard*.

(ii) Spoken materials, even academic lectures, are normally much less densely packed with information than written texts.

(iii) It is more difficult to remember material heard in a FL than in the MT.

(iv) If people are forced to pay attention to and try to remember *everything* they hear they will probably end up remembering very little.

(v) There is a difference between teaching and testing.

(vi) Many students need guided practice in making notes while listening.

Student C's teacher was probably trying to make things *too* easy for his students and had failed to relate their listening practice to the real-life situations in which the students would actually want to use the skill. By always speaking so slowly and clearly and by not exposing them sufficiently to recordings of a variety of native English speakers, he had failed to prepare them to cope with normal spoken English.

Why does listening comprehension get neglected?

(i) Despite their own experience in learning foreign languages many people, like student B's teacher, seem to think that listening, and comprehending generally, is fairly easy – certainly much easier than speaking or writing.

This may be because, in most circumstances, the 'act of comprehending' causes us much less anxiety. It is much less public than speaking or writing, where our performance, mistakes and all, is available for inspection. It is much easier to cover up or be unaware of our errors of comprehension. For the most part we can imagine to ourselves that we have understood the gist of what we heard and as long as we smile, nod occasionally and look generally attentive, no-one else is likely to know how much or how little we have actually understood.

This probably explains why many teachers over-estimate their students' abilities in listening comprehension. The process of comprehension, being a part of learning, is invisible; all we can observe is evidence that it has or has not taken place. In many circumstances such evidence is easy to fake; and in the classroom it is particularly easy to copy it from others who *have* understood, or to work out what we are supposed to do from the general situation.

To take a simple example: you go into a beginners' class at the start of a lesson and say, 'Please sit down everyone, and listen to me.' Immediately, everyone sits down and looks attentive. Does this mean they understood what you said? Maybe.

Or maybe a few did and the rest followed their example. Or maybe nobody understood *what* you said but they understood that you were a teacher, that you had said *something*, that therefore the lesson was about to begin and that they should behave as they normally would at the beginning of a lesson. I am saying, not that it is a waste of time to give such instructions in English, but that the response to classroom instruction is not always evidence of comprehension of the language used.

In fact when we are faced with situations where a great deal depends on accurate comprehension, we realise that it is not easy at all. Most people who have had to operate in a FL overseas can recall incidents which brought this truth home to them. My own moment of truth – and panic – came in a French suburban station when I just didn't know whether the announcement was telling me to change trains or stay on the one I was on. Such incidents should remind us that our students too may well need much more specific, concentrated listening practice.

(ii) Another reason why specific practice in listening comprehension may be neglected is that some audio-lingual courses appear to give a great deal of incidental practice through pattern drills and dialogues. Yet if we examine these activities we find that many of them demand very little in the way of 'real' listening. Once the pattern in a drill has been established, the learner often has to listen for only a single cue word in order to produce the required response. Much traditional dialogue work is even less demanding, as each participant knows exactly what the other is going to say. All he has to listen for is the silence that tells him it is his turn to speak. Again, I am saying, not that such activities are worthless for developing other skills, but that we should not imagine that they provide adequate comprehension practice.

Recent emphasis on the use of communication games, information gap activities and dialogues with cue cards (see Chapter 5) is partly an attempt to give more realistic practice in comprehension as well as production.

Part 2: The process of comprehension

In this part I want to look at some of the common factors involved in comprehending both spoken and written material. Part 3 will deal with differences between listening and reading.

Our knowledge of the process of comprehension is sketchy; so indeed is our knowledge of the total learning process, as outlined in Chapter 1. We cannot be sure that we know about *all* the factors involved but we can make some reasonable guesses about some of them. What happens when we comprehend a written or spoken message in our MT? The process is probably something like this:

A Perception – cracking the code

First we have to be able to recognise and discriminate between contrasting sounds or letter and word shapes. This aspect of the perception of speech is dealt with in Chapter 2; the code-cracking process for reading is discussed in Chapter 4.

B Decoding – making sense of the message

Each short stretch of meaningful material which is read or heard has to be

(i) recognised as meaningful and understood on reception
(ii) held in the short-term memory (STM) long enough for it to be
(iii) related to what has gone before and/or what follows.

Out of this process come pieces of information which can be stored in the long-term memory (LTM) for recall later.

As pointed out in Chapter 1, what we remember later, and presumably what is stored in the LTM, is this more general information – the gist of the message, not a whole sequence of the short stretches of material which we held briefly in the STM.

We can show the whole process in the form of a model.

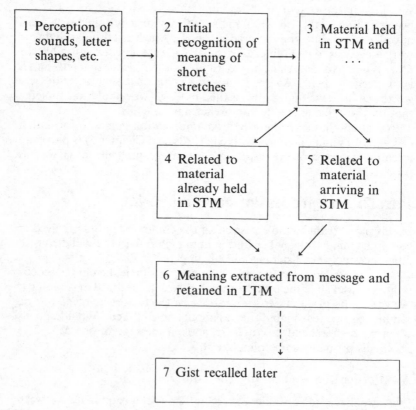

It must be remembered that stages 1 to 6 follow each other with extreme rapidity and that the processing time available within the STM may be very short indeed.

Stages 2, 3, 4 and 5 in the model involve not only the recognition of lexical meaning but the perception of grammatical relationships as signalled by such things as word order, tense markers and various 'structure' words whose function it is to show such relationships. We also have to recognise the relationships between various substitute forms and the items they refer to. Pronouns are the obvious example, but auxiliary verbs are frequently used to refer back to quite long stretches of material.

e.g.   Sam promised to give me a lift down to Brighton at the weekend but last night he rang up to say he *can't* now.

Demonstrative pronouns, like 'this' often refer back to whole arguments or concepts discussed earlier. (This means we need to give students practice in *this*!)

C   Prediction and selection – redundancy to the rescue

Although the process just outlined sounds and is complex, our task is made easier by our ability to *predict* what is likely to come next and our ability to *select* which stretches of material we will pay maximum attention to and which we need not bother too much about.

Prediction and selection are both possible partly as a result of what is known as redundancy. When we talk to someone, there are many things which may cause the hearer to lose part of the message e.g. fatigue, noise, distraction. Languages protect messages against such loss by giving more information than would be necessary if transmission and reception were perfect. This provision is called 'redundancy'. Thus in *normal* circumstances of noise, etc., 'redundant' information is *vital* for the protection of the message. In everyday use, the word 'redundant' means 'unnecessary', but in the scientific use employed here, it means 'necessary as a safeguard for communication'! For example, suppose a speaker says:

She   put on   her   gloves to keep   her self warm.

The competent hearer may miss any one or even two of the three boxed items and still understand the message. Thus any two of the three are 'redundant'. This is why we can understand telegrams, messages distorted by loudspeakers or faulty telephone lines, and stretches of terrible handwriting. Some people can apparently read a newspaper and listen to a radio programme at the same time and get the main points from both sources of information.

We can often predict specific items with a high degree of accuracy. For instance, in a British setting there is little doubt about the missing items in the following:

> As we hadn't eaten all day we were really _____.
> Fortunately the chip shop was still open so we bought two big bags of fish __ _____.

If we *know* what is coming we have, in a sense, already understood it before we hear it. This ability to predict is invaluable in listening.

We can also make predictions which are much less specific but which are still helpful, as they prepare us for what follows. For example, many words and phrases used to link sentences and clauses lead us to expect that the next thing we hear or read will be a reason (*because*), a contrasting statement (*but, however*), a result (*so, therefore*), an addition (*also, not only that*), a rephrasing (*in other words, that is to say*), or an example (*for instance*).

Similarly (What does 'similarly' tell you?) words like 'secondly', 'finally', tell us that a new point is about to be made and openings like 'I'd like to make three points . . .', or 'There are four stages in the process' give us some idea about what to expect.

In speech we get additional cues from intonation and stress. If we hear:

> 'I'd like to help you . . .!',

we need hardly wait for the 'but' or the excuse which will certainly follow.

Selection is possible, then, partly because of our ability to predict; we can momentarily 'switch off' if we are convinced that we know what is coming. But efficient listeners and readers never switch off completely, because they have learnt that their predictions are occasionally wrong; the unexpected sometimes happens and we have to be prepared to modify our expectations in the light of what we actually hear or read.

> A: I'm just going down to the pub for a quick . . .
> B: Pint?
> A: No, a quick word with the landlord.

We can also read or listen selectively in a more general sense if we have a specific purpose in mind and are interested only in information on a particular topic. We have the ability to filter out, if listening, or skim over, if reading, sections which are not relevant to our particular purpose.

When comprehending material in our MT, then, our task is made easier by this ability to select and predict; we can to a certain extent relax, let our attention wander slightly, ignore some of the incoming signals and anticipate others. All of this imposes less of a strain on the STM; it has less material to process and a little more time in which to process it.

D   Comprehension of FL material

With material in a FL the general process of comprehension is, presumably, similar but with the following factors making it more difficult:

(i) All the stages in the process are likely to take longer; it takes us longer to recognise 'familiar' elements as familiar, and longer to see the relationships between the successive short stretches of material. When reading, we may want to keep looking back to check that our initial assessment of such relationships is correct, and this will slow us down further; when listening, we cannot do this easily.

(ii) At each stage we are much more likely to make mistakes: to fail to discriminate correctly between contrasting forms; to confuse one word with another that looks or sounds similar; to misunderstand or fail to see important grammatical relationships. This can be a cumulative process so that we end up getting a completely wrong idea or getting completely confused.

(iii) We are very much more likely to come across stretches of language which we do not understand at all. We have then either to devise ways of working out their meaning from context or to train ourselves to ignore what we cannot understand, in the hope that we will still get the gist of the message or that the full meaning will become clear later.

(iv) As we are much less familiar with the FL it is more difficult for us to anticipate and predict and we cannot select with the same degree of confidence. We are less sure what is important so we try to pay equal attention to everything. Thus more processing time is taken up, and less remains in which to attempt to predict and select.

(v) Our STM for FL material is likely to be much less efficient. All the factors mentioned above place extra burdens on it. It may, not surprisingly, stop working altogether from time to time, resulting in that complete lack of comprehension which is familiar to all FL learners.

We shall return to these difficulties in Part 4, where I shall suggest ways in which we can help learners to overcome them.

Part 3: Some differences between reading and listening comprehension

So far we have been looking at comprehension processes common to both reading and listening. But there are some important differences which should be remembered when choosing or devising listening exercises. The first six differences mentioned below tend to make listening more difficult than reading:

(i) Initial perception may be more difficult as there is the possibility of a greater range of variation in the way different speakers produce the 'same' sounds. Think of all the varieties of vowel sounds used by speakers with different accents and compare this with the much narrower range of variation in types of print. This is an important point to consider if your students are going to come into contact with a variety of English speakers, not only native speakers of English but others whose pronunciation of English is affected by their own MT.

(ii) Speech is much more likely to be distorted by various types of noise. Think of telephone conversations, announcements over public address systems and conversations in crowded, noisy places. If we are really interested in written material we can shut out many distractions but this is more difficult with speech, and it demands a greater degree of concentration.

(iii) The listener has little or no control over the speed of the input of spoken material. He can occasionally ask someone to slow down but in most circumstances his comprehension just has to try to keep pace with the speed at which the message is being delivered.

(iv) Spoken material is usually heard only once. There are a few exceptions to this (see point (vi) below), but in most cases we cannot go back and 're-hear' material in the same way that we can re-read it and we certainly cannot keep going back and checking that we heard correctly while the message is still coming in, because we just cannot stop the flow.

(v) As we cannot stop the inflow of information we have very little time in which to try to work out the meaning of unfamiliar stretches of material. (See page 63, Part 2, D(iii).) We just have to keep on paying attention to the new material coming in and hope that we will get the general idea.

(vi) The listener sometimes has to deal *simultaneously* with another task. This applies not only to formal note-taking but to other tasks like taking down directions or messages from telephone calls.

The next four differences can make listening easier than reading.

(vii) Spoken material is normally much less densely packed with information than written material. I am talking here about genuine spoken material, not written texts read aloud. There is usually much more repetition, not necessarily exact repetition but rephrasing and recasting. Sometimes this is marked by such phrases as – 'I mean . . .', 'What I'm trying to say is . . .'; but we also often hear or read the same idea simply repeated in slightly different words. This, of course, is only a help to the listener if he *recognises* it as repetition. For the learner who has not reached the stage where he can readily recognise the same idea in different words, this aspect of spoken material may be an added difficulty.

Another thing which makes the information less dense and which, like repetition, partly compensates for the listener's lack of control over speed, is the number of pauses and hesitations in normal speech.

(viii) If he knows how to interpret them, the listener gets considerable help in comprehension from such aspects of speech as intonation and the placing of stress. These are not available to the reader, who has to rely on the hints provided by such devices as punctuation. Through intonation and stress the speaker can make grammatical relationships clearer, and emphasise what is important or new. At the same time he de-emphasises asides, parenthetical remarks and less important material and this helps the listener in the process of selection.

It is important to remember, however, that all this help is available only to those who have learned how to use it. Learners whose MTs have very different intonation systems and stress patterns from those of English may need considerable help and practice in this area.

(ix) In many circumstances, the listener gets additional cues to meaning from outside the language itself. These may come from his knowledge of what to expect in the general situation (see Part 1), from various gestures made by the speaker, and so on.

(x) In conversation the listener can ask for clarification of something he is unsure of. Students need to be taught appropriate ways of doing this so that they will be able to ask for further explanation confidently and without causing offence.

Part 4: Developing listening skills

A Types of listening material students may need to be able to comprehend

If we are going to help learners to develop listening skills we need to consider what types of material they will *ultimately* want or need to listen to. Of course, it is not always possible to predict this with any accuracy, especially if you are teaching in a TENOR situation. (See Chapter 1.)

However, you may be able to make some reasonable guesses. The following should serve as a check-list to help you to ensure that you have not left out something that may be of real importance to your students in the future.

1 Dialogue

(i) Unscripted, spontaneous conversations and discussions between (a) the learner and other FL speakers, (b) the learner and native English speakers, (c) other FL and/or native speakers without the learner participating.

Such material may contain a great deal of repetition, rephrasing and hesitation. (There will, that is, be a high degree of redundancy.) There may be a variety of accents to cope with. Speed of delivery will vary greatly and may sometimes be rapid. There will be many 'short forms', unstressed words, elliptical sentences and perhaps unfinished sentences.

(ii) Scripted conversation, e.g. dialogue in plays and films, usually between native speakers. This often tries to simulate authentic conversation and many of the characteristics will be the same. In fact there is

65

usually much less redundancy, though it may be easier to follow than authentic conversation as it tends to be better organised.

2 Monologue

(i) Prepared but unscripted talks such as lessons and lectures delivered from outline notes. This will contain some repetition, rephrasing and hesitation, but not as much as spontaneous conversation. Accent and speed will vary, though very rapid speech is unlikely.

(ii) Spoken instructions and public announcements. These tend to be high in information density but usually fairly short and often repeated in identical form. If public address systems are used or there is a lot of general noise, they may be difficult to hear. Accents may vary but speed will be fairly uniform and moderate.

(iii) Formal scripted talks, lectures and news bulletins read aloud (sometimes called 'spoken prose'). These are very similar to written texts. They have high information-density and little repetition. They are usually delivered at moderate speed in a fairly deliberate style. The speaker will most frequently use whatever accent is considered standard in his part of the world.

There is no suggestion that we should expose learners to all these varieties from the beginning, but if we are aware of our ultimate aims and of the potential range of listening materials, we may avoid some of the mistakes of the teachers of students A and C referred to in the introductory examples.

B Ways of developing skills

There are basically two ways of helping people to develop skills. One is just to give them plenty of graded practice and hope that they will work out for themselves the most efficient way of coping with it. This can be a useful method but it may be inefficient, as it is time-consuming and it assumes that everyone will in fact arrive at the most satisfactory solution of their own accord. Unfortunately not everyone does; many learners become addicted to rather inefficient ways of doing things quite early on and never abandon them.

The other way is to try to find out how efficient practitioners of the skill operate, to isolate the more specific sub-skills which the process entails, then to devise activities and exercises which focus on the development of these sub-skills.

This may well be a more efficient method, provided that we do, in fact, know what the process entails. As I said in Part 2, we can make reasonable guesses about the process of comprehension but we certainly do not know everything about all the factors that may be involved. For this reason, I think we need to use both methods of developing listening (and reading) skills.

We need to give both general practice and exercises which focus on such things as developing the ability to listen selectively, to recognise repetition and rephrasing, to make predictions and modify predictions, to make use of the information provided by linking words and markers of grammatical relationships, to extract the gist of a message without necessarily understanding every word of it. We also need to give practice in such a way that the whole process of FL comprehension is gradually speeded up.

Older established procedures for developing comprehension tend to emphasise general practice; a text is presented, followed by questions, often on matters of detail. More recently developed procedures emphasise the second, skills analysis, approach and of course such exercises do give general practice as well. It is on this latter type of exercise that I will concentrate in the rest of this chapter.

C Making the learner's task easier

The type of practice you give to any particular group of learners will obviously be influenced by the types of material you think they will eventually want to listen to. But neither the material nor the circumstances in which they listen to it need be exactly like the 'target' situation right from the start. In view of all the learner's difficulties outlined in Part 3 you will have to use a more gradual approach to 'the real thing'. The learner cannot really control his FL listening experiences but you can control them for him in various ways.

(i) You can select material of appropriate interest level. Students perform better with material they *want* to listen to because they enjoy it. Apart from catering for any specialist interests you may know about, you should find the following generally useful: jokes, personal anecdotes, human interest stories, material containing some puzzle to be solved, and serialised stories.

(ii) You can use your prior knowledge of the material to guide the listeners. This may be done in two ways:
    (a) You can introduce the topic with a short discussion; for example you could announce the title or say the first sentence and ask what they think it will be about. This arouses certain expectations and makes the students mentally prepared for the topic; it may also activate latent knowledge of vocabulary associated with the topic. Some teachers use this time as an opportunity to ensure that vocabulary *essential* to an understanding of the exercise is known. Only essential items whose meaning cannot be worked out in any other way should be dealt with like this, however, as one of the important skills learners must develop is how to deal with 'new' vocabulary themselves. It is sometimes useful to prepare students by *mentioning* a particular word first and saying, 'You will hear this word in the exercise. I don't think you know it but you should be able to work out what it means.'
    (b) Perhaps most important of all, you can help students to be

selective by giving them a purpose for listening. Give *a few* questions *before* the first hearing, or ask them to pick out the 3 main points, or the main steps in a process. Set tasks which entail concentrating on certain features and filtering out irrelevant information. (See examples in Part 5, B.)

(iii) You can select material at an appropriate level of linguistic difficulty as regards syntax and vocabulary.

(iv) You can control the length of the material. Listening exercises should be shorter than reading texts, especially in the earlier stages. If you want to use a longer exercise, split it up into short sections and ask questions appropriate to each short section as you go along.

(v) You can repeat the material. This is obvious but needs to be done with care. In most target situations material will be heard only once. It is, therefore, a good idea to give students something specific to listen for, even on first hearing, to prove that they can get some information from a single hearing. It may be something very simple like the number of people involved or 'what happened to X in the end?' It is amazing how often students are prepared to listen to the same thing over and over again provided that they are given a good reason for doing so, like trying to answer specific questions or solving some sort of problem.

(vi) You can control the speed of delivery and clarity of diction. This again is obvious but it is very easy to take it too far. Students who will eventually have to listen to speech at full speed and with native-speaker fluency (with short forms, unstressed words, etc.) should be weaned off careful, slow speech as quickly as possible. Another important reason for not going too slowly is that in very slow speech the useful cues to grammatical relationships provided by intonation are obscured, and extremely slow speech actually places a greater burden on the STM because by the time the voice reaches the end of a sentence the learner may have forgotten how it started. If you want to make things easier in the early stages by controlling speed, it is better to deliver each sentence at a moderate speed but pause rather longer than you normally would, *between* sentences. This gives the listener a little more time to process the information without distorting the normal speech patterns.

(vii) You can control the variety and types of accents and the amount of noise and other distortions.

D Providing feed-back

Students need to be given some idea of how well they have understood something they have listened to. Of course, they have their own personal assessment but, as we have seen, this may be unreliable. Part of a teacher's job is to provide some form of outside, objective assessment. This is, of course, similar to testing; but it should be a form of testing which puts the interests of the learner first rather than those of the test or the administrator. There are in fact many problems involved in the assessment of comprehension; some of them were touched on in Part 2 of this chapter, and others are dealt with in Chapter 7.

Basically the problem consists of finding a way in which the student can demonstrate how well he has understood the comprehension material without this being obscured by other factors. Thus a student may have understood the material while he was listening to it but be unable

(i) to understand the question (this applies particularly to multiple-choice questions); or

(ii) to formulate and produce a satisfactory answer; or

(iii) to remember the answer.

Obviously, full comprehension requires an ability to remember the information received; it is pretty pointless listening at all if you are going to forget everything immediately. But the LTM for FL material may be quite short in the earlier stages and may take some time to develop, so if we want to provide students with feed-back on their powers of *comprehension* we should not set tasks which rely too heavily on memory.

E Information transfer exercises

Information transfer exercises are very useful here. These involve *receiving* information in one form, e.g. verbal, and transferring the information, or selected pieces of it, to another form, e.g. diagrams, graphs, lines on maps, labels, etc. The same technique can also be used for reading comprehension.

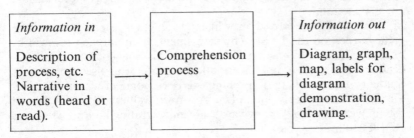

Information in		Information out
Description of process, etc. Narrative in words (heard or read).	Comprehension process	Diagram, graph, map, labels for diagram demonstration, drawing.

Here is an example:

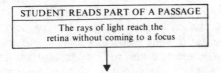

STUDENT READS PART OF A PASSAGE

The rays of light reach the retina without coming to a focus

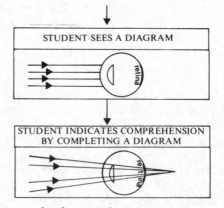

The information can also be transferred in the opposite direction, i.e. you can *start* with a diagram, or graph, etc. and transfer the information into spoken or written form. Or you can use a cyclic principle and incorporate some written work as demonstrated in the 'Weekday Islands' exercise on page 72. In this example the non-verbal response to the listening exercise provides a convenient prompt for the composition process, leading to a written summary.

The advantages of using information transfer exercises in listening comprehension are:

(i) Straightforward non-verbal responses, such as the drawing of lines on a diagram, can be carried out and assessed without any interference from the student's ability to *produce* samples of language. Recognising or writing short labels involves an absolute minimum of linguistic production. We can fairly claim that we are assessing comprehension, not production.

(ii) As the tasks are carried out while the student is listening, there is no great burden on the LTM. Any assessment of comprehension will be uncontaminated by memory factors. (This, of course, can be a disadvantage if you use information transfer exercises *exclusively*. Students need a variety of listening exercises, some of which will bring the LTM increasingly into play. As most well-established types of listening exercise do this anyway, I am concentrating here on what may be a less familiar type.)

(iii) The fact that the student has to do two things at once – listen and perform a simple task – is valuable preparation for the much more complex task of note-taking later. (See Part 5 below.)

(iv) To perform the task, the student has to select the relevant information and filter out the rest. He knows in advance what type of information he is listening for and will be constantly trying to anticipate whether what he wants is likely to be in the next stretch of language or not. Thus this type of exercise helps to develop the ability to *select* and *predict*, two of the important sub-skills discussed in Part 2 above.

Part 5: Examples of exercises

A Exercises with focus on anticipation and prediction

1 Short completion exercises.   Students are asked to provide (orally or in writing) a likely ending to the unfinished final sentence. They have no idea how long the text you are reading to them will be or when you will stop so they are constantly trying to predict what will follow. Do not let them shout out.

---

e.g. 1 Last night there was a story on the news about a monkey that escaped from a zoo. It did quite a lot of damage to some vegetable gardens and it frightened several children playing in the park. They caught it in the end in a house not far from the zoo. They think it got into the house by . . .

Conversations, which are best taped, are useful for this type of exercise.

---

e.g. 2 A: What are you looking for?
      B: The screwdriver.
      A: What do you want the screwdriver for?
      B: I was feeling cold and we can't use the electric fire until I fit a new plug. But I can't find the screwdriver anywhere.
      A: Well why don't you . . .

Such exercises can also be used to draw attention to the significance of various linking devices. If the last word is 'because', a reason is expected, if it is 'but', 'however' or 'on the other hand', a contrasting statement is likely.

---

e.g. 3 A: Would you like to come round for a drink tonight? We could look at my slides of our trip to Wigan.
      B: I'd love to but . . .

The significant word is not necessarily the last one of course.

---

e.g. 4 Although the dealer told Sam that it would be easy to get spare parts for his car, when it needed a new clutch plate he . . .

An alternative form of this type of completion exercise provides the student with a choice of possible endings on the BB or on a handout. For instance, for e.g. 2 the choice might be:
    Well why don't you:
    (i) buy a new plug?

71

    (ii) use your pocket knife?
    (iii) just stop shivering?

2 Longer completion exercises.   For these a longer spoken text is used with a number of stopping places, at which predictions can be elicited; then the 'correct' completion is given so that the story can continue. Some texts, with suggestions for their use, will be found in *What Next?* (See Further Reading.)

B Information transfer exercises with focus on selection, anticipation and the modification of expectations

1 The Exploration of the Weekday Islands
Notes on presentation
(i) Make sure that students understand the points of the compass as this is *essential* to the exercise.
(ii) Try to make it sound as though you are *telling* a story rather than reading it aloud. You may find this easier if you do not keep exactly to the text but change the wording in places and perhaps add a few extra little details. This increases the redundancy, reduces the density of relevant information and gives students more time to carry out their task. But do not read it slowly.

THE EXPLORATION OF THE WEEKDAY ISLANDS

You've got a map † of the Weekday Islands. They were discovered in 1720 by Captain Short. I'm going to tell you about Captain Short's voyage in the islands and about how the main islands got their names. As you listen, I want you to draw a line on the map showing the way his ship went. Draw a small circle at the places where he anchored and write the name of each island on it or near it. All right?

First, draw a compass like this in the top right hand corner of the map. (T draws compass on BB and if necessary establishes that major points are known.)

Captain Short came from the north of the group of islands, so start your line at the top of the page near the centre. The first land he saw was the large, circular island in the north of the group. He anchored in the large bay on its west coast and went ashore. As it was a Monday, he called this island Monday Island.

The next day, he sailed along the south coast of Monday Island and in the distance he saw the coast of a long, narrow island to the south east. He landed at its northern end and noticed that the island was very fertile. There were fruit trees and herds of wild pigs. It was Tuesday when he landed so he called this island Tuesday Island.

† The map on p. 73 is the *solution*. The students' maps would not show the route or the islands' names.

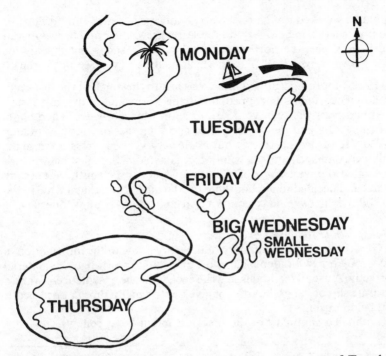

The following day, he sailed south along the east coast of Tuesday Island, but it was very cloudy that day so he didn't see the small island to the south west of Tuesday Island. He continued sailing south until he came to two small islands. He anchored in the narrow passage between these two islands and named the larger one Big Wednesday and the smaller one Small Wednesday. He called the narrow passage between the two islands the Midweek Straits.

While his men were looking for fresh water on Big Wednesday, they met some of the inhabitants, who spoke a language similar to the language of Spring Island where Captain Short and his crew had recently spent several months. The inhabitants of Big Wednesday said there was a large mountainous island to the south west.

Captain Short set sail for this island and soon sighted its northern tip. But he couldn't find anywhere to land, so he sailed west along its northern coast; then south along the west coast; then he sailed east along the south coast; but the island seemed to be surrounded by high cliffs. Then he turned north and sailed along the east coast until he came to a small, rocky bay. He anchored there and named the island Thursday Island.

But Captain Short and his men didn't stay long on Thursday Island. A storm arose early in the evening and the Captain was afraid that his ship

73

would be wrecked on the rocks. So he sailed east, intending to ride out the storm in the open water. But the storm grew worse and he was driven north west, past the northern tip of Thursday Island and, luckily for him, between five small islands which he didn't even see in the dark.

By Friday morning Captain Short was just to the north of the five small islands. The wind had dropped, but in the storm a lot of the ship's fresh food had been washed overboard or ruined by salt water. Then Short remembered about the wild pigs and good supplies of fruit on Tuesday Island. He turned north east but made very slow progress because his sails were damaged and the wind was against him. Still, just before dark he sighted the west coast of the small island to the south of Tuesday Island and decided to anchor there for the night. And that's why, in the Weekday Islands, Friday comes between Tuesday and Wednesday.

Some possible follow-up exercises
(i) Give the students a summary of the story but with the information in the wrong order. Students can work in groups to arrange the material correctly. A useful method is to write each sentence or sentence-part on a separate slip of paper; but do not give out too many slips at once as this can be confusing.

A jumbled summary of the first part might be as follows.

---

1 This is because Captain Short did not discover it until Friday,
2 To the south east of Monday is Tuesday Island which was discovered the following day,
3 The Weekday Islands were discovered in 1720 by Captain Short.
4 This is a large circular island in the north of the group.
5 but the small island to the south of Tuesday is not called Wednesday as might be expected.
6 The first to be sighted was Monday Island.
7 as it was covered in cloud when he was first in the area.
8 They are named after the days of the week on which they were discovered.

(ii) In addition or as an alternative to the above, students could be given a writing task based on the listening exercise. The following is an exercise I have used. It avoids getting involved in the technicalities of latitude and longitude which an 'authentic' ship's log would entail:

On Captain Short's ship there was a young sailor called Fred. He could read and write and he kept a diary. He did not write very much each day and he knew very little about navigation. This is what he wrote on the evening of Monday January 11th 1720.

We continued sailing south and came to an island. We anchored in a large bay and some of us went ashore. When we asked Captain Short what he was going to call the island he couldn't think of a name at first. Then he said, 'Well, today's Monday; let's call it Monday Island'.

Now write down what you think the sailor put in his diary on the other days of that week.

2 The Millers' Family Tree

Notes

(i) This can only be done with students familiar with kinship terms in English. It was originally written to help to revise such terms.

(ii) Make sure students understand the symbols for male and female or use others they are familiar with.

(iii) Quite a lot more padding can be usefully added.

(iv) Further notes on this exercise are given in brackets.

T: This is the family tree of the Miller family. (Puts it on BB and gets class to copy.)

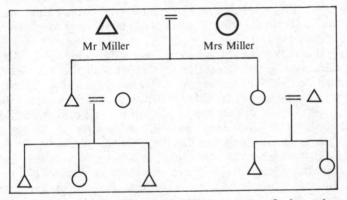

T: I'm going to tell you a story, and I want you to find out the names of the Millers' children, their son-in-law, their daughter-in-law and their grandchildren.

(Note: Expectation created. Purpose in listening and therefore task of selection clearly defined.)

THE MILLER FAMILY

Many years ago when Mr Miller was a young man, he enjoyed playing tennis. There was a girl called Ruth who also went to the tennis club. Mr Miller and Ruth fell in love. They became engaged and not long afterwards they got married. About a year later their first child was born.

(Note: Attention aroused, relevant information expected.)

75

He was a boy and they called him Sam. A few years went by before they had any more children. They hoped they'd have a little girl next time and they did.

(Note: Expectation aroused.)

Mr Miller wanted to call her Margaret but Mrs Miller said it was an unlucky name in her family. They talked about it for several days and in the end they chose the name Mary.

(Note: Listeners need to modify expectations and 'filter out' the section about Margaret.)

The two children, Sam and Mary, grew up.

(Note: Confirmation of correct answers.)

They both did well at school and later Sam went to a teachers' college. While he was there he became a very good friend of the Principal's daughter who was also at the college. Her name was Liz. They became engaged and

(Note: Expectation aroused. Shortly to be confirmed.)

as soon as they were qualified they got married.

About a year later, old Mr and Mrs Miller were delighted when their first grandchild was born. It was a boy and his parents named him Jack.

(Note: variation between 'chose the name', 'called him', 'named him'. This is deliberate here but could be reduced to one form to simplify the text.)

The year that Jack was born was a very busy and exciting one for Mr and Mrs Miller because at Easter their daughter Mary also got married – to a boy called Bert she had met at school. Mr and Mrs Miller thought she was a little young to get married, but Bert was a nice boy so they didn't really mind. They were very happy when at the end of that year Mary and Bert also had a son. They called him Alan after Mr Miller.

The following year Liz and Sam had their second child, a daughter who they called Ruth after old Mrs Miller; and it wasn't very long before Bert and Mary also had a daughter who they decided to call Freda.

(Note: In this section the vital information is made much more dense and students have to work more quickly.)

When Liz and Sam's third child was born they couldn't decide on a name for him for a long time. At first, they thought of Alexander, a name they both liked, but it seemed such a long name for such a little baby. One of their friends suggested Francis but Mr Miller said it was also a girl's name. In the end they asked Bert and Mary to choose a name for the little boy and they chose one very like their own daughter's name. They called him _____?

(Note: In this section expectations are again aroused and have to be modified. In fact there are various signals which indicate 'this is not the final answer yet'. These could be focused on in this and subsequent exercises at a fairly advanced level. In this case the signals come mainly from 'At first' and intonation cues.

The final name could, of course, be given depending on the group's knowledge of related names.

Obviously the whole exercise would be better with local names and the story modified to suit local culture. It can be followed up with a 'find their ages now' exercise. This has denser information and revises kinship terms. You may have to repeat it several times.

e.g. *Find the ages*

Mr Miller is 63 and his wife is 61.

Their son is 40.

He has a nephew aged 17.

Jack is 18 and one of his cousins is 15.

Fred's mother is 37 and her sister-in-law is 36.

Mary has a niece aged 16.

Mr and Mrs Miller's other grandson is 14 and his uncle is 44.)

C Listening games, competitions, problem solving exercises, etc.

These activities provide general listening practice. The element of competition or problem solving increases motivation.

1 Spot the change.   A text is read aloud, then read a second time with alterations of meaning. Students have to spot the changes in the second version. This can be made into a team game with points awarded along the following lines:

1 point for spotting a change.

2 points for remembering the original version.

Lose a point for saying there is a change where there isn't one.

This is a very easy exercise to prepare and can be based on newspaper articles, sections of reading exercises, etc.

As a variation you can use part of a reading text which you have just dealt with. There may then be no need for a first reading.

2 Spot the contradiction.   A similar game can be played by making changes in a text so that there are internal contradictions in it. This is more difficult to prepare.

In the following example the 'correct' version is given in brackets.

Robert was a wealthy young farmer. He was about 85 (35) years old and still a bachelor. His father was dead but his mother-in-law (mother) was still alive. His only brother was called Fred.

Robert had a big house, hundreds of cows, a big blue Rolls Royce car but no wife and this made him sad. His mother, a kind old man (woman) aged 17 (70) said he should go away for a holiday. She said his father (brother) would look after the factory (farm) while he was away.

A few days later Robert woke up early in the morning, just after 6 p.m. (a.m.). He ate his supper (breakfast) quickly, said goodnight (goodbye) to his mother and spoke for just a few hours (minutes) to his brother George (Fred) who was already milking the hens (cows). Then he set off in his beautiful yellow (blue) Rolls Royce, etc.

3 Who lives where?   This is a frequently-used exercise which calls for attentive listening. Very few students can solve it on first hearing, so on each repetition they have to listen selectively for the information they require to complete their own diagram. The exercise also revises certain prepositions.

Bird Lane
T: Six people live in Bird Lane. Their names are:
       Mrs Rook, Mr Sparrow, Miss Robins, Mr Hawk, Miss Starling and Mrs Crow.
(T writes these names on the BB in random order.)
Here is a plan of the lane. Copy it down and then we'll see if you can work out who lives in which house . . . Ready?

Plan and main text:

1	3	5
BIRD LANE		
2	4	6

Mrs Rook lives in number 1 and Mr Hawk lives in the house opposite to her. Miss Robins lives between Mr Sparrow and Mrs Rook. Miss Robins often visits Mrs Crow, the old lady who lives between Mr Hawk and Miss Starling.

When this has been completed they can go on to note down the inhabitants' pets, their jobs, the colours of their curtains, etc., etc. Here is an example.

Additional text:

Mrs Crow has a black cat. It is very frightened of the big dog that belongs to the man who lives next door. This big dog often barks at the parrot that lives in a cage in the window of the house opposite. The woman in the house next door to the black cat had two white mice but now she has only one because the cat caught the other one one day when she left the window open. The cat would also like to eat the goldfish which lives between the parrot and a white rabbit.

You will find other ideas for listening games and puzzles in Wright et al.

D Note-taking exercises

Note-taking is a complex activity which combines listening, selecting, summarising and writing skills. It is best approached gradually by way of exercises which help and guide the process of selection, summary and organisation. Many information transfer exercises are in fact highly controlled note-taking exercises and are very useful in the earlier stages.

You can also prepare short talks and give students incomplete outlines of the main points, which they can complete as they listen to the talk. As they become more proficient you can reduce the amount of support by, for example, giving only occasional headings and the *number* of points to be noted.

A good source of ideas for note-taking practice at more advanced levels is the course by James, Jordan, and Matthews.

E Other sources of material

Apart from using published material, which is often in the form of a text plus a tape or cassette, you can make up exercises of your own by adapting material from newspapers, magazines, and textbooks. You have to be careful *not* just to read out the written material, however. (See 'Weekday Islands' exercise.) Always try to make it sound like a talk, rather than a text read aloud. If possible, record the material sometimes, trying to get a variety of voices and accents if appropriate.

If you have a radio cassette, the radio is a very good source of varied listening material. This is usually better than listening to direct broadcasts in class as it gives you a chance to listen first and prepare suitable questions and exercises.

F Extensive listening

I have been concentrating in this chapter on what some people would call 'intensive' listening, i.e. the students listen to fairly short 'texts' and carry out specific tasks set by the teacher, such as answering questions or making some non-verbal response. Extensive listening activities use material which is usually longer and easier. Detailed tasks are not set, though the teacher may indicate broadly what to listen for and ask one or two questions at the end to check that the main points have been understood. Extensive listening gives students general practice, increases their exposure to the language and ought to be enjoyable.

In the early stages of a course, jokes and personal anecdotes are useful for this; they are enjoyable and you can tell if at least some people have understood by their response to the humour.

At more advanced levels, radio plays, films, and stage plays are excellent but it can be discouraging if full length plays and films are introduced too early. Authentic conversations, with background noise as in real life, should also be used when possible.

Listening to pop songs is also a form of extensive listening and can be a powerful motivating factor in some situations.

If facilities are available, much extensive listening can be done individually, either in a language laboratory or at home using borrowed cassettes. Some teachers make their own recordings of 'talking books', reading aloud the texts of books known to be popular with students. The students then either just listen, or listen and follow the text at the same time. This is an excellent way of reinforcing and extending knowledge of the language. 'Talking book' cassettes are also available commercially.

Further reading

RIVERS, W. *Teaching foreign language skills.* University of Chicago Press, 1968.
> Chapter 6 deals with the stages of development of listening abilities for FL material and suggests activities for each stage.

HEATON, J. *Writing English language tests.* Longman, 1975.
> Although this is concerned primarily with testing, many of the wide variety of suggested tests can be adapted as practice exercises. Do beware of simply testing your students. See especially Chapter 5.

JAMES, K. and MULLEN, L. *Inspector Thackeray calls.* Longman Structural Readers, 1974.
> Short plays useful for extensive listening at intermediate level. The listener is invited to spot the criminal's mistakes and beat the detective to the solution.

UNDERWOOD, M. *Listen to this.* Oxford University Press, 1971.
> Short recorded conversations about people's jobs. A variety of accents is used.

UNDERWOOD, M. *What a story!* Oxford University Press, 1976.
> Unscripted recordings of anecdotes, followed by questions. You could, of course, adapt these by asking some questions first.

ABBOTT, G. *What next?* Longman, 1976.
> A collection of stories arranged as anticipation exercises (see Part 5, Section A 2 above).

WRIGHT, A. et al. *Games for language learning.* Cambridge University Press, 1979.
> Contains ideas for listening games and puzzles (see Part 5, Section C 3 above).

JAMES, K., JORDAN, R. and MATTHEWS, A. *Listening comprehension and note-taking course.* Collins, 1979.
> Material for note-taking practice (see Part 5, Section D above).

Chapter 4: Comprehension and reading

by John Greenwood

EXAMPLE 1

T:	Turn to page 103. Look at the reading passage. Maria, start reading.
Maria:	In one nine and four . . .
T:	No. Nineteen -oh-four.
Maria:	In nineteen-oh-four Mr Smith . . .
T:	No. *Mrs* Smith . . .
Maria:	. . . Mrs Smith died.
T:	Sirio, go on with the next sentence.
Sirio:	After ten years . . .
T:	No, we've read that sentence already. Wake up. We're up to line 18 . . .

EXAMPLE 2

The learners are silently reading a text in order to complete a worksheet which the teacher has given them. Since they are working independently of the teacher, the teacher is able to circulate round the class, helping individual learners on occasion and checking that the reading task is being tackled adequately by all.

Part 1: What is reading?

Confronted with two such contrasting situations, most teachers would agree that **EXAMPLE 2** shows the more desirable and effective teaching. However, I believe it is fair to claim that the activity in **EXAMPLE 1** is a more common practice than the purposeful silent reading activity in **EXAMPLE 2**. Many a teacher has asked me on a teacher-training course: 'What is wrong with getting the learners to read aloud? It's good pronunciation practice.' Asking your learners to read aloud is of little value in helping them to develop into efficient readers. Normally, reading is a silent and individual activity, since the writer's expectation was that the text would be read, not heard. There are indeed some written texts which are meant to be read aloud and listened to, such as news bulletins on television and radio. These are relatively few, however, and the vast majority of learners will not need to learn how to be competent news-readers. Of course, you as a teacher of English need a high level of skill in reading aloud, since you need to provide a good model of the written language for your learners to listen to.

As **EXAMPLE 1** above shows, learners are usually very poor at reading aloud: mistakes and hesitations provide a bad model for the other learners to listen to. As for the unfortunate victim who is forced to read aloud, he is often merely mouthing meaningless language because of lack of rehearsal and time to comprehend what he has to read aloud. No wonder the learners become bored and the teacher soon gets irritated.

The use of reading aloud for pronunciation practice bears little relationship to silent reading. Moreover, if the teacher really wants to do pronunciation work, it is spoken, not written, material that is needed. If it is the pronunciation of separate words that is concerned, then pupils need practice of each word, either in isolation or in a phrase, but not 'lost' in some long text; I outlined some techniques for pronunciation practice in Chapter 2. If oral fluency is the aim, then again, reading aloud will at best achieve reading aloud fluency, which is quite a different skill; and more useful techniques for training oral fluency are given in Chapter 5.

Unfortunately reading aloud is often done simply because the teacher wants a change of activity or a rest. Variety of activity for both teacher and learner is essential – so is a rest! However, it seems a pity that such an ineffective activity as reading aloud should be used so often for this purpose. The later chapters 'Planning your teaching' and 'The teacher and the class' will suggest how variety of activity can be achieved.

So far, I have been negative in my remarks in order to state what reading is not; or rather, what I intend to exclude in this chapter on reading. Now let us look at the nature of silent reading. I have already made certain assumptions about the nature of reading, that is, about the behaviour of a reader. If we have a reasonable idea of what is involved in the reading process, then we are more likely to be in a favourable position to help our learners by

(i) determining the types of reading matter our learners should be exposed to; and

(ii) choosing appropriate teaching techniques so that our learners read efficiently the material presented to them.

Many attempts have been made to define or describe the nature of reading. It is generally agreed that there are two broad aspects or levels. First there is a basically visual task, that of deciphering the marks on the page, the brain receiving signals from the eye. This mechanical level includes eye movement, from left to right for English, to be learnt by a learner who does not use a left-to-right script in his first language, or who is illiterate in his first language. Secondly, there is a cognitive task, that of interpreting the visual information, so that one is not simply 'barking at print' as Maria was probably doing in **EXAMPLE 1**. Here we are concerned with thinking skills, since some kind of reconstruction takes place in the reader's mind: he attempts to build up the meaning the writer had in mind when he wrote the text.

Part 2: How do you teach reading?

Some differences between the spoken and written forms of a language have already been outlined in Chapter 3. If we accept that the written form is different from the spoken form and not a mere copy, then it follows that the ability to read will have to be specially taught, since it will not automatically follow on from oral work. Many learners of English will, after leaving their language classes, come in contact largely – and sometimes solely – with the written form. It would seem sensible to teach them to read efficiently.

The task of teaching reading is not an easy one. For one thing, if your learners are reading silently, you are to a certain extent excluded. The teacher-pupil interaction of oral activity will be lacking. Nevertheless, you can help your learners in many ways, as I will indicate in this chapter.

We should bear in mind these questions in our teaching of reading:
(i) Am I teaching my learners or testing them? That is, is this material or activity a means of helping my learners to improve their reading ability, or does it assume they already have the ability to deal unaided with the text? In short, does my reading comprehension *lesson* differ from the end-of-year comprehension *test*?
(ii) How can we help our learners not merely to cope with one particular text in front of them but with their reading ability in general? Can we encourage them to use reading strategies which will enable them to tackle further texts?
(iii) Are we helping our learners to read on their own? We should aim at gradually withdrawing our guidance as our learners progress, so that they eventually become independent readers. While endeavouring to provide sufficient guidance, we must avoid spoon-feeding our learners.

A   Reading with a purpose

Efficient reading depends first of all on having a purpose for reading, knowing why you are reading a text. The purpose could be a very general one like reading a novel for pleasure or escape; on the other hand, it could be very specific like looking up a telephone directory for somebody's number or address. The purpose will usually determine the appropriate type of reading and the relevant reading skills to be used.

Let me give an example. If the purpose is to find out which clauses of an Act of Parliament are mentioned in a chapter of a history text-book, slow and intensive reading of the whole text would be inefficient reading. What is needed here is *scanning* for the relevant details; i.e. the eye, directed by the brain, runs down through the lines on the look-out for the relevant details. When these are recognised, the brain will tell the eye to slow down for closer scrutiny. And usually, at this point, another type of reading (intensive reading) may operate, since the purpose will now have changed.

You may say this is all very obvious. It is; but it is so often ignored by teachers. One result is that many a postgraduate overseas student at a British or American university has difficulty keeping up with his reading programme because at school he was conditioned, by so many years' practice of reading English without a purpose, to read everything in the same way and at the same speed.

So here is a golden rule for any reading activity: learners should know the purpose for their reading before they actually read. However simple and obvious this may seem, it rarely happens. The normal procedure is that the students are required to read a passage and then answer the questions that follow. Their reading is usually purposeless because they have not read the questions first, and so have no idea what they will be asked. Inevitably they try to retain all the information, some of which could be irrelevant. No wonder a uniform slow pace develops, together with boredom from a lack of challenge and interest. A minimum improvement would be to set the questions before the text, thus using them as a learning device, that is, a means of developing certain skills in reading comprehension. Questions set afterwards act as a testing device, since by their very position such questions cannot help the learners during the initial reading.

Two examples will perhaps show more clearly what I mean. First let us take a text for beginners. Like so many such texts, it is far from inspiring and far from authentic; and, as sometimes happens, we are even left in some doubt as to what is intended.

Text 1

Mr Smith's house has got four bedrooms, a living-room, a dining room, a kitchen, a bathroom and a lavatory. There is a lavatory in the bathroom too. The bedrooms and the bathroom are upstairs, and the living-room, the dining-room, the kitchen and the lavatory are downstairs.

The first bedroom is Mr and Mrs Smith's, the second one is John's, the third one is Mary's and the fourth one is Anne's. Catherine's bed is in Anne's bedroom too.

Go into Mr Smith's house now. The room on your left is the living-room, and the room on the right is the dining-room. Where is the kitchen? It is behind the dining-room. And where is the lavatory? It is in front of you. There is a garden behind the house, but it is not big. Is

there a garden in front of the house too? Yes, there is, but it is very
small.

Go upstairs now. Which is Mr and Mrs Smith's bedroom? It is on
your left. The bedroom on your right is John's and the bathroom is
between his bedroom and Mary's. Anne's bedroom is behind Mary's.

There is a big bed and two big cupboards in Mr and Mrs Smith's
bedroom, and there is a small bed and a cupboard in John's room.
John's bed and Mary's bed are the same size, but her cupboard is
bigger than his, because she has a lot of clothes. Anne's bed is small,
but it is not as small as Catherine's.

Anne's room has got blue walls, and there are white ships and green
islands on them, because it is a children's bedroom. John's bedroom
has got white walls, and Mary's has got grey walls. John has got
pictures of horses on his walls, and Mary has got pictures of beautiful
clothes.

I doubt whether you bothered to read right to the end of that. But
what happens when the learner is given the text and simply told to read
it? He reads(?), yes, silently, but at a depressingly slow pace because he
expects to be tested afterwards and he does not want to be 'caught out'
by any question. All six paragraphs are given equal attention, since no
purpose has been given. Furthermore, by the time the learner reaches the
multiple-choice questions at the end (in the book from which the text
is taken there are ten such questions to each text), he is very confused
and perhaps bored, finding the test-type questions a hindrance, rather
than a help, to his understanding of the passage. Perhaps your reaction
will be the same:

Choose the correct statement from each set:

1a Three of Mr Smith's bedrooms are upstairs and one is
    downstairs.
1b Mr Smith's four bedrooms are downstairs.
1c Mr Smith's four bedrooms are upstairs.

2a There is one lavatory in Mr Smith's house. It is downstairs.
2b There is one lavatory in Mr Smith's house. It is upstairs.
2c There are two lavatories in Mr Smith's house. One of them is
    upstairs.

3a John's bedroom is behind Mary's.
3b Mary's bedroom is in front of John's.
3c Mary's bedroom is in front of Anne's. etc.

Suppose, on the other hand, that I started by telling the class that they
are going to read a text in order (here's the *purpose*) to complete two
plans, one of them showing the ground-floor rooms and the other the
upstairs rooms:

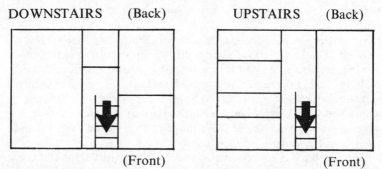

DOWNSTAIRS   (Back)   UPSTAIRS   (Back)

(Front)   (Front)

The situation is immediately changed. The bored, uninterested expression on many faces is replaced by one of interest; on some, consternation – if not panic – may appear. However, I first ask them to scan the whole passage to find only those paragraphs which must be read carefully in order to find out the arrangement of the rooms and which paragraphs can be ignored after skimming through them. Obviously paragraphs 3 and 4 are the relevant ones. This conscious separation of the relevant and the irrelevant is important training for our learners and can start even at this fairly elementary level. Notice that if the purpose had been to find out what the rooms looked like, paragraphs 5 and 6 would have been the relevant ones. Then I give the class a few minutes to complete the two floor plans, as I circulate to see where the difficulties are.

I have used this with groups of learners who were given no floor-plans but were asked to draw them. In every group keen discussion between neighbours developed. A lot hinged on the single preposition 'behind' in paragraph 4 in working out the direction of the stairs. I finally *supplied* the un-labelled floor-plans *and* the arrows on the stairs, because otherwise the passage left too many doubts. But in a multilingual class, one might preserve the doubts and welcome the ensuing discussion in English of the merits and demerits of various solutions to the problem. In either case, the following is usually accepted in the end:

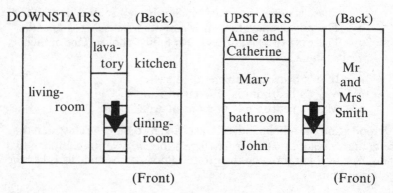

DOWNSTAIRS   (Back)   UPSTAIRS   (Back)

| living-room | lava-tory | kitchen |
| | | dining-room |

| Anne and Catherine |
| Mary |
| bathroom |
| John |

Mr and Mrs Smith

(Front)   (Front)

Text 2

London Transport
CHILDREN. On the Underground, children under 3 are carried free and children between 3 and 14 pay half fare.
On buses and coaches one child under 3 years of age, accompanied by a fare-paying adult or child passenger and not occupying a seat, is carried free. Additional children under 3 years and all children of 3 years and under 14 years of age are carried at half the adult single fare.
DOGS. You may take your dog on the top of a bus, or in a Green Line coach, or on a single-deck bus, only if the conductor or driver/operator agrees. You may take your dog on the Underground (and must buy a ticket for it) but you *must* carry it on escalators – it is a punishable offence not to do this.
FARES AND TICKETS. A list of fares is in every ticket hall on the Underground, and in every bus and coach. You must not board a train without a ticket, or leave a bus or coach without having paid your fare. You cannot buy ordinary tickets in advance or in a 'carnet'. Return tickets are available on the Underground, for use on day of issue only.
QUEUES. When waiting at a bus stop or coach stop always form a queue – then everyone gets on in turn. Please allow passengers to get off before you try to get on.

The traditional way of treating this text would be to ask the class to read it and then answer questions like:
(i) Are children under 3 years carried free on the Underground?
(ii) Can you take your dog on the top of a bus?
etc, etc.
Instead, the following procedure would seem more appropriate:

Step 1   The teacher distributes the text face down so the learners do not read the text. The teacher writes on the BB: M (20p) + 15 + 8 + 2

Step 2   T explains: A mother (M) wants to go somewhere in London by bus with her three children, aged 15, 8 and 2. How much will it cost her, if the adult bus fare is 20p? I'll give you 40 seconds to find the answer. Turn over the paper. Start now.

Step 3   After sufficient time (not necessarily 40 seconds) the teacher elicits answers.

Another question – one designed to lead to discussion – would be:
A woman wants to travel on the Underground with her three large dogs. Can she do so? Give me a reason for your answer. Various answers may be offered by the class:
– Yes, because she can use stations without escalators.

87

– Yes, because she can ask other passengers to carry two of the dogs on the escalator.
– No, because one lady cannot deal with three big dogs.
– etc.

I have said that such a procedure is more appropriate, because I put the learners as readers in a situation that they might encounter. Why and when would they read such a text? Presumably, when they were wanting to travel in London by bus or Underground with a family, etc. That is an authentic reading situation. What does the mother with three children read? The whole text and then a string of comprehension questions? Certainly not. Precisely because she has a purpose before reading, she reads only that part of the text which is relevant. Obviously she begins at the beginning and scans until she reaches the word 'children', then she prepares to read carefully but notices that the first sentence deals with the Underground, so she scans on until she sees 'buses'. Now she realises she is at the relevant section. Having read carefully up to 'single fare', she leaves the rest of the text as irrelevant.

It is such purposeful authentic reading that I want to develop as the norm for my learners. Why should we inflict post-text comprehension questions on our learners when we do not inflict them on ourselves? I am of course referring to the teaching of reading, not the testing of it.

To go back to our two examples at the beginning of the chapter, **EXAMPLE 2** is more satisfactory and appropriate, not only because it is silent reading that is being practised, but also because the learners have been given a specific purpose to their reading in the form of a worksheet, which is an aid during the actual reading of the text.

B Transfer of information

By asking my class to draw a plan of the two floors, I was asking them to translate, not from one language to another (a verbal translation) but from a verbal form to a largely non-verbal form. This sort of activity has already been mentioned in Chapter 3. It has been used for generations in geography and science textbooks. So, once our learners are familiar with its use in school books, we can exploit it for learning purposes. Not all reading matter lends itself to such exploitation, but here are a few well-tried types:

(i) Information from any account of a journey can be transferred to a map with a route marked. Verbs, nouns and other items can be inserted at the appropriate points on the map. An example of this is shown later with the James Cook text (pages 103–106).

(ii) Information from a text which compares the activities, possessions, etc. of two people can be transferred to two separate lists or columns.

(iii) A set of instructions for making or operating something simple (e.g. following a recipe or operating a telephone or cassette recorder) can actually be carried out.

(iv) A description of a process (e.g. how clothes are made or how cocoa is produced) will include the features of sequencing, so a flow-diagram provides a good visual translation. I will illustrate this later when I deal with the structure of texts (pp. 98–99).

As well as helping the learner to understand a text, this transfer of information technique has another advantage. It gives you instant feedback, since you can see immediately whether the learner has read correctly. This is much more reliable than asking the usually useless question: 'Do you understand?' since you can *see at a glance* how much or how little has so far been understood.

C Cognitive skills of comprehension

One possible way of establishing a purpose for reading is by focusing the learner's attention on a particular cognitive skill. In fact, a change in the purpose usually entails a change in the cognitive reading skill, and therefore the type of reading done.

What are these cognitive skills? Many lists have been suggested, but they all include most of the following abilities:
(i) to anticipate both the form and the content;
(ii) to identify the main idea(s);
(iii) to recognise and recall specific details;
(iv) to recognise the relationship between the main idea(s) and their expansion (examples, etc.);
(v) to follow a sequence, e.g. events, instructions, stages of an argument;
(vi) to infer from the text ('read between the lines');
(vii) to draw conclusions;
(viii) to recognise the writer's purpose and attitude.

So we can help the learners by saying to them: 'I want you to read this text in order to state the main idea', or 'in order to list the sequence of events', or 'to identify the writer's attitude'. But before I give some examples, let us consider the nature of authentic reading material.

D Types of text

'The reader of certain foreign language texts often gets the impression that Frenchmen are strictly systematic beings who one day speak merely in futures, another day in *passé défini*, and who say the most disconnected things only for the sake of being able to use all the persons in the tense which for the time being happens to be the subject for conversation.' (Jespersen, *How to teach a foreign language*. Allen and Unwin, 1904.)

The unit of written language – what we read and write – is not usually the isolated sentence, but a combination of sentences linked together by cohesive ties. This combination ('discourse') is so basic and expected that the reader takes for granted the means by which the coherence and cohesion of a text are achieved. I will return to this later (see page 100). Here I merely point out that we should avoid presenting our learners with lists of thematically unconnected sentences – either for reading or for writing purposes:

> Bill comes to school on a bicycle every day.
> There is a bottle of water on the floor.
> I often throw a ball into the air.

However, there are indeed instances of an isolated sentence (often without a finite verb) which we read in everyday life, e.g. an entry in a telephone directory, a street sign, a public notice in a building, newspaper headlines. So some practice of this specialised format is desirable, though it will be limited, reflecting the relative infrequency of occurrence of an isolated sentence. (See the useful book by Pearce in Further Reading.)

Another format is of course the semi-verbal one, like diagrams, charts, tables and maps. Such reading is now quite common. Here are typical examples, not specially prepared for language teaching use. Note that all these could be well exploited in terms of the transfer of information technique.

Text 3

Casualties

Div.	District	QUARTERLY TOTAL 1979			QUARTERLY TOTAL 1980			TOTAL FROM 1.1.80		
		Fatal	Serious	Slight	Fatal	Serious	Slight	Fatal	Serious	Slight
A	Manchester	1	6	86	1	12	69	1	30	246
B	Manchester	1	24	157	4	26	126	10	81	397
C	Manchester	3	20	101	1	27	100	3	73	321
D	Manchester	1	28	176	–	20	145	4	75	477
E	Manchester	1	16	146	4	27	141	10	67	411
F	Salford	3	62	256	4	72	274	11	189	742
G	Tameside	1	43	184	2	42	172	8	130	503
J	Stockport	5	85	258	3	45	311	8	138	840
K	Bolton	1	94	278	6	86	280	14	214	818
L	Wigan	7	65	247	4	52	275	23	157	856
M	Trafford	7	41	235	1	29	217	10	107	655
N	Bury	2	28	154	3	33	163	11	81	501
P	Rochdale	9	41	223	2	41	214	12	118	634
Q	Oldham	2	51	250	6	41	221	12	146	717
	TOTAL	44	604	2751	41	553	2708	137	1606	8118

Text 4

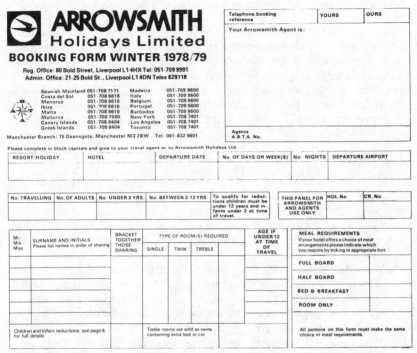

Text 5
In the diagram below, the influence of climate on the generalised crop rotation can be seen by the dominance of grass and the small proportion of crop land. The grass sward usually degenerates after several years due to impeded soil drainage and the dying out of the better grasses. Ploughing, with the cultivation and manuring required for cereals and root crops, restores soil condition and the crops give a cash return and

ROTATION OF CROPS

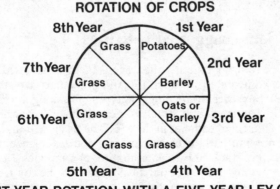

AN EIGHT YEAR ROTATION WITH A FIVE YEAR LEY OF GRASS

fodder for stock. Potatoes are the chief cash crop and a fraction are retained for domestic use. Seed potatoes, a third of the £6 million crop, are widely exported.

Oats, formerly the chief cereal crop, now has only one third the acreage of barley which has a greater yield and feed value, especially for pigs. The new varieties of barley are more resistant to disease and weather damage and formerly carried a subsidy advantage. Oats are still dominant on the acid soils and on the hills. All other crops have a negligible acreage by comparison. Flax, which had disappeared from Ulster farms, due to low returns and high labour costs, has been revived on a trial basis.

E Types of reading

As I have implied already, the type of reading (sometimes called reading strategy) will be determined predominantly by the purpose for the reading. Some important categories are:

1 Skimming. The eye runs quickly over the text to discover what it is about, the main idea(s), the gist. Thus, skimming occurs in the following.

(i) When the reader looks quickly at the contents page of a book, or at the chapter headings, subheadings, etc. This is sometimes called previewing. Another example is when the reader glances quickly through a newspaper to see what are the main items of the day. This will often mean just glancing at the headlines.

(ii) When the reader goes through a particular passage such as a newspaper article merely to get the gist.

2 Scanning. Here the reader is on the look-out for a particular item or items he believes is in the text; for example, the name of the scorer in a football report. Again it is fairly fast reading with instant rejection of all irrelevant data, perhaps most of the text.

3 Intensive reading. Also called study reading, this involves close study of the text. As the amount of comprehension should be high, the speed of reading is correspondingly slower.

Part 3: Some suggested activities

It is now time to bring together the various factors discussed in Parts 1 and 2 which contribute to the act of reading: the nature of the reading process itself, purposes for reading and types of reading. I will now give examples of various ways in which you can help the reader become as mature and efficient a reader as in the MT. These suggestions are neither exhaustive nor mutually exclusive in any one text, since a text can sometimes be best tackled by a combination of strategies. My aim is to help the learner by using an analytical approach, i.e. by focusing his attention on one aspect at a time, as preliminary reading activity.

Gradually, it is hoped, the learner synthesises these aspects as he becomes a more independent reader.

A Before-reading activity

The overriding aim in doing any class work with our learners before they begin to read a text is to create a positive attitude in their minds towards the text to be read. In short, we are concerned with motivation.

You will obviously attempt to provide texts that are interesting, but this will not always be easy. For one thing, what interests one learner may not interest another learner, even of the same age, sex and cultural background. There have been surveys of topics of interest for boys and girls of different ages. You may find these of some help, but beware of the cliché topics like sport for boys, cooking for girls. You yourself are perhaps the best judge of what topics seem most interesting and appealing to your particular group of learners.

However, there is something else to bear in mind. While not failing to exploit the fact that an interesting topic may contribute towards enjoyable reading, we have a duty as teachers to train our learners as efficient readers of many types of texts even if these have no special interest; in this case, interest can be created in other ways. Your learners can be motivated, as I have already indicated in Part 2, by being challenged in some way, by having a purpose to their reading. Although your learners are set a task before they begin reading, the task remains relevant during the actual reading, as we saw with the example of the house-plan and with the London Transport regulations.

Furthermore, you can motivate a class by encouraging some anticipation. Here are two examples:

1 Anticipating the content. If the text has sections with headings, the learners can be asked to read only these headings and then say or write down what they expect the text to be about. However, not all texts are so obliging as to provide such convenient clues.

More often, the text will have only one heading. Here the teacher can say before the learners look at the text:

> T: You're going to read something about 'Our Town'. What things do you think you might read about?

Learners give their suggestions which are written up on the board, e.g.

Our Town		
Shops	–	types and place
Schools	–	size and place
People	–	jobs, homes, hobbies

It is better not to extend this preliminary work until all items in the text are listed, since two initial activities in reading the text can be:

First reading: scanning the text to see if all the items listed on the blackboard do actually appear in the text, and

Second reading: listing items in the text which they had not predicted.

A variation of this is to give the class the first paragraph or two and then ask them what is likely to follow.

2 Anticipating both content and form. As an example of this, imagine that the teacher distributes copies of this set of pictures (magazine pictures might be passed round instead, or blackboard drawings used):

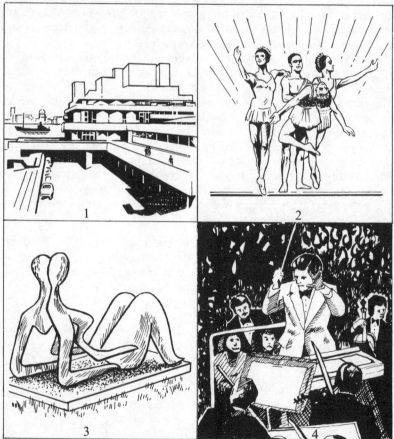

In this case the learners are told not to look at the text on the reverse side. (If forbidding them is a guarantee that they will, then make sure they are all looking at the pictures by a quick start on the following.)

T: Now, what can you see in Picture 1? Yes, there's a building near a river. Anybody know where the river is? No, not Paris. Yes, London. Now, the building. Yes, Anna; it's the National Theatre. What do we see in a theatre? Yes, plays. Who are in plays? Yes, actors and actresses. They act in a play. What part of the theatre do they act on . . .? . . . Picture 4. What do you see? Yes, an orchestra. Who are the people in the orchestra? Yes, musicians – yes, or orchestral players. Where do they play? A new word for you. In a concert hall.

etc., etc.

This is merely an indication of what would actually occur. The point I want to make is that I am not only anticipating the content of what the learners will shortly read on the reverse side but I am also rehearsing the vocabulary, most of which is already known to this group of learners. My aim here is to recall known language and activate language the readers may expect to come across; such words as *act, play, theatre, stage*, and so on.

This anticipation work is exploiting the well-known and obvious phenomenon that we understand the familiar better than the unfamiliar. With familiar material we find it easier to predict what will occur – or is likely to occur. This applies to form as well as content. Such work is especially helpful in dealing with texts that contain a high proportion of new words.

3 Vocabulary work.   Even if your learners are interested in the subject matter of the reading text you have chosen, they will soon lose interest if they find the vocabulary too difficult. If the majority of words are unknown to your learners, you would be wise to discard the text and choose another one more appropriate to their linguistic level. However, a few unknown words – say, five – in a short text of about 300 words should be acceptable. You may decide during your lesson preparation that the meanings of these new words can be derived from the text itself when your learners are reading it. Alternatively, you may consider the words as unimportant for the reading purpose. In both cases, you will deliberately exclude any preliminary vocabulary work.

However, you may judge some or all of the unknown vocabulary as key words whose meaning is crucial to the understanding of the text. This is where some preliminary vocabulary teaching could help your learners. Your aim will often be limited to developing your learners' receptive vocabulary so that they will recall the meanings when reading the text themselves. You will not therefore need to spend a lot of the lesson on preliminary vocabulary teaching to establish a productive knowledge. By the usual means of illustrations, demonstrations, synonyms and definitions, your teaching will remove much of the uncertainty and frustration your learners feel when meeting new words

95

in a text. But remember: a short preliminary session to the reading activity, not a protracted session on the dictionary meaning of words.

B While-reading activity

1 Identifying the main idea

(i) Read the passage in order to give a title.

(ii) Read the passage in order to select the most appropriate title from those given. Discuss rejects.

The type of reading used for such practice will be *skimming*, since the aim is to avoid close and slow reading of the text for all details.

(iii) Identify the topic sentences, i.e. find and underline.

A paragraph will often, but not always, have a topic or key sentence. This is often a generalisation or summary, exemplified or expanded in other sentences of the paragraph. It helps a reader to understand a text if he can identify topic sentences because obviously these will indicate the main ideas, thus acting as markers to the organisation of the text. Unfortunately, not all paragraphs have a topic sentence at the beginning, though this is a very common position. The teacher could collect examples of texts where the first sentence of each paragraph is the topic sentence. Thus learners would develop the habit of being on the look-out for this useful clue to the gist of the text. Here is an example:

Text 6

PLANNING AND THE ENVIRONMENT

<u>The growth of towns and cities in Britain is subject to careful planning control.</u> Green belts, within which all building is severely restricted, prevent the sprawling of larger towns and ensure that their inhabitants have ready access to 'lungs' of parkland or countryside. Within the towns building is also subject to controls, which are designed to maintain aesthetic and safety standards, to protect existing amenities and to preserve a balance between residential, commercial and industrial development.

<u>Not only towns and cities, but also roads, industries, airports and, indeed, all construction work is subject to close public scrutiny.</u> Plans must be presented for approval to local authorities which, in turn, must submit their broad proposals for development within their areas to the appropriate government department. Plans must also be made available for examination by the general public. In addition, important new schemes are usually the subject of discussion in both local and national press and broadcasting programmes.

Other legislation, some of it long-standing and some of it passed recently to deal with newer threats, is designed to protect the environment against pollution by industry or by any other source, including the general public. Various regulations limit the emissions of noxious chemicals into air and water, whether by factories, aircraft or motor traffic, or by private householders – many urban areas are now smokeless zones. Other laws control the amount of noise that may be made by industry and traffic.

Britain is a nation that is proud of its heritage of landscape and of history and great efforts are made to protect it. Large areas of the countryside, including forests, and of the coastline are set aside as national parks, within which construction and other works are either expressly forbidden or strictly controlled. In addition, many rights of way are preserved, sometimes across private land, to form long, continuous footpaths and bridleways through areas of outstanding natural beauty. Other areas are protected as nature reserves and many species of plants and animals are also protected by law throughout the country.

2   Finding details in a text

(i) Telephone directory: Find somebody's number in, say, 20 seconds.

(ii) Newspaper article: Who scored the second goal?
How many people were injured in the explosion?
Who met X at Y?

(Aids: pages from an old telephone directory; newspaper articles stuck on card; a worksheet.)

The type of reading practised here is *scanning*. One useful technique to use for this work is the information-gap technique, whereby the reader has to fill in the missing information on a work-sheet by scanning a text which has the required information. The teacher can often use texts from the class course-book, which must not be ignored or totally replaced by supplementary material; and can manage without sophisticated aids. To illustrate, I have chosen a short text from a well-known course-book used in many countries.

(iii) The teacher writes the following on the blackboard:

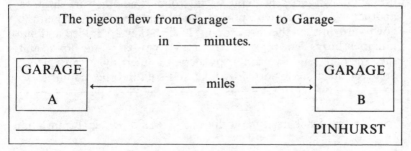

D

The class is told to copy it down quickly. Then the teacher asks them to open their books at the following text in order to fill in the gaps on the worksheet:

Text 7

NO WRONG NUMBERS

Mr James Scott has a garage in Silbury and now he has just bought another garage in Pinhurst.

Pinhurst is only five miles from Silbury, but Mr Scott cannot get a telephone for his new garage, so he has just bought twelve pigeons. Yesterday, a pigeon carried the first message from Pinhurst to Silbury. The bird covered the distance in three minutes. Up to now, Mr Scott has sent a great many requests for spare parts and other urgent messages from one garage to the other. In this way, he has begun his own private 'telephone' service.

---

3 Following a sequence. The learner who realises that what he is reading involves some form of sequencing (i.e. related items in a particular order) is able to understand a lot of the text, even if there are some unknown words. An example at the elementary level would be a route from A to B, a familiar favourite with course-book writers. Here, the reader is usually required to indicate the sequence of moves by plotting the route on a street-plan.

At a much more advanced level an example would be a text describing some kind of process, where sequence is also important. Again, I take a text from a published course-book:

Text 8

Cloth is brought to the factory and examined. If it is torn or dirty, it will not be used. The cloth is taken to the cutting room. Here a special pencil is used for drawing on the cloth, and then it is cut. Boxes of dressing-gowns are sent to the sewing room where they are sewn. In another room the sleeves, pockets and belts are put on. When the gowns are finished they are examined. Then they are folded and put into their boxes. The price and the size are written on the boxes, and then they are sent, by train or by lorry, to other towns in England. Some of them are exported by boat and sold in other countries.

Such a text lends itself naturally to some kind of visual translation.

The text-book provides a series of pictures:

These pictures obviously assist with vocabulary as they show various stages in the process. But this can be represented also as a flow-diagram:

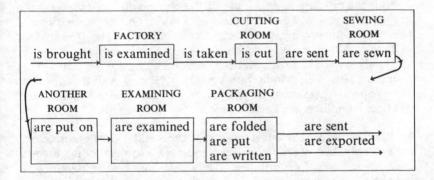

Learners can be asked to read the description of how clothes are made in order to fill in missing information in the flow-diagram.

Here, the reader is likely to read more intensively than in my previous examples. What is important is that the reader, through focusing on the use of the passive in a sequence, is helped to read other process texts more efficiently, even though the words will vary from text to text. That is, to a large extent he will be on familiar ground. After all, our main concern as teachers is not so much: 'How can I help my learner to cope with this particular text he has in front of him at the moment?', but rather: 'How can I help my learner to cope with this type of text, so that when he comes across a similar text he will be able to read it with confidence?'

4 Inferring from the text. Together with identifying the main idea, the ability to infer ('reading between the lines') is sometimes called a manipulative thinking skill. Whereas reading for literal meaning focuses on what is explicitly stated, we often go beyond the explicitly stated; we want (or we are led by the writer) to make conjectures, to work out what is implied in the text. In short, we think when we read. Of course, inferring presupposes literal understanding of the text. It is not an alternative, but a higher level of comprehension. Furthermore, it is not fair to expect our learners to infer beyond their own knowledge of the world.

5 Recognising the writer's purpose and attitude. This can be difficult even for the native-reader, since a good writer will often prefer to be subtle and indirect in his intentions and attitudes. Therefore we are here concerned with reading by the advanced learner.
(i) The writer's *purpose*: It could be any of the following or a mixture of them: to ridicule, to amuse, to protest, to accuse, to teach, etc.
(ii) The writer's *attitude*: It will be determined by his purpose. It could be: serious, superficial, sympathetic, angry, etc.

Both the purpose and attitude of the writer will usually reveal the prejudices, the bias, he has towards his subject. One of the marks of a mature, sensitive reader is the ability to recognise such bias. The student of English Literature will spend a lot of his time interpreting attitudes and analysing the linguistic means by which a literary writer achieves his purposes. However, non-literary texts may be used with our learners. Newspapers, magazines, advertisements of all kinds, religious and political pamphlets are good sources.

6 Recognising discourse features. A text will consist of discourse, i.e. a combination of interrelated sentences. This combination is formed in various ways. For instance, the words will belong together as members of the same lexical field, so that a text on football will have words like *goal, foul, off-side, kick, head, pass.* But a text is held together by other cohesive means. Let us look at a short text which illustrates some of these:

> Mary was feeling very unhappy. There were several reasons for this. First, she had lost her purse. Secondly, she had just missed the last bus. Thirdly, her father had insisted that she should be home before 10.00 p.m. and it was now 11.00. Fourthly, she had not liked the film. But just then, she remembered that she began her holidays the next day, so she felt a little better.

We can identify discourse features here as:
(i) *this, she, her* as substitutes refer back to previous statements.
(ii) *first, secondly, thirdly, fourthly* signal a list of some sort.
(iii) *but* indicates a change or contrast relative to some previous statement.

(iv) *so* introduces a consequence or result of previous events.
This subject is further discussed in Chapter 6.

A good reader knows the significance of these markers which help him understand the text. For instance, on encountering the sequence marker *first* the reader expects some kind of listing to follow. The learner can be helped to react in the same way by having his attention drawn to such discourse features. One exercise could be to identify such features in a text; another exercise could require filling in the missing features; or the teacher could provide the opening sentences of a text indicating a sequence and the learners be asked what the next word will be. *Then*, *next*, *afterwards* etc. would all be acceptable.

7 The teacher's role. While your learners are busy with their silent reading, you yourself will be very active. Not only have you provided the texts and suggested ways of treating them, but you will be there in the class, ready to help both individual learners with their particular difficulties and the whole group if a general difficulty arises. You will very likely be asked the meaning of an unknown word in the text and you may be tempted to give an instant translation. In certain circumstances you may be justified in doing so, but you will usually wish to train your learners to derive the meaning of the word from the context itself. I illustrate this in Part 4 where I treat in detail a full text. In Part 1, I criticised the use of comprehension questions after the text as often an inadequate learning device because such questions come too late. On the other hand, you may find it very effective to question your class while they are tackling a section of the text. A short question and answer session may clarify some point which your learners find difficult.

C After-reading activity

While your learners are reading purposefully, you can gain a good idea of how they are coping with their reading because you will be able to circulate round the classroom, seeing how well the reading tasks (e.g. filling in a worksheet) are being done. However, some kind of follow-up should be valuable – both for you and your learners.

To begin with, I would hope that your learners were still interested enough in their reading to want to check the results of the reading task. For example, in the lesson illustrated in Part 4 the teacher needs to check that the learners have drawn the correct route of Cook's journey. In Part 2 we saw the room plan of the two floors. We would need to check that our learners had plans that were acceptable according to the text.

However, checking on the reading activity is only the first step. We can exploit the learners' experience in reading by means of further activities. For instance, we may now consider it valuable language work to deal with some of the unknown words which we had deliberately chosen not to consider at the pre-reading stage. Or we may now want to go from the receptive stage to the productive stage of learning certain words.

And we must not forget that reading is often a preliminary to some other language work like writing. What your learners have been reading can sometimes be used as a model for their own writing. For instance, having read the text on page 98 which dealt with the process of making dressing gowns, your learners could attempt to write similar descriptions of processes, e.g. how bread is made, how a car is manufactured, how coffee beans are treated. The vocabulary will of course vary according to the subject matter but the structure of the discourse will be similar, with the dominant feature being a sequence of passives. I recently found useful a six-paragraph text on the British education system as a model for my class of Italians to follow in writing a parallel description of the Italian education system. Each paragraph had an opening topic sentence and each paragraph dealt with a different topic, so that my learners had a clear framework, viz.

Paragraph	Topic
1	Compulsory education
2	Types of schools
3	Facilities
4	Examinations
5	Universities
6	Adult education

This particular example is obviously suitable only for advanced learners, but appropriate texts can be found and exploited in this way even for the less advanced learner.

Part 4: Exploiting a reading text

After all the analysis of Part 3, you may well feel that the reading activity is in danger of becoming so compartmentalised that the learner will lose sight of the whole process. Obviously we will have failed as teachers if our learners remain at the analytical stage. Focusing attention on specific skills is not an end in itself, but an attempt to help the learner to cope with what otherwise could well be too difficult. The ultimate aim is a synthesis, so that the learner becomes an efficient reader on his own. The teacher's guidance through analysis will gradually be withdrawn as the reader progresses.

To bring together some of the aspects of reading considered in Part 3, I will now illustrate how I would treat a particular text. This treatment is not meant to be definitive, since it will be obvious that there are various ways of exploiting the text. I may only touch upon, or even ignore certain aspects that another teacher would wish to highlight. Nor do I wish to imply that such a treatment is suitable for all texts, though I would hope that my treatment is generalisable to a certain extent, and not merely idiosyncratic. For instance, the learners in **EXAMPLE 2** at the beginning of the chapter might well be purposefully engaged in reading such a text as the following and working silently on it.

Text 9

James Cook is perhaps the greatest English explorer, not only because of his discoveries in Australia and New Zealand, but because he set new standards in the accuracy of charts and in the preservation of the health of seamen.

5   Cook was the son of a farm labourer at Marton, in the North Riding of Yorkshire, and as a young boy he worked on a farm, receiving little education. He served for a short time in a haberdasher's shop and then ran away to sea. He started as an apprentice at the age of seventeen to a Whitby firm of coal-shippers,
10 and during this period he learned the art of navigation. It was in small ships of the collier type that he made all his voyages of discovery and exploration.

At the outbreak of the Seven Years' War, Cook volunteered for the Royal Navy. The captain of his ship soon realised that this tall, silent,
15 modest North-countryman was not only strong and handsome but also a dependable and efficient seaman who would make an excellent master or navigating officer. Cook was promoted and as an officer he served in a number of line-of-battle ships. In one of these he helped to pilot the fleet which took General Wolfe to Quebec.

20 The charts that Cook made in Canada won him a high reputation as a surveyor. As a result, in 1768 he took command of the *Endeavour*, the ship chosen by the Admiralty and the Royal Society to go on a scientific expedition to the newly discovered island of Tahiti. The supposed purpose of the expedition was to observe the astronomical
25 transit of the planet Venus: its real purpose was to beat the French in the discovery of a continent called Terra Australis Incognita which was believed to exist in the South Pacific.

Cook found no land to the south of Tahiti, so he turned west to discover and chart the east coast of New Zealand, the west having
30 been discovered by Abel Tasman in 1642. In six months Cook charted 2,400 miles of coastline with extraordinary accuracy. He then continued west, and reached the eastern coast of Australia (which he called New South Wales), the north-western parts having been discovered, but not settled, even before Tasman's time, and named
35 New Holland. On 29th April 1770, Cook landed at Botany Bay, the place to which the first fleet of convicts was sent a few years after his death. From New South Wales, Cook sailed north, but the *Endeavour* ran aground on the Barrier Reef. Cook calmly organised the refloating and repair of the ship, and then continued the voyage to
40 Java.

Stage	Teacher	Learners	Comment
1	Tells the class they are going to read about James Cook. Asks them what they know about him.	Respond with a few details about Cook.	Anticipation work. A few details are sufficient for this preliminary work.
2	Tells the class to find the following key phrases which will help them to get the gist of the first four paragraphs: —the greatest English explorer —worked on a farm —ran away to sea —learned the art of navigation —the Royal Navy —he took command of the *Endeavour* —a scientific expedition —the supposed purpose —its real purpose	Find the key phrases.	Highlighting key phrases as a help to identifying the main ideas.
3	Asks the class now to read quickly the first four paragraphs in order to give a title to each paragraph.	Read lines 1–27 and write down four titles.	Practice in identifying the main ideas. Type of reading: skimming.
4	Discusses with learners the suitability of titles, e.g. Paragraph 1: A great explorer Paragraph 2: His youth	Give titles.	To confirm or revise learners' understanding of the gist of these four paragraphs.

104

Stage	Teacher	Learners	Comment
	Paragraph 3: Life in the Royal Navy *Paragraph 4*: The *Endeavour* expedition		
5	Provides on **BB** or on a handout a simplified map of the South Pacific area (Australia, New Zealand, Tahiti, Java).	Copy map from **BB**, if no handout provided.	A preliminary to some transfer of information work.
6	Asks class to read the last paragraph and draw the route Cook took. Circulates round the room to check on performance.	Draw the route by extracting information from last paragraph.	Type of reading has changed from skimming (lines 1–27) to study reading. This is to provide: 1: a change of activity and 2: practice in another reading skill. Note that a specific purpose has been provided before learners read the paragraph.
7	Now asks one learner to draw his route on **BB** and checks its accuracy. Refers class to the text if there is any doubt, discrepancy, etc.	One learner draws his route on **BB**. Other learners comment on its accuracy, and, if necessary, provide the correct version.	Confirmation or revision of learners' comprehension. Constant reference back to the text itself.
8	Asks class to read the last paragraph a second time and	Read a second time and write in the verbs.	A second reading requires a different purpose, to be effective.

105

Stage	Teacher	Learners	Comment
	write in all the Simple Past Tense verbs at the correct points on the route map.		Further study reading.
9	Elicits verbs from learners while he writes them up on **BB** at the appropriate points. As he writes the verbs, he utters a full sentence, e.g. Yes. He turned west.	Provide verbs for **BB**. Check the points where verbs are written.	Immediate feedback. Learners hear as well as see the sequence of events on Cook's voyage.
10	Asks individual learners to recount the events of the voyage by looking either at **BB** or their own version, but with the full text covered.	Different learners recount the voyage orally.	Not memorisation of the text, but an oral account of part of the last paragraph. The transfer of information work provides adequate stimulus/cues. Note here, and in other stages, practice of the listening and speaking skills in a subordinate role.
11	Asks class to write out the account, with reference only to the information on their maps.	Write the account of the voyage.	Initial written follow-up. Further work could be provided by writing a similar report of another voyage.

Part 5: Additional aspects

A Vocabulary

One obvious assumption I made in the treatment of the Cook text was that the words were known by the class. However, comprehension work will often include tackling problems of lexical difficulty. We must not forget that a learner may be able to work out the structure of a text and to transfer information into another form, and yet have difficulties at the end with certain words. Conversely, a learner may fail to leave the starting point because of not knowing two or three crucial nouns and verbs in the opening sentences. In fact, if a text has too many unknown words, it is unsuitable for that learner. I have already mentioned one way of dealing with some vocabulary before getting students to read the text.

But a basic assumption underlying this whole chapter is that reading involves much more than simply knowing the dictionary meaning of individual words. As for coping with unknown words, the learner has to develop strategies which will allow him either to discover the meanings of the words or at least to proceed further with the text in spite of not knowing the meanings of certain words.

Let me illustrate from the Cook text, used in Part 4. In the second paragraph, the word 'haberdasher' may be a new word to the class. To know the meaning of this word is not essential in this paragraph, so it is enough if the learner replaces 'haberdasher's' with 'kind of . . .' This is often quite adequate for unknown adjectives or other modifiers. An unknown noun can often be read as 'a something'. Learners could be encouraged to use this strategy as a first step, which may be sufficient for some reading purposes.

Learners can also be given practice in deriving the meaning from the context, i.e. looking for clues in the rest of the sentence(s), so that an intelligent guess is likely to be correct. Again, in paragraph two of the Cook text, the word 'collier' may be new. The reader might manage to guess that it had some connection with '*coal*-shippers' in the previous sentence.

Work on word-formation and derivation can help the reader to decipher at least something. For instance, it is useful and fairly easy to remember the significance of certain prefixes, such as the negative meaning of *dis-, un-, im-*.

B Extensive reading

This is often associated with supplementary reading books read outside the classroom. Its main value is to foster fluency – and, let us hope, pleasure in reading. As this type of reading (of short stories, novels, magazine and newspaper articles) is usually a very private matter,

107

teacher-free and below frustration level in difficulty, it is desirable for learners to aim at a fairly good speed. There is plenty of material available for extensive reading. Supplementary readers of varying levels of difficulty are published in large numbers by the leading publishers. (See Brumfit in Further Reading.)

Newspapers and magazines have been used for a long time. A favourite with many teachers – if not learners – is to compare and contrast two newspapers. Depending on the task given, this could easily become very detailed study reading. It is a mistake to consider newspapers and magazines easy reading just because of the topicality of the news items. To counteract this, special magazines at different levels are now on the market. (See Mary Glasgow publications in Further Reading.)

With extensive reading, we are on the borders of teaching Literature with a capital 'L', and no clear division is practical or desirable. It is not by accident that so many supplementary readers are simplified versions of literary works of merit. However, as the teaching of Literature is not of importance to all teachers, but specialised and restricted to certain situations, I will not discuss it here. Those interested in teaching Literature – or even compelled to do so! – will find useful references in Further Reading.

Conclusion

I have attempted in this chapter to indicate some of the factors involved in reading. As I have focused on the reading process itself, I have not included the traditional comprehension questions, whether open-ended or multiple-choice, since these are part of testing, assessing the amount of comprehension achieved by the reader. This aspect belongs to the chapter on Assessment. Nor have I dealt with what are called study skills or search skills, which are basic requirements for most of us; for example, using an index and a dictionary. Special English courses for students undertaking university courses in the medium of English will often include a study skills component, so that the learner can cope with the reading requirements of university work.

To end on a note of encouragement: from the comments I hear from teachers and learners and from the number of recent books whose suggestions, ideas and approaches are discussed in this chapter; from all this it would seem that we may be witnessing a marked improvement in the reading ability of many of our learners. There is no hard documentary evidence from longitudinal research studies, and my impression may include a substantial element of wishful thinking. Nevertheless, I would like to think that of the two examples at the beginning of the chapter, **EXAMPLE 2** is becoming the norm, rather than **EXAMPLE 1**.

Sources of the texts in Chapter 4.

Text 1. HILL, L. *A first reading book.* Oxford University Press, 1969.
Text 2. Text displayed in London Transport bus and Underground stations.
Text 3. *On the road.* Summer issue 1979. Volume 2, No. 2. The Greater Manchester Police Traffic Department.
Text 4. *Arrowsmith holiday brochure 1978–79.* Arrowsmith Holidays Ltd.
Text 5. SMITH, R. *Northern Ireland – a regional geography.* Northern Ireland Government Information Service.
Text 6. *Planning and the environment.* HMSO, 1978. For British Information Services.
Text 7. ALEXANDER, L. *Practice and progress.* Longman, 1967.
Text 8. *Majid in England.* Course-book used in Algerian secondary schools.
Text 9. Adapted from *The Oxford Junior Encyclopedia.*

Further reading

1 English as a first language

It is significant that most of the research on reading comprehension has been done with native-readers in mind. The Open University has produced an excellent course and two collections of articles:

Reading development course. Open University, 1977.
MELNICK, A. and MERRITT, J. *Reading: today and tomorrow.* University of London Press, 1972.
MELNICK, A. and MERRITT, J. *The reading curriculum.* University of London Press, 1972.

Many definitions of the nature of reading appear in the Melnick and Merritt books. Two particularly good articles are:

CLYMES, T. 'What is reading?'
STRANG, R. 'The nature of reading.'

Any book by F. Smith is stimulating and perceptive. The latest is:

SMITH, F. *Reading.* Cambridge University Press, 1978.

2 English as a second language

Among the many general methodology books, these three give interesting studies:

BRIGHT, J. and MCGREGOR, G. *Teaching English as a second language.* Longman, 1970.
RIVERS, W. *Teaching foreign language skills.* Chicago University Press, 1968.
ALLEN, J. and CORDER, S. *Edinburgh course in applied linguistics, Volume 3.* Oxford University Press, 1975.

A good collection of public signs and notices seen throughout Britain is:

PEARCE, M. *English sign language.* Harrap, 1977.

Three books which exploit well the semi-verbal format used in the transfer of information technique are:

JORDAN, R. *Looking for information.* Longman, 1980.

THOMAS, B. *Practical information.* Arnold, 1977.

DAVIES, E. and WHITNEY, N. *Reasons for reading.* Heinemann, 1979.

A popular book used on study skills courses is:

YORKEY, R. *Study skills for students of English as a second language.* McGraw-Hill, New York, 1970.

Information on available extensive reading material appears in:

BRUMFIT, C. *Readers for foreign learners of English* (ETIC information guide 7). British Council, 1979.

and Mary Glasgow Publications publish many magazines, e.g. *Click, Crown, Clockwork, Catch, Club, Fusion.*

3 Literature

For those who are concerned with the teaching of literature, I have found the following books very useful:

WIDDOWSON, H. *Stylistics and the teaching of literature.* Longman, 1975.

MOODY, H. *The teaching of literature in developing countries.* Longman, 1971.

HINDMARSH, R. *Passing in literature* (Stage 4 of the Cambridge course for African secondary schools). Cambridge University Press, 1972.

4 Initial teaching of reading and writing

'Cracking the code' is obviously the first step for any learner of English who does not know the Roman script. As this is the main area of teaching in the primary schools in Britain and the United States, there is a vast literature on the subject. The following book gives a survey of the different methods of teaching reading and writing, and contains a good bibliography:

SOUTHGATE, V. and ROBERTS, G. *Reading – which approach?* University of London Press, 1970.

Chapter 5: Oral fluency

by Gerry Abbott

EXAMPLE 1

T:	(Pointing to BB) Now look at the beginning of the chart again. Step one, Dokmai?
P_1:	First, the teak trees are felled.
T:	Good. One *and* two . . . Chardchai?
P_2:	First the teak trees are felled. Then the branches are removed.
T:	That's right. Good. Now, Somchit. First . . .?
P_3:	First the teak trees are felled. Then the branches are removed. The trees . . .
T:	Trees?
P_3:	Logs. (T nods.) The logs are dragged to the nearest river.
T:	Thank you. Wanlee?
P_4:	First the teak trees are felled. Then the branches are removed. The logs are dragged to the nearest river and floated down to the sawmill . . .

EXAMPLE 2

P_1:	Have the Boltons got any children?
P_2:	(looking at his own handout) Oh yes, three.
P_1:	Are they boys or girls?
P_2:	Two boys and one girl.
P_1:	(noting this on her handout as T arrives and watches) And . . . have they yet a house?
T:	Have they got a house yet? Have they got a house yet?
P_1:	Have they got y- . . . a house yet?
P_2:	Yes.
P_1:	Is it large, or small?
P_2:	Large. (P_1 notes this, too.)
P_1:	And have they got a car?
P_2:	Yes . . . (T moves on to another pair.)
P_1:	Is it British or foreign? . . .

If you think for a moment about what was going on in those two episodes, you will see that there were at least four fundamental differences between them in spite of the fact that oral fluency was the main object of each. For a start, in the first episode the type of language being spoken was what we could call 'monologue' – the sort of prose used either in a lecture or in a book – whereas the language of the second example was definitely intended to resemble dialogue. In fact the former was an oral preparation for closely-guided writing; this sort of work will be discussed in the next chapter, and I shall deal mainly with the teaching of what we can loosely term 'conversation'. Returning to our examples, you may also have noted that whereas the teacher was in an obviously dominant position in the first episode (nominating speakers, interrupting and acting as arbiter of correctness the whole time), he was in the second case a much less obtrusive figure, checking and correcting briefly in a brisk tour of the class. Thirdly, the learners in the first episode were giving a solo performance in front of the whole class (*and* the teacher), whereas in the second episode most of the speech was one-to-one, face-to-face, as in normal conversation. And finally, one pupil spoke at a time in the first episode; in the second, the whole class was practising at the same time.

The first part of this chapter is concerned with how physical and other factors – the limitations of time, class size and so on – affect the activities that we organise. The second part will consider some oral activities ranged on a scale from the least to the most 'conversational'. Finally, I illustrate some activities involving the use of audiovisual aids.

Part 1: Some facts of life

At any given moment in a real conversation, one person is talking to another, or to others, in a small group. Our classes, however, are seldom small groups: a class of forty or more is by no means unusual in many countries. At a cocktail party to which forty people have been invited, the guests break up into more and more groups as the numbers increase and the party gets under way. A similar sort of break-up has to take place in a lesson if oral practice of sufficient quantity and quality is to be achieved. But it is of course no use breaking up your class into pairs or groups until you have given everyone sufficient preparation as regards what to say and how to say it. Two major problems, then, are:-
(i) how to ensure that everyone gets adequate preparation; and
(ii) how to ensure that everyone gets adequate practice.

In effect, this is to say that there is a tension between, on the one hand, the teacher's desire to exercise strict control in order to ensure accuracy of grammar and pronunciation, and on the other hand the need to relax control in order to allow the class to use newly-acquired language in a conversational way.

Practice takes time; and a further problem is how to give forty pupils sufficient oral practice in forty minutes. If you were to teach them individually and equally the whole time (and assuming that they were angelic learners!) each would get only one minute's worth of oral practice, the rest of the time being thirty-nine minutes' worth of listening. Inevitably, then, some oral practice has to be done simultaneously instead of consecutively. This has one advantage: in simultaneous practice, the timid learner can make his first mistakes privately, without fear of making a fool of himself in front of the whole class. It is just like being a member of a choir rather than a soloist.

Summarising what I have said so far, then, we can account for most of the major types of oral work in this fairly simple table:-

		1 CONTROLLED	**2** RELAXED	
A	**S I M U L T A N E O U S**	*Choral work:* Class or group repeats, in unison, sentences of a specified pattern. Teacher 'conducts' from the front.	*Pair/group practice:* Pairs or small groups converse independently, using newly-introduced language. Teacher circulates and helps.	**P R I V A T E**
B	**C O N S E C U T I V E**	*Individual work:* One pupil (or pair) produces specified sentence(s). Teacher nominates speakers and corrects as much as possible.	*Dramatisation:* Pairs or groups perform one at a time. Teacher intervenes as little as possible.	**P U B L I C**
		CORRECTNESS	**COMMUNICATION**	

The amount of choral work that has to be done will largely depend on the size of your class: with a group of a dozen you may not need to do any at all, whereas with a class of fifty such work may occupy five to ten minutes. Also, consider the amount of pair/group practice you can allow: you may not want to risk letting a large, unruly class of young teenagers do any at all, whereas an adult class – even quite a large one –

may do such work quietly and efficiently, and might reject choral work as babyish.

The amount of 'public' individual work you can get students to do may depend on the culture of the learner. For example, you should not expect South-east Asian students (especially girls) to be as ready to contribute as North-west Europeans. I used to have some difficulty in breaking through one cultural barrier in Thailand: my students did not find it easy to practise contradicting me. If I said 'I'm from New York', instead of retorting 'No, you're not! You're from London!' they would tend to grin knowingly, not wanting to tell their teacher that he was wrong. (I did not at the time have the sense to see that they would cheerfully have contradicted *each other*!) Chinese students tend to be retiring, preferring not to participate in oral work but to get on quietly with other tasks. Japanese students may avoid committing themselves to a public oral contribution for fear of making a mistake and losing 'face' among their peers. In North-west Europe, Finns are said to be reluctant to contribute orally to the lesson, apparently because of a natural reticence that is part of their cultural background. Expatriate teachers and those teaching foreign students in Britain have to become sensitive to such facts and adjust their teaching accordingly.

As I mentioned in Chapter 1, there is also a developmental factor to be taken into account. Young adolescents are often too self-conscious to take kindly to the production of the strange sounds of English. Such factors, both cultural and developmental, may affect both the amount and the quality of 'public' practice that your students can achieve, whether individual or as part of a dramatisation. (A dramatisation is simply a relaxed performance of a dialogue, with the rest of the class as audience, in which the speakers are encouraged to use appropriate facial expressions, tones of voice, gestures and even simple 'props'. I do not mean readings or performances of plays.)

So far we have considered the limitations of time and class size and some cultural/developmental inhibitions. There are further practical difficulties. For example it is an awkward fact that, though you may want to teach spoken English, your textbook is a written document. If you are lucky it will contain printed dialogues of reasonable quality which you can use; if you are not quite as lucky as that, you may be able to produce dialogue material on a duplicated handout; if, like most school teachers, you cannot even do that, you can (provided you have enough time before the lesson and the right sort of blackboard, e.g. sliding blackboards, blackboards on easels and the kind that are made of flexible material and can be rolled round and round) write your material on it and then conceal the dialogue until you want it to be seen; and if you have the wrong sort of blackboard, you can either write up your material beforehand and sellotape old newspaper over it or write the dialogue when you reach the point of the lesson when you want the class to see it. The point is that as soon as you let them *see* it, they are engaged

114

in reading rather than oral fluency-practice. The printed or written dialogue is best used as a visual follow-up to oral work. (One exception to this rule is the 'disappearing dialogue' technique illustrated later in this chapter.)

Since the dialogue is to be dealt with purely orally at first, you have a further problem: the dialogue demands two voices, yet you are normally the only teacher in the class. You therefore have to present your material in one of two ways: either

(i) by talking to yourself, i.e. playing both parts yourself; or
(ii) by using a pre-recorded tape.

Playing two parts yourself can provide humorous and memorable episodes for your class. One technique is to write the names of the two dialogue characters on each side of the blackboard and to stand by the appropriate name as you play each part; one teacher I watched also changed hats as she went from one side of the blackboard to the other, and her class (lower secondary EFL) loved it. Another teacher stood on the dais looking downwards when playing the part of a policeman, then stepped down and looked up at where he had been in order to play the part of a little boy who was lost. This, too, delighted a class of European beginners aged about twelve.

However, there are several advantages in presenting a dialogue by means of tape or cassette if you can. If you are not a native speaker of English, you may want to use dialogues recorded commercially and in this way bring native speakers' voices into your classroom. If you are a native speaker, it is important to provide a variety of voices and regional accents for your class to adjust to. (If you find pre-recorded tapes unsatisfactory for your purposes, or not available, expatriate native speakers will usually help to record a dialogue occasionally; when you do use their services, it is wise to impress upon them the need for natural English spoken at or near normal speed – not the slow, over-enunciated English-For-Foreigners that the British sometimes employ!) It is also possible to 'converse' with a tape-recorder, a routine which I will illustrate later in this chapter.

These, then, are a few of the facts of life to be faced when teaching conversational English: the fact that a class may be so large and time so limited that some work has to be done simultaneously; the fact that you may have to turn yourself into two 'characters' in order to present a dialogue; the fact that cultural and/or developmental inhibitions may militate against the production of fluent English; the fact that a textbook dialogue should be heard and not seen during oral practice. To these I would add what in Chapter 1 I called 'Abbott's Paradox': the fact that, the more a student wants to say something, the more liable he is to resort to use of the mother-tongue or of 'stem-form English'. We now have to consider this tension between formal accuracy on the one hand and, on the other, the ability to communicate successfully, however inaccurate the forms used.

Part 2: Correctness and communication

As teachers, we are reasonably happy with the concept of 'correctness' in English. It is, of course, a Good Thing. It is obviously our job to know what is and is not correct; and it is clearly our duty to make our students similarly aware. However, teachers who are non-native speakers may not be able to detect all errors; and even native speakers disagree on points of correctness, especially concerning certain features of everyday English which do not get into textbooks, e.g. the use of *they* meaning *he* or *she*: *If anyone hasn't got their passport, they'd better go and get it now.* Teachers, whether native speakers or not, may regard such a feature as incorrect because it is not found in textbooks and does not seem 'logical'.

Furthermore, we would agree (probably no language teacher has ever disagreed) that languages are for communicating with. We are aware that linguistic communication is the transfer of *meaning* from one person to another, and that a meaning can be expressed in various ways, as we saw in Chapter 1:

> Why not forget all about it?
> I'd forget about it if I were you.
> etc.

What makes us uneasy is the fact that

> *I suggest you to forget it, OK?

also communicates just as effectively, if said with a reasonable pronunciation.

If we take effective communication in English as our aim, then, are we to accept utterances which are incorrect? The answer, of course, is No. How on earth could you be seen to accept an incorrect sentence offered by a student, when another student – or indeed the same student, after a quick glance at his notes – is likely to challenge you? And how could we happily allow our students to go on using forms which an outside examiner is going to mark wrong? On the other hand, mistakes are inevitable: they occur and recur, sometimes with a frequency that we find alarming. Does this mean that we are to spend all our time pouncing on mistakes? Again, the answer must be No. What attitude are we to take, then?

In the last two or three decades, there has been an increasing concern with communication in English language teaching. What is meant by 'communication' in this context? Does it mean 'passing information to somebody'? Yes; but this can be done without the use of language at all in many everyday situations, and – as we have seen – can be achieved without linguistic accuracy. Does it mean 'saying what one wants to say, instead of what one is told to say'? Yes; but again we have seen that in a TENOR situation a pupil may not truly want to say anything in English, though he may be coaxed into willing co-operation. Does it mean 'saying what is true rather than just what is linguistically correct'? Yes; but this clearly cannot be done all the time. Does it mean 'producing authentic English rather than stilted textbook-ese'? Well, yes again, if possible; but while the use of authentic English conversations has value for listening comprehension practice, I doubt whether such unedited material is of much use to beginners. Or does communication mean 'paying attention to what people mean rather than how they express what they mean'? Certainly; but people sometimes express themselves so badly that we do not know what they mean, and so we come back to the need for accuracy. All of the above ideas are part of the recent 'communicative' movement; and I have had to qualify each of them with a 'but . . .'!

The growth of this movement is reflected in the materials for oral activity developed in the last twenty years or so. Let us now have a brief look at some of these. In order to avoid criticising other people adversely, I shall take examples only from my own work:

Text 1: 1962

Make sentences of the same pattern as the given examples:
FLOUR	a	FLOUR IS MADE INTO BREAD.
BREAD	b	BREAD IS MADE FROM FLOUR.
WOOD	a	WOOD IS MADE INTO PAPER.
PAPER	b	PAPER IS MADE FROM WOOD.

sand   1 a _____

glass   b _____

This drill in its full form contained five pairs of items. It was intended to be done orally, with repetitions when pronunciation was not good enough, and then the answers were to be written in. It is not difficult to find fault with it. To spare my blushes, I will confine myself to two major defects:

(i) Given the examples, it is quite easy for a student to go all through the drill correctly without knowing what he is saying. In substitution drills of this sort, the teacher usually provides the pronunciation of the 'cue' words, so the student's utterance often sounds very good.

(ii) It is difficult to imagine the four sentences (those given in the examples) as a part of a conversation. There is no attempt here to tackle the business of dialogue; there is merely a catalogue of similarly-constructed sentences.

There is also a transformational element in the drill: A . . . B is

117

transformed into B . . . A. Other possible types of transformation are active ←→ passive, positive ←→ negative, positive ←→ interrogative, and so on. Like substitution drills, transformational drills require little or no attention to meaning. Secondary school students themselves, brought up on a diet rich in such exercises, have told me: 'We can do them, and we get them right. But we often don't know what they mean.'

There is one thing to be said in favour of simple substitution drills, however. At the stage when a learner is just beginning to grapple with the oral expression of new sentences, when his STM must not be overloaded and when his tongue sometimes refuses to do what he wants it to do, the repetitiveness of substitution drills has a place. As soon as the pupil has perceived meanings, he concentrates on forms and needs to practise on simple materials such as the above for a while.

Text 2: 1969

EXAMPLES

bicycle	If she were to see the bicycle, she'd certainly want to ride it.
books	If she were to see the books, she'd certainly want to read them.
car	If she were to see the car, she'd certainly want to drive it.
shoes	If she were to see the shoes, she'd certainly want to wear them.

1 piano	4 chocolate
2 parcels	5 letters
3 dress	6 toy

This drill has all the failings of the previous one, except that in order to perform accurately the learner cannot forget all about the meaning of what he is saying: he has to bear in mind the noun given as a cue, and provide a suitable verb and pronoun himself. Again, in spite of the fact that it is totally 'non-communicative', it has one valid use: it is a good way of revising vocabulary in a brisk and quite enjoyable way. (I had not intended it for that purpose, though!)

A development of the substitution drill is the 'guided conversation'. This is an attempt to use a short model dialogue as a basis for variations. Substituting one word often entails making further changes, so there is some need for the student to keep in mind the meaning of what he says:

Text 3: 1971

A   How's your mother?

B   Not very well, I'm afraid. She's going to a new <u>doctor</u>.

X

A   Oh? What's <u>he</u> like?

B   Well, she says *<u>he's</u>* very <u>capable</u>.
                           Y

X	Y
dentist	clever
specialist	knowledgeable
hospital	efficient
clinic	well-run

One of the main difficulties with this type of work is the heavy memory-load required and the consequent dependence on looking at the text in the book or on the blackboard. This can turn the drill into a mere reading-aloud exercise. However, see the 'disappearing dialogue' technique in Part 3 of this chapter.

A similar sort of drill is produced, for use in language laboratories mostly, which places less strain on the memory:

Text 4: 1969

Aim To practise clauses with **WHO** as subject relative pronoun.
  Here are some examples. Listen.
e.g. (a) A   Did you steal this money?
             B   No, sir. The boy who stole it has run away.

    (b) A   Did you hit this little boy?
             B   No, sir. The boy who hit him has run away.

    (c) A   Did you throw those stones?
             B   No, sir. The boy who threw them has run away.

Now you do the same with these:

1   A   Did you break this window?
    B   No, sir. The boy who broke it has run away.

2   A   Did you hurt this little girl?
    B   No, sir. The boy who hurt her has run away.

3   A   Did you start this fight?
    B   No, sir. The boy who started it has run away.

4   A   Did you pick these flowers?
    B ·No, sir. The boy who picked them has run away.

5   A   Did you spill this ink?
    B   No, sir. The boy who spilt it has run away.

Here we see clearly one major development: there are two speakers, and each exchange does resemble dialogue. It is also a little less mechanical than the previous examples since the student (B) has to bear in mind not only the pattern as a whole but also has to supply

(i) the past tense of the verb used by A; and

(ii) the correct pronoun for the object of the verb.

Though this drill was produced for use in language laboratories, such practice is just as well done – and in some ways, I think, better done – in class. The teacher can take the part of A first, addressing one individual at a time. A certain number of students can then be given a slip of paper each; each slip contains a cue-word (e.g. *window*, *ink*) and these students can then engage their neighbours in brief exchanges as the slips are passed round.

Nevertheless the drill is highly artificial; the main trouble is that it is a series of separate dialogues of minimal size, each with a different context, so that the learner has continually to imagine fresh situations: 'some money has been stolen' – 'someone has hit a little boy' – 'some stones have been thrown', and so on. One attempt to overcome this drawback has produced the contextualised drill, in which there is only one context:

Text 5: 1975

Aim   To practise questions beginning with HOW.

Note   Usually, Daddy tells little Bobby a bedtime story about a spy called Captain Wonder. Last night, Daddy didn't finish the story, so Mummy (A) is finishing the story. But little Bobby (B) keeps asking questions.

Listen to these examples.

e.g. (a)   A   Captain Wonder escaped from his cell.
             B   How did he escape from his cell?
             A   Well, I'll tell you.

      (b)   A   He dug a tunnel.
             B   How did he dig a tunnel?
             A   With his spoon.

      (c)   A   Then he climbed over the wall.
             B   How did he climb over the wall?
             A   Well, he was very clever.

Now you ask the questions.

1   A   He made a rope.
      B   How did he make a rope?
      A   By tying two sheets together.

2　A　Then he reached the border.
　　B　How did he reach the border?
　　A　Oh, I forgot to tell you something.

3　A　First, he got a car.
　　B　How did he get a car?
　　A　He stole one, and he drove it to the border.

4　A　Then he hid it.
　　B　How did he hide it?
　　A　He pushed it into a river.

5　A　Er . . . Then he got on a train.
　　B　How did he get on a train?
　　A　He jumped from a bridge.

6　A　Then . . . he crossed the border.
　　B　How did he cross the border?
　　A　Well, he stayed on the roof of the train.

7　A　And in the end, he went home.
　　B　How did he go home?
　　A　Ask Daddy tomorrow. Good night, Bobby!

This 'contextualised' drill shows one or two improvements upon the non-contextualised variety: it is recognisable as *one* dialogue (not several short ones in succession) and it contains some of the features of a conversation such as the pieces of information that link the exchanges and 'fillers' such as *well, oh* and *er*. Students seem to enjoy such drills, perhaps because there is more motivation to listen and take part until the end, and I suspect that some learners enjoy the ingenuity of such a drill as much as its linguistic value. Such drills are indeed difficult to devise, especially when designed to elicit practice of question forms. (Most drills in which questions occur simply make use of the question to elicit a response.) Whatever its merits, the contextualised drill nevertheless smacks of artificiality. For instance, in real conversation, the question forms would be elliptical, e.g.

　　A　He dug a tunnel.
　　B　How? (*not* How did he dig a tunnel?)

　Also enjoyable in spite of some artificiality is the sort of dramatised story in which, because of its repetitiveness, much of the dialogue becomes predictable and can therefore be provided by the learners. We are probably all familiar with such stories from the days of our childhood. There is one about a kind but unintelligent boy who on Monday is sent by his mother to work on a farm. The farmer has no money and every day he pays the boy by giving him food to take home; and every day the boy, Charlie, loses it in some way or another. By

Thursday, all the dialogue shown in brackets can be contributed by the class, and students can be selected to act it out:

Text 6: 1976	
	On Thursday (*Charlie went to the farm and worked hard.*) At the end of the day, he asked the farmer
Charlie	(*Can I have some money, please?*)
Farmer	(*I'm sorry. There isn't any.*)
Charlie	(*Can I have some eggs?*)
Farmer	(*I'm sorry. There aren't any.*)
Charlie	(*Can I have some butter?*)
Farmer	(*I'm sorry. There isn't any.*)
Charlie	(*Can I have some biscuits?*)
Farmer	(*I'm sorry. There aren't any.*) But here's some milk. Charlie took the milk, poured it carefully into the basket and started to walk home happily. But as he was walking home, the milk ran out of the basket. (*When he arrived, there wasn't any milk left.*) His mother opened the door.
Mother	(*Hello, Charlie! What did the farmer give you?*)
Charlie	(*Some milk.*)
Mother	(*Good! Where is it?*)
Charlie	It ran out of the basket. (*There isn't any left. It's all gone.*)
Mother	(*What? You stupid boy!*) *I'm* going to work on the farm tomorrow!

So far, we have noticed an increasing concern to find ways of eliciting 'communication-like' behaviour, conversations that sound as natural as possible given the student's need for clear guidance. We must remember, incidentally, that the simple imitation of a dialogue is mere production by rote learning and remains so however authentic the material is. Some provision for systematic variation of a model dialogue is necessary if the student is to be helped to transfer his skills from the classroom into 'real life'.

Although I have apologised for the artificiality of the materials illustrated so far, we have also to bear in mind that artificiality is inherent in the learner's situation. Students are no fools: they are probably more aware of the social constraints of the classroom than we are, and know that artifice is unavoidable. Besides, some form of repetition is necessary for memorisation; and authentic language is not sufficiently repetitive.

Nevertheless, the persistent concern with communication has produced one technique which will have many useful applications in our classrooms. Communication being, by definition, the transfer of information from a source to a receiver; and information being, by definition, not already known by the receiver; a 'communicative' exercise can be devised simply by ensuring that person A has some information which person B has not, and then prompting an exchange of information. This sort of activity can be done in two ways:

Procedure 1: The teacher knows what his students do not know.
(Consecutive) They elicit the information from him. This can be done when demonstrating the activity to your students before going on to procedure 2. It is also safer than procedure 2 in a large monolingual class that might become noisy and unruly if not closely supervised.

Procedure 2: In each pair, Student A knows what Student B
(Simultaneous) does not know, and vice versa. Each pair works independently.

For example, let us suppose you have an up-to-date Football League table (this one is fictitious):

Text 7: 1980   Teacher's version

Team	Games played	Games won (2 pts)	Games drawn (1 pt)	Games lost (0 pts)	Points scored
Manchester United	12	9	2	1	20
Arsenal	11	9	2	0	20
Liverpool	12	9	1	2	19
Nottingham Forest	12	8	3	1	19
Tottenham Hotspur	11	10	0	1	20

You can (i) get your class to copy from the blackboard a table with no results recorded in it and then get students to ask you and jot down the answers (*Procedure 1*);
or (ii) having briefly started them off in this way, issue to pairs of students the following complementary sets of information, on duplicated sheets:

Student A's card

Team	Games played	Games won (2 pts)	Games drawn (1 pt)	Games lost (0 pts)	Points scored
Manchester United	(12)	9	2		
Arsenal		(9)			
Liverpool	12	9	(1)		
Nottingham Forest				(1)	
Tottenham Hotspur	11		0		(20)

Student B's card

Team	Games played	Games won (2 pts)	Games drawn (1 pt)	Games lost (0 pts)	Points scored
Manchester United	(12)				
Arsenal	11	(9)	2		
Liverpool			(1)		
Nottingham Forest	12	8	3	(1)	
Tottenham Hotspur		10			(20)

(Students can work the last two columns out by themselves.)

The shared information (circled on each card) is used by the teacher at the start of the practice, for the purpose of providing model questions. (*How many games have Manchester United played?* etc.) Students get the rest of the information from each other. If they want to find out who is top, second, and so on, further empty columns can be put on the blackboard, and the class can elicit from you the information necessary for establishing the position of the teams:

Goals scored	Goals conceded	Position
21	8	2nd
22	10	3rd
18	6	5th
20	7	4th
17	3	1st

It is quite likely, though, that you have no access to duplicating facilities. In this case, students can be asked to copy a blank framework from the blackboard and fill in their own details, taking care not to let their neighbours see. For example, suppose your students have been practising some simple 'social' English such as:

> What's that man's name?   Pablo.
> Where does he come from?   Venezuela.
> What does he do?   He's a student here.

You can now ask everyone to copy this from the board:

Text 8: 1980

Person	Name	Country	Occupation
Man			
Woman			
Old lady			
Boy			
Girl			

(The headings are not necessary, of course, and you may want to do without them.)

You then ask the class to fill in details of their own choosing. As soon as each pair is ready, simultaneous pair-practice can begin and you can 'listen in' as you move around. One or two particularly good (or particularly funny!) examples can be identified for public performance later.

125

The element of problem-solving (finding out the positions of the five football teams) provides good motivation for pursuing the exercise. Simple detective work is always popular. Here, as a final example, is one which works well when done using just the blackboard, from which the class copies the empty table, with the teacher holding the completed table in his hand to begin with. Earlier, I said that in real conversation many questions are elliptical. (A: He dug a tunnel. B: How?) This final example shows how such forms can be given deliberate practice.

Text 9: 1980

Name	Eyes	Hair	Age	Height
Anderson	brown	fair	40	very tall
Jackson	(blue)	fair	20	very tall
Johnson	blue	(fair)	39	very short
Richardson	blue	fair	(41)	very tall
Robinson	blue	white	70	(very tall)

Providing a model:
The table is originally empty except for the parenthesised items. Also on BB is the problem:

> 'One of these men is a murderer. The police know that he is very tall, is about forty years old and has blue eyes and fair hair. Which man in the murderer?'

T: What colour is Mr Jackson's eyes?   C: Blue, etc.

Providing practice:
PP ask T – or other PP who have been given the information. At the appropriate times, T encourages PP to say, e.g.:

> It can't be Mr Anderson, because he's got brown eyes.
> It might be Mr Jackson because he's got fair hair.
> It must be Mr Richardson!

Notes: Any eliminated suspect is ignored, there being no purpose in asking useless questions. Working column by column (vertically) and across (horizontally) elicits two forms of textuality:

	What colour are	Mr. Anderson's	eyes	
And	what about	Mr. Jackson's	( )?	*Vertical*
And	( )	Mr. Johnson's	( )?	

	What colour are	Mr. Anderson's	eyes?	
And	what about	his	hair?	
	How *old* is	he	?	*Horizontal*
And	how *tall* ( )	( )	?	

In the above 'information-gap' exercises I have concentrated on the practice of questions because in my opinion the teaching of question-use is generally poor. This technique is ideally suited to the practice of questions; but its usefulness does not end there, as we have seen in previous chapters. Any of the 'information transfer' techniques illustrated earlier for use in comprehension work can be reversed and used for oral practice. For example, after doing the 'Weekday Islands' exercise (Chapter 3), students can be required to narrate the main details of the sea journey using only their maps as cues. However, this sort of exercise practises monologue rather than dialogue, and will be dealt with in the following chapter.

There is one other recent technique which should be briefly mentioned but which does not strike me as very useful in most teaching situations. Pairs of students are given cards on which the roles they are to play are indicated as in this fictitious example:

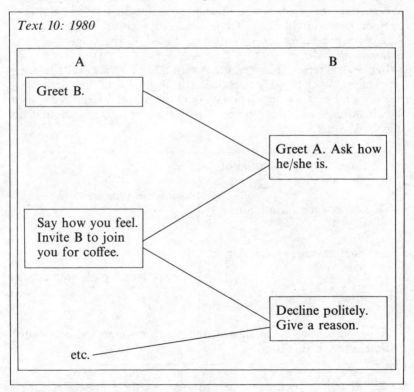

Text 10: 1980

A   B

Greet B.

Greet A. Ask how he/she is.

Say how you feel. Invite B to join you for coffee.

Decline politely. Give a reason.

etc.

One assumption of such exercises is that the students will already be familiar with the labels for various functions (*greet, invite, decline*). This might be true in the case of students who have studied English for some considerable time in a rather bookish way but who need to be shown

127

how to operate in conversation; it is not true of the majority of learners. If both of the students know *greet*, for example, there is no problem at this stage. If they do not, then either the exercise is useless or the teacher must teach the meaning of *greet*; and it is a strange form of grading which puts *greet* before *hello*. Furthermore, it is dangerous to give the instruction 'Ask how he is'. It will quite often lead to the production of **How you are?* In any case, there is nothing very 'communicative' in acting under instruction in this way.

Our brief survey has covered the period from 1962 to 1980. Though I recorded the dates of materials for the sake of interest, it must not be thought that, like archaeologists digging deeper, we can (or should) date techniques so that we know which is the most old-fashioned. Quite the contrary. I suggest that, within the space of one lesson (i.e. class period), we could well follow the course that we have just been surveying: the journey from 'concern for accuracy' to 'concern for communication'. We should not reject the old-fashioned (or even think in terms of 'fashion'); we should rather retain it and supplement it with the new. Again, the prevailing *either-or* attitude should, I suggest, give way to a *both-and* attitude.

In practical terms, this means that we might want to use all the major types of oral work roughly classified at the beginning of this chapter (see p. 113), and that we could well employ them in the sequence 1a, 1b, 2a, 2b, so that within the space of half an hour in class our students might participate in:

1a	simultaneous imitation of model	'correctness' desirable
1b	consecutive variation of model	
2a	simultaneous † extension in pairs	'communication' desirable
2b	dramatised public performances'	

† but consecutive if the class is difficult to manage and/or totally uninterested in English.

I would hate it to be thought that this was my definitive recipe for all circumstances. I am thinking mainly of the fairly large secondary school class of zero-motivated learners, but even here I am just offering a suggestion, not a prescription; one of the stages could be omitted in small classes and in those that are easy to manage.

In any case, no activity – least of all the oral part of a lesson – should degenerate into mere routine. The next and final section contains a few ideas, some of which will, I hope, stimulate you to provide a variety of further activities of your own devising; the ones that I offer can be slavishly copied if you like, but normally any other person's ideas will benefit from some adaptation to your own particular circumstances. I do not claim that they are particularly novel or startling, and I shall not make use of very unusual, too expensive or otherwise 'impossible' aids. I realise that in some places even the simplest materials and facilities are hard to find. I shall confine myself to the blackboard, the flannelboard and the tape recorder.

Part 3: Some ideas to consider

A   The questionnaire

Before going on to teaching activities, I have one suggestion which (I confess) I have never used myself, but which now strikes me as potentially very useful as a way of ensuring that some of what is said in class is true of, and relevant to, our students. At the beginning of the school year or course, they could complete a questionnaire (typed in the mother tongue if necessary) designed by you to elicit the sort of personal information that you expect will be useful during the coming session. For example, if the Present Perfect is introduced in the textbook, some of your questions could elicit information about your students' travels and experiences; or, in readiness for the Present Simple, you might want to ask about likes and dislikes in music (*likes, plays*), reading-matter (*reads, buys*), sports (*plays*), and so on. These simple questionnaires would be completed and handed in to you. You would use them when deciding what particular model sentences to use, or when devising some model dialogues, or choosing vocabulary items for an exercise about the students' experiences: 'Pietro has been to Paris. He has eaten snails. He has seen the Eiffel Tower' . . . etc. (others can say 'I've never . . .' or 'I haven't eaten snails but I have eaten frogs' legs') . . . or preferences: 'Nikos likes folk music. He plays the guitar' . . . etc. Students are usually more interested in each others' lives than in those of textbook characters. Some teachers prefer to issue little questionnaires while such linguistic topics are being dealt with, rather than at the beginning of the year. You can, of course, do either – or both.

B   The blackboard

(i) If you cannot (or will not?) draw pictures on the board, you will at least admit that there are some visuals which you can draw: street-plans, maps, tables of information, road-signs, charts, ground-plans and graphs do not require drawing-ability. Here is the blackboard table

129

E

copied down and used by the students in **EXAMPLE 2** at the beginning of this chapter. Remember?

Mr & Mrs	*Children*		*House*		*Car*		*Television*	
	boys	*girls*	*large*	*small*	*British*	*foreign*	*b/w*	*colour*
Aston	2	1	1	—	1	—	—	1
Bolton								
Chilton								
Dutton								
Easton								

The teacher went through the given examples (i.e. details about the Astons), drilled the class on these questions and answers and then allowed students to make up and fill in the other details themselves. Students on the left did the Boltons and the Chiltons, their neighbours did the rest, and neither saw the others' table. Then, as in **EXAMPLE 2**, neighbouring students asked each other about 'their' families.

(ii) Here is a simple street plan which can be built up as you get increasingly more complex practice of asking for and giving directions.

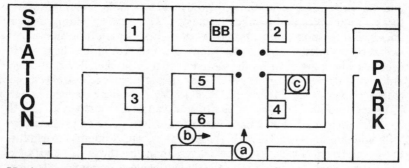

Having established a simple enquiry, e.g. *Excuse me, where's the Bank of Britain, please?* the teacher indicates various starting-points which involve journeys of increasing length. Those marked on the above plan will elicit directions such as the following:

    ⓐ   Go straight on. It's on your left.

    ⓑ→   Turn left and go straight on. It's on your left.

    ⓒ   Turn left outside the door, turn right at the traffic-lights and then go straight ahead. It's on your left.

(However, you would be unlikely to do all of this in one lesson!)

At the right time you can tell the students, working in pairs, that the ones on the right take even numbers and the ones on the left take odd numbers. They quickly copy the plan if they have not already done so, and you explain that a student can locate each of his places in any of the three numbers available to him on his plan, taking care not to let his neighbour see. The places are indicated on the blackboard (but not on the map, of course):

Evens	*Odds*
the library	the museum
the bus station	the police station
the mosque	the market

Starting at the gates of the park, students ask each other the way. Directions must always be given from the place just reached. At the end, street plans are compared.

There are all sorts of variations of this; but care must be taken not to overdo this or any other form of practice. I have heard learners mutter (in their mother tongue, not knowing that I understood) 'Oh, God, not *another* map!'

(iii) The 'disappearing dialogue' is a surprisingly popular technique, considering that it is founded on sheer memorisation. It consists mainly of the cumulative rubbing-out of bits of a blackboard dialogue. The erasing can be done at random; but I find that the simplest way is to write it in (say) three imaginary columns, so that erasing from right to left is done quickly and easily. You challenge pairs of students to remember it as you successively rub out column 3 and column 2:

A:	Can I	help you	madam?
B:	My	car was stolen	last night.
A:	Where	was it	parked?
B:	In	my garage,	of course.
A:	Was	your garage	locked?
B:	No,	it wasn't.	

Column 1	*Column 2*	*Column 3*
Not erased, but left for 'substitution' work.	Erased after second period of practice.	Erased after first period of practice.

Then you get a different dialogue to appear.

When only Column 1 is left, you change *car* to *gun* and give the pairs enough time to plan what they are going to say. They can vary whatever they want to, e.g.:

131

A: Can I help you, *sir?*
B: My *gun* was stolen *this morning.*
A: Where was it *kept?*
B: In my *desk.*
A: Was *your desk* locked?
B: *Yes, it was.*

Then you can change *gun* to *jewels* . . .

(iv) If you can draw simple stick figures and shapes, you can slowly build up a picture. At first there is no detail, no context: at the beginning, therefore, it is necessary to use expressions of uncertainty. Expressions of certainty appear as the context becomes clearer. An example of this is given on the facing page.

Of course, this does not have to be as complex as I have made it; and of course you could use four large pictures on card consecutively. You could go on to encourage your class to write the story of how the poor fellow met his death.

Oral practice of a very similar kind can be achieved using a problem in written form. Look at Chapter 11, page 270, for example: by putting the empty table on the BB, you can get individuals to contribute steps to the solution, using *might be/can't be/must be* followed by a *because*-clause.

C The cheap flannelboard

This is an underestimated aid and is my favourite. Let me tell you how to make and use one that is cheap, easy to make and efficient.
You need:-
(i) a piece of wood or soft man-made board, 1m × 75cm or thereabouts, not too heavy; one side of a large box will do, as long as it is fairly flat.
(ii) a piece of flannelette or brushed cotton material (not of man-made fibre) which is 4 or 5cm longer and wider than your board. I prefer white material.
(iii) some drawing-pins.
Simply stretch the material over the board and pin it down at the back. (Some people like to glue the material to the board.) If you need to carry it around a lot, you might want to make it a little narrower and give it some sort of grip or handle; this will largely depend on the weight of your board. So much for the board. What about the materials to use on it?

Find an old newspaper, some old used duplicating paper and a piece of fairly fine sandpaper (glasspaper). Put a sheet of newspaper on your table to protect it. Put a sheet of duplicating paper on top and sand it. Stroke with the sandpaper from the middle to the right only (assuming you are right-handed). Hold the sheet in position with your left hand. Do *not* go backwards and forwards, as this will crease and tear the paper. Soon, this sanding will make the paper slightly furry. Turn the duplicating paper 180° and sand the other half of the same side in

Step	Accident . . . Murder? . . . or Suicide?		
	Picture on BB	What you do/say	What students practise
		'He's lying on the ground. Why?'	He might be dead/sunbathing hurt/resting ill/falling drunk/asleep.
		Add rain and pavement; invite suggestions.	He isn't sunbathing/falling. He can't be resting/asleep. He might be dead/drunk/ ill/hurt.
		Add house, blood, back of car. Tell the class what it is as you add detail. e.g.: 'There are windows. . . . here's some blood . . .' etc.	He might have fallen over. / fallen out of a window. / been run over. / been pushed out of a window.
		Add broken window, glass on pavement.	He can't have been run over. He might have fallen through the window. He might have been pushed.
		At this point, say 'There is a small hole in his head. There is no gun, here or in his room.'	He must have been shot/murdered. He can't have shot himself committed suicide. He must have fallen when he was shot, etc.

133

exactly the same way. If you now place the furry side of the sheet against your flannelboard, it should stay there. If all is well, you can now practise with clean paper or cheap card.

Always sand your paper before turning it over and drawing/writing on it. Your pictures can be kept easily in folders or envelopes and will last literally for years.

(i) The advantage of the flannelboard over the blackboard is the mobility of the visuals and the fact that they can be manipulated by the student. It is helpful in formal grammatical work, providing a handy introduction, a reminder or a remedial aid. Here is a set for use when dealing with Present Simple statements and questions:

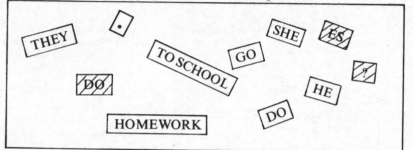

You can use these yourself in an explanatory way when introducing this grammatical topic; but I would prefer to get the students to use them a little later on. Start with the board empty, then proceed as follows, for example:

Start with: | THEY | GO | TO | SCHOOL | . |

Teacher's move   *Student's move*

Replace full-stop with question mark. | ~~DO~~ | THEY | GO | TO | SCHOOL | ~~?~~ |

Replace *they* with *she*. | ~~DO~~ ~~ES~~ | SHE | GO | TO | SCHOOL | ~~?~~ |

Replace question-mark with full stop. | SHE | GO ~~ES~~ | TO | SCHOOL | . |

Replace *to school* with *homework*. | SHE | DO ~~ES~~ | HOMEWORK | . |

Replace full-stop, etc. | ~~DO~~ ~~ES~~ | SHE | DO | HOMEWORK | ~~?~~ |

This can easily be made into a team game, but the visuals do suffer from over-eager handling! You could make similar sets for negatives and for practice of the Past Simple forms.

(ii) For the more advanced students, you can use your flannelboard for teaching sensitivity to and production of appropriate intonation patterns. The following sentences, for example, have different implications depending on where the main stress (white arrow) falls. (The black arrow, indicating a rising intonation, remains constant.)

Sentences					*Typical implications*

| PETER | DIDN'T | BREAK | JOHN'S | WATCH | FRED DID. |

| PETER | DIDN'T | BREAK | JOHN'S | WATCH | HE LOST IT. |

| PETER | DIDN'T | BREAK | JOHN'S | WATCH | HE BROKE MARY'S. |

| PETER | DIDN'T | BREAK | JOHN'S | WATCH | HE BROKE HIS CLOCK. |

You will need: the five words of the sentence; the four implications; and just three arrows, all sanded, of course. There are various ways of proceeding, depending on how aware of intonation your class has become. Here is one way.

(a) You put up just the sentence; then say it in the four different ways, adjusting the falling arrow each time.

(b) Do the same, this time without the falling arrow, getting students to tell you which word you stressed.

(c) Say again, this time putting up (and then removing) the implication.

(d) Say again at random; a pair of students respond, one by placing the falling arrow on the right and the other by putting up (or holding up) the right implication.

(e) Pairs of students come to the front. One speaks, the other holds up the implication; then vice versa.

Finally, you can forget the board and practise dialogues:

Peter didn't break John's watch. Well, who *did* then? *Fred.*	Peter didn't *break* John's watch. Well, what *did* he do with it? He *lost* it.
Peter didn't break *John's* watch. Well, whose *was* it then? *Mary's.*	Peter didn't break John's *watch*. Well, what *did* he break? His *clock*.

(iii) In English, as in all languages, we do not normally use longer forms than we need to use. *The man in the corner* is fine unless there happen to be two men there, one standing and one sitting. In this case we have to say, e.g. *the man standing in the corner* in order to avoid ambiguity. But if there were two men standing there a moment ago and we want to refer to the one who has just gone away, we have to say *the man who was standing in the corner*. Prepositional phrase → participial phrase → relative clause: we use the shortest possible. Many learners need to have this

135

explained and to practise these forms carefully, since their languages have a different system. Your flannelboard can help you. This is what you need:

1 These people are at a party. Put Jack and Jill on the board, standing by the door. ('Who's that man over there by the door?' . . . 'Jack'.)
2 Put Jim in Jill's place.
('Who's that man over there by the door?' . . . 'Which one?')
Show how the question was inefficient this time.
3 Go through the other examples ('by the window/table'), using first man-woman couples, then single-sex pairs, and get students to volunteer the most efficient sentence in each case.
4 Now take away one of the pairs that you put up, saying 'He's/She's gone home'. Show that it is now necessary to say:

Who's that	man woman	who was	standing sitting	by the	window? door? table?

Start again and get pairs of students to ask and answer.
A game could be set up, so that a team lost points for inefficient questions that made the opposition ask, 'Which one?'

D The tape-recorder

I shall confine myself to a few brief suggestions here.
(i) Firstly, try talking to the tape-recorder. If you want to present a dialogue and cannot (or do not want to) use a commercial one, get a friend, colleague or relative to record just one speaker's part, with very brief pauses between each 'turn'. For example it should be no trouble to get someone to record:
Tape: That's twenty-five pounds, sir (madam) . . . At nine o'clock.
In class, using the *pause* mechanism, you speak to the voice on the tape:

136

You	The tape
Two singles to Manchester, please.	
	That's twenty five pounds, sir.
Here you are. When's the next train?	
	At nine o'clock.
Thanks.	

If you 'learn your lines' you can hold quite lengthy and very lifelike conversations with your machine!

(ii) Secondly, your students can talk to the machine:

You	The tape
Listen . . .	(sobbing noises)
It's Flo, She's crying. Why? I don't know. Ask her.	
Students	
Why are you crying?	Because I fell over.
Why did you fall over?	Because I was running.
Why were you running?	Because I'm late for school.
Why are you late?	Because I got up late.
Why did you get up late?	Because I went to bed late.
Why did you go to bed late?	Because I was studying.
Why were you studying?	Because I've got an exam today . . . And
	I'm late! (sobbing noises)

(iii) Lastly, I would suggest that recording the voices of students in class is not done as much as it could be. Now that very light portable cassette recorders are made which can be carried with the strap slung over a shoulder and the microphone held in the hand, the 'walkabout' or 'man-in-the-street interview' technique should be used as a means of giving the learner the feedback he needs. If during pair-practice you were to get recordings here and there, you could later provide different and less embarrassing public performances which would sooner or later include every voice in the class.

Sources of the texts in Chapter 5, Part 2

Text 1. ABBOTT, G. and KRUATRAUCHUE, F. *Towards better reading and writing,* Workbook 3. Social Sciences Press, Bangkok, 1962.
Text 2. ABBOTT, G. *Conditionals.* Longman, 1969.
Text 3. ABBOTT, G. Unpublished handout material, Dip.TEO Course, Manchester University.

137

Text 4.　ABBOTT, G.　*Relative clauses,* Teacher's book.　Longman, 1969 for the British Council.

Text 5.　ABBOTT, G.　*Question-word questions,* Teacher's book.　Longman, 1975 for the British Council.

Text 6.　ABBOTT, G.　*What next?* Teacher's book.　Longman, 1976.

Texts 7, 8 and 9.　ABBOTT, G.　'Teaching the learner to ask for information'　*TESOL Quarterly,* 14, 1, 1980.

Text 10.　ABBOTT, G.　Unpublished. 1980.

Further reading

Books

Probably the most useful single book to turn to for practical help is:
BYRNE, D.　*Teaching oral English.*　Longman, 1976.

If you want to read more about the theoretical and recent historical background without getting bogged down in theory, you should dip into the relevant sections of:
RIVERS, W.　*Teaching foreign language skills.*　University of Chicago Press, 1968.

An excellent book on aspects of learning and teaching oral fluency – whether or not you use a language laboratory – is:
DAKIN, J.　*The language laboratory and language learning.*　Longman, 1973.

For further help and inspiration with audio-visual aids, try:
LEE, W. and COPPEN, H.　*Simple audio-visual aids to foreign language teaching.*　Oxford University Press, 2nd edition, 1968.

or, if you need more sophisticated suggestions, these:
HOLDEN, S. (Ed.)　*Visual aids for classroom interaction.*　London: Modern English Publications, 1978.

WRIGHT, A.　*Visual materials for the language teacher.*　Longman, 1976.

Articles

ABBOTT, E.　'Communicative exercises: a problem and a suggested solution'　*ELTJ,* 33, 3, 1979.

ABBOTT, G.　'Teaching the learner to ask for information'　*TESOL Quarterly,* 14, 1, 1980.

Chapter 6: Writing

by Peter Wingard

EXAMPLE 1

First, turn back to page 111 and read Example 1. After such oral pre-paration, the class goes on to produce a written account of the process. To remind them, they have diagrams of the five steps. They also have the following **BB** table, shown to them before they start, hidden while they write, then shown again to help them check their work:

First		trees		fell-	-ed
	the		are	float-	
Then		branches		remove-	-d
—		logs		drag-	-ged
		they		sawn	

Work produced by Dokmai, a fairly good pupil:
(errors underlined)
First the trees are felled. Then the branches are removed. The logs are dragged <u>into a</u> nearest river. They are floated down to a sawmill and sawn <u>to the</u> planks.

EXAMPLE 2

Now imagine another class which, after practising the oral use of the Passive, is given a formal written drill as a follow-up. The BB has:

Turn these sentences into the Passive.
1   They fell the trees.
2   A raft floats on a river.
3   They remove the hair from the skin with a knife.
4   The carpenter saws the planks into sections.
5   A beaver drags heavy pieces of wood to build a dam.

Work produced by Chardchai, a fairly good pupil:
(errors underlined)
1   The trees were <u>fallen</u> by them.
2   A river is floated on by a raft.
3   The hair is <u>remove</u> from the skin with a knife.
4   The logs are <u>saw</u> by the carpenter into sections.
5   Heavy pieces of wood <u>dragged</u> by a beaver to build a dam.

Part 1: Preliminaries

Dokmai and Chardchai have each made four obvious mistakes. Dokmai's mistakes are not concerned with the Passive, but with prepositions and articles. She uses the sequence adverbs *first* and *then*, and does not over-use them. She uses *they* instead of repeating *the logs*, and she leaves out the unnecessary repetition of *they are* after *and*. She seems capable of using the Passive to recount a simple process. Such basic skill is capable of further development towards more sophisticated accounts of more complicated processes.

Chardchai has been made to concentrate more narrowly on practising the Passive, but he has made four errors with the Passive itself. Dealing with single sentences, he has no thread of meaning to guide him. So he tends to concentrate his attention on linguistic forms themselves. *Fell* strikes him as a past tense – the most common use of this form – so he transforms that past tense form into the Passive form *were fallen*. The form *remove* sticks in his mind and he reproduces it, omitting the redundant *-d*. In the case of *saws*, he remembers to take off the *-s*, but again forgets the *-d*. In the case of *drags*, he again remembers to take off the *-s* and add *-ged*, but this time forgets the redundant *are*.

You may feel that these manufactured examples are unfairly weighted against Chardchai's exercise. Perhaps Dokmai too would have made mistakes with the Passive. Both experience and research, however, show that errors are more numerous when attention to meaning is weaker. Apart from the question of errors, Dokmai has at least done an exercise which takes her a few steps on the road to communicating in English about processes, whereas Chardchai is still doing knees-bend exercises indoors and has not begun to face the problems of actually walking.

This chapter will emphasise three aspects of the learning and teaching of written English:

(i) Writing as a *channel* of FL learning; that is, the use of writing alongside listening, speaking and reading in the process of learning important elements of the language and developing command of the language;

(ii) Writing as a *goal* of FL learning; that is, the development of writing skills to fulfil such purposes as note-taking, summarising, narrating, reporting and replying required for various real-life situations.

(iii) Writing with *cohesion*; that is, employing the various linguistic means by which the parts of any written text are made to relate to one another and to constitute a continuous, organised whole.

These three aspects are really inseparable, and any piece of written practice may be expected to contribute to all of them. But it may assist clarity of thinking if we consider them one at a time, and any particular exercise may emphasise one of them more than the others.

In recent years there has been a healthy tendency for written exercises to show an increasing concern with communication rather than with mere practice of linguistic forms. This has meant a greater emphasis on whole texts of paragraph or greater length, and on the cohesive devices by which such texts are articulated. This is all to the good. But we must remember that whole texts are constructed of sentences, and that we have to find ways of making sure that the sentence grammar is well known as well as ways of practising putting sentences together for communicative purposes. You cannot make bricks without straw, and you cannot build houses without bricks.

When we come to consider whole texts, the matter of appropriateness for communication is so important that it should be kept in mind throughout this chapter.

Before he starts writing, and from time to time as he writes, the student should be asked, and encouraged to ask himself: 'What is the purpose of this communication? To tell a sequence of events? To explain how something is made up? How something works? The reasons for something? To compare? To advise? To seek advice?' etc, etc. If the student has received a firm grounding, this highlighting of the function of what he is writing will help call to mind the appropriate grammar and vocabulary he has previously learned and used in relation to that function.

But the function should not be considered in abstraction. The writer should also be asked, and encouraged to ask himself: 'Who is my potential reader? What will he reasonably expect to find in my message? How can I make it clear, unambiguous and readable for him?' This will help the writer to select the most appropriate language and present it in the most appropriate way.

There must also be some plausible reason (apart from the need to exercise writing skill) why the communication is being made in writing rather than orally. This may be obvious. Perhaps the addressee is at a distance, and cannot be spoken to. Or the communication is intended to be used by many different addressees over a period of time. Or it is important for the addressee to have a precise record so that he can refer back to it in detail. Having asked: 'Why does this communication need to be in writing? What is the advantage of making it in writing?' the writer will be led to think about the difference between spoken and written language.

Writing can often be more concise, but it must be fully explicit, whereas spoken communication can often be sketchy and leave things to be clarified later in reply to questions. Writing sometimes, but not always, needs to be more formal and more impersonal. In writing there are ways in which you can help the addressee's understanding through visual layout – through punctuation, for example. In written communication, also, more care can be devoted to making things easier for the addressee through effective ways of arranging and connecting up what you want to say. If a student has received a good grounding, thinking about this will call to mind the basic cohesive features he needs to compose a good written text.

Thus we should constantly keep to the forefront the purpose of communication, the needs of the addressee, and the requirements of the written medium. This calls for imaginative effort on the part of the teacher and the students. The teacher cannot just say 'Write' but must discuss with the students the occasion and setting of each piece of writing. This will add interest to the writing task and effectiveness to the product.

This book does not deal with handwriting. For learners already literate in a language using the Roman alphabet, handwriting presents few serious problems. For illiterate learners of English, and for learners literate in a non-Roman script, it demands more space than could be given in this book. For such learners a systematic handwriting course should obviously form part of the early stages of learning English. Often the course-book in use does not give sufficient guidance, and supplementary material on handwriting is necessary. In this situation teachers are recommended to consult Bright and Piggott (1976).

Spelling can be touched on very briefly here. Its problems are more complex than those of handwriting, and comprehensive guidance cannot be found in any one source. Clear thinking on teaching English spelling to foreign learners starts with the division of the problems into two groups:

(i) Problems arising from complications and irregularities in the English writing system. These are the same for foreign learners and native speakers alike, and lead to such errors as *nessessary, *hopefull, *seperate*, etc, etc. For such problems we may get help from material intended for native speakers of English. A variety of practice techniques – visual, auditory, kinaesthetic and cognitive – may prove helpful. For a good brief guide see Moorhouse (1977) in Further Reading at the end of this chapter. Try to show students that there *are* regularities in the system. Wherever possible, find a *group* of words having the particular spelling pattern which is giving trouble. For example, *c* before *e, i* or *y* represents /s/ in *centre, cedar, city, civilised, cycle* and *cylinder*. Learning spelling rules can be interesting and useful. Do you know, for instance, why we write *cat* with *c* and *kitten* with *k*? If not, turn to page 168.

(ii) Problems connected with MT interference are special to foreign learners, and vary according to their MT. They lead to errors such as the following:

– *seating* for *sitting* (MT having only one sound unit in the area covered by the two English sound units /iː/ and /ɪ/).
– *hole* for *hall* (MT having only one sound unit in the /o–ɔː/ range).
– *librairy* for *library* (MT using *ai* spelling in cognate word or words; e.g. French *librairie*).

It is clear from these examples that there can be interference from MT pronunciation and/or MT spelling. In the biggest number of cases pronunciation is the basic difficulty. Wherever you identify a spelling problem linked to MT interference in pronunciation, teach the spelling in immediate connection with the pronunciation. An example of variation in the manifestation of a problem according to the MT is spelling error associated with the English phoneme /ʌ/. Many languages lack a central vowel comparable to this. In certain types of West African English the English phoneme tends to be replaced by an MT sound approximating to /ɒ/. This naturally produces spelling errors such as **hont* for *hunt*. In certain types of East African English, however, the replacement made is an MT sound approximating to /a/. This is associated with spelling errors such as **hant* for *hunt*. In all such cases careful analysis of the pronunciation problems (see Chapter 2) is the teacher's first move.

Part 2: Writing as a channel of FL learning

A   The contribution of written work

There are good psychological and practical reasons why writing (W) should be fully integrated with listening, speaking and reading (L, S and R) in a FL course, and not treated in isolation or neglected. Even where the main goal is spoken skill, W can be of great assistance. Let us look at some of its contributions.

(i) If we analyse L, S, R and W we find a large overlap among the component skills involved in them. There are differences, of course, but there are many elements in common. Thus to teach L, S, R and W in close association makes for economy in learning. This applies right from the early stages, and we can regard with suspicion any suggestion that the introduction of R and/or W should be substantially delayed. We can also ignore dogmatic arguments to the effect that, in introducing a new linguistic item, the order of practice must always be L, S, R, W.

(ii) In real-life communication there is of course frequently *alternation* between receptive and productive activity, and between the use of spoken and written channels. For instance, a businessman reads a letter he has received, jots down notes about it, makes a phone call to check an important point, and finally drafts his reply in writing or dictates it on to a tape. L, S, R and W all contribute and mesh together in his activity. There seems good reason to think that similar alternation and inter-mingling are appropriate in FL learning.

(iii) People do differ, of course, in their ability to learn through the ear, through the eye and through muscular movement. Some pianists, for instance, get help in memorising a piece of music by being able to call up a visual image of the printed page of the score. Others completely lack this ability. All pianists, however, depend on the memory of a series of muscular movements and, most of all, the memory of a complex pattern of sounds. In FL learning, some learners are more dependent than others on the visual and muscular memories associated with W. In any class, different students will have a different balance in their ability to learn aurally, visually and kinaesthetically (that is, through movement). Thus the safest approach to the class as a whole is one which employs all three.

(iv) When we write in our MT, we often rehearse as we go along, in the form of 'inner speech', what we intend to put down on paper. Sometimes we need to discuss orally with someone what we are going to write and the way we are going to put it – when planning an important letter or a serious written proposal of some kind, for example. If this is so in the MT, how much more important is oral preparation, both of the audible and of the inaudible kind, when writing in a foreign or second language. Without it, the learner is much more likely to take refuge in mental translation from the MT. His writing will be less fluent and more prone to MT interference errors. A written exercise without oral preparation tends to be more of a test than a training exercise. Oral preparation should thus be the rule rather than the exception, so that when the learner begins to write he has a clear idea of the format and content, and a ready flow of suitable 'inner speech', which he can transcribe with suitable editing into the written text he wants to produce.

(v) What is taken in through more than one channel is more likely to be learned well. That is, the channels can reinforce one another. They can of course interfere with one another too. For example, we have already noted how pronunciation problems can lead to spelling problems. Another obvious case of mutual interference is when a teacher interrupts students' concentration on a piece of written work by giving a stream of spoken instructions. However, provided we can minimise interference, practice in L, S, R and W can be mutually reinforcing.

(vi) W is especially suited to a reinforcing role, as it is done relatively slowly, should involve close concentration, and leaves a record which can be used later. Its potential for reinforcement is not achieved unless conditions are right, however. Too often we see the written exercise relegated to the fag-end of the lesson, done hastily, and not even completed by most of the class. Perhaps the earlier part of the lesson was not finished on time for some reason, so the teacher squeezes the written work into the last few minutes, when everyone is tired and waiting for the bell. Concentration is close to zero, the work is scrappy, and there will not be an orderly written record for later reference. It is true that written work, because of the concentration and attention to detail it requires, should be done in fairly short spells. But these must be adequate in length for the task in hand, and must not be given when students are tired. For some readers, my reference to 'an orderly written record for later reference' may arouse unhappy memories of copybook notes to be learned by heart and regurgitated in a test. This is not at all what I have in mind. Properly considered, the idea of a cumulative written record is not to be despised. If written work is done on pieces of paper which are not then filed, or if it consists merely of 'first drafts' in a 'rough notebook', without a 'fair copy' ever being produced, its value is much diminished. I am not suggesting that there must be a 'fair copy' stage for every exercise, but that there sometimes should be one.

(vii) W lends itself more easily than L, S or R to *individualisation* of learning. There are two aspects of this. The first is variation to suit different levels of ability in a class. It is quite difficult to carry this out in the average class in the case of L and S, somewhat easier in the case of R, and easiest for W. Without changing the nature of the exercise, we can set work at a basic level for everyone, and extra work at a more extended and sophisticated level for the better students.

(viii) A second aspect of individualisation to which W lends itself is *self-dependence* in learning. With regard to S practice in the language laboratory, a frequent cause of complaint is students' failure to notice the difference between their own performance and the model. In W practice it is easier to train students in self-checking and correction, and such training is essential from the beginning stage. Nevertheless, individualisation can be overdone, and students should also be trained to co-operate by checking each other's work. We all find mistakes more easily in other people's work than in our own. If we have been led to think of mistakes as part of the process of learning rather than a sign of moral turpitude, and if the classroom atmosphere is not excessively competitive, students will gratefully accept each other's help in this respect.

(ix) Thus time spent on written work *in class* is not wasted, and teachers should not feel guilty about it, provided of course they are not inactive while it is in progress. It permits *immediate* checking of individuals' work, and the possibility of reminding the whole class at a suitable point to check for a particular type of error which is found to be occurring. This immediate feedback is of great assistance to teaching and learning.

B The nature and grading of written exercises

Different written exercises have different purposes, and many will be multi-purpose. Sometimes a major purpose may be the practice of a particular grammatical form, or of a way of expressing a particular function or notion. For example, you may wish to exercise the use of relative clauses, or ways of expressing duration, etc, etc. But wherever possible an exercise should have some intrinsic function or interest which is real for the students – describing something which the reader does not already know, giving an opinion, solving a problem, etc. I am not suggesting that you will *never* give exercises involving mechanical drill or isolated sentences. But most exercises should involve effort to express meaning, selection of meaning to be expressed, and production of a complete text.

A complete text does not mean a *long* text, of course. One way in which written work can be graded is in length. Exercises for near-beginners and 'false beginners' should be limited to texts of about half a dozen sentences. Quality is of paramount importance. Several short exercises will generally produce more learning than one long one. Even at the intermediate stage one should concentrate first on exercises requiring production of a 'basic minimum' text for a given purpose. Once this has been achieved, students may be encouraged gradually to produce longer, more elaborate and more ambitious texts.

Another important dimension of grading is the degree of control over the student's expression exercised by the material. At one extreme is copying and dictation, where the intention is to exercise total control over what the student writes. The other extreme would be free creative writing, but we can assume that this is not appropriate (except in the final stages of a course geared to an examination requiring it). Practically speaking, the other extreme is an exercise where students are guided through subject-matter or data, given in such a form as to direct the student to particular areas or functions of language – for example, a route on a simple or simplified map leading him to produce a set of instructions for getting from A to B.

Between these extremes we have exercises where the student is provided with all or some of the language he needs, but has to select, re-arrange, alter or add to it in various ways to produce his written text. Such techniques are often referred to as controlled or guided composition, and some examples follow. These are placed in approximate order of the degree of freedom or control they provide. This does not necessarily correspond to the relative difficulty of the exercise, of course, which also depends on other factors. The important thing is to adjust the exercise to the class so as to strike the right balance between predictability and unpredictability. Too much predictability means dullness, too much unpredictability means confusion.

1 Copying. Source of exercise: article by MCGRATH, A. in *Modern English Teacher* Vol 3 No. 2, 1975. Level: elementary.

Instructions: (i) to students in monolingual classes – given in MT: The following sentences are from reports to police by a witness regarding two suspects. The sentences have been mixed up by a secretary. Sort them out and write them under the appropriate picture.

Instructions: (ii) to teacher of multilingual class: Demonstrate, by questioning and by providing the first sentence in each case, that two appropriate descriptions are required. (In the rest of the exercises below, only the instructions to students in monolingual classes will be given.)

He was about 40.
He was about 60.
He was thin.
He was fat.
He had a beard.
He had long hair.
He was wearing glasses.
He was wearing a hat.

....
....
....
....

Comment: mindless mechanical copying is clearly of little value. But selective meaningful copying may be useful at an elementary stage. The student has to make sense of each sentence, relate it to a context, then copy it. The finished product is a pair of very short, very simple but cohesive texts. The broad language function being practised is description in relation to a narrative of past events.

2 Selection.   Level: 'false beginners' to intermediate. The exercise includes quite difficult vocabulary and 'pseudo-passive' verbs.

Instructions to students: we are going to describe a hen's egg, using the diagram. All the sentences we need can be built just from the table. Make the sentences you need. Then decide what order to put them in. Then join them up into a paragraph.

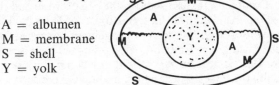

A = albumen
M = membrane
S = shell
Y = yolk

A/The hen's egg		circular.
A/The yolk		white in colour.
A/The membrane		surrounded by the albumen.
It	is	a thin skin.
It		connected to the membrane.
which		protected by the shell.
and		oval in shape.

Comment: the students may well need much more help than merely the above instructions, which could well be given in the students' mother tongue. Among points which might be discussed with them in the MT are:

147

– How shall we begin our description? From the middle? From the outside? Or by mentioning the egg as a whole?
– When can we use *it*?
– How can we use *which*?

Perhaps all or part of the exercise might first be worked on the BB, as the task of selection is quite complex. Students might perhaps be left to make the selections between *a* and *the* unaided, though even this is not as simple as it may appear. The language function is description, of a kind extremely common in academic language. The most frequent verb form in such language – here the only finite verb form – is the Present Simple tense of the verb *to be*.

A possible solution:

A hen's egg is oval in shape. The membrane is a thin skin which is white in colour. It is protected by the shell. The yolk is circular. It is surrounded by the albumen and is connected to the membrane.

---

3   Re-ordering.   Level: elementary.

Instructions to students: put the sentences in an order which makes good sense. Use *and* and *then* where convenient, and leave out any unnecessary repetition.

> He arrived there at 8 o'clock. He put on his clothes.
> John woke up at 7 o'clock. He ate his breakfast. He cooked his breakfast. He set off for the factory. He washed himself.

Comment: in a sense both the egg exercise and this one are 'copying' exercises, in that nothing has to be added which is not given. But the tasks of selection and re-arrangement vary greatly in complexity. The broad language function being practised here is simple narration, using the Past Simple tense, without any complications of out-of-order items using the Past Perfect, which a similar exercise at a more advanced level might include.

A possible solution:

John woke up at 7 o'clock. He washed himself and put on his clothes. Then he cooked and ate his breakfast. He set off for the factory and arrived there at 8 o'clock.

---

4   Conversion.   Source of exercise: Gerry Abbott. Level: intermediate to advanced.

Instructions to students: rewrite using *if* in each sentence. The first is done for you.

148

Fred's plane landed at Manchester because it was foggy.	If it hadn't been foggy Fred's plane wouldn't have landed at Manchester.

He went into the city because the plane had been diverted.

He stayed at the Midland Hotel when he went into Manchester.

He met Flo because he stayed at the Midland Hotel.

He fell in love with Flo when he met her.

So Fred and Flo got married because it was foggy.

Comment: textbooks often contain mechanical exercises in conversion or transformation from one grammatical format to another. We should seek a *purpose* for conversion if we wish to use it. Thus conversion exercises from active to passive are undesirable if they give the impression that the two forms are equivalent alternatives. But re-writing, say, from a personal narrative of a visit to a factory to an impersonal account of the industrial process observed there could be a useful exercise.

The Fred and Flo exercise is something of a *tour de force*. Normally we do not tell a story by means of a string of *if* clauses. And yet for this particular story, where the point is that of coincidence or 'fate', the string of *if* clauses maintains narrative interest. The exercise may provide an enjoyable way of practising the rather difficult '3rd conditional', used to refer to what might have happened but did not, and what might not have happened but did.

5 Transfer of medium.   Level: intermediate to advanced.

Instructions to students: (exercise to be done in language laboratory) Listen to the tape, which gives a running commentary on an incident, seen by Granny as she looks out of the window into the street. You can play it several times if you wish. Then write an account of what happened. As far as possible, write the whole account without playing the tape any more. You can play it again afterwards to check your account and compare it with the running commentary.

Tapescript: (not to be supplied to students)

Oh look! What's that man doing? He's going up to Fifi. Ha ha! He's trying to stroke her. (Sound of dog growling.) Oh, hark at her! She's growling at him. I think she's going to bite him. Come here, Fifi! Bad dog! (Sound of running footsteps and barking.) Now he's running away and she's running after him. Now she's got him by the leg. He's fallen on the ground! What shall we do?

Comment: it would not be a realistic exercise to transform the commentary sentence by sentence into a narrative, and it might be expected to encourage verb errors. But to attempt to re-tell the whole incident, with opportunities to refresh the memory if necessary, does seem valid. Various spoken English elements are omitted in the re-telling, and some changes of lexis seem desirable. The students could be asked to make a summary account in about four sentences, and/or a more expanded one giving more detail, e.g. in a letter to a relative. But in any case the re-telling should be more concise than the spoken commentary, and this in itself provides a useful lesson for the students. A possible solution (summary version):

> A man tried to stroke our dog Fifi. She tried to bite him. He ran away but she seized him by the leg.

6 Completion.   Source of exercise: adapted from an exercise by Gerry Abbott. Level: intermediate to advanced.

Instructions to students: study the short articles on diamond and lampblack. Then fill in the missing half-sentences, so that each sentence shows one or two differences between the two substances.

Diamond
Carbon occurs in nature in practically a pure state as diamond. Diamond is a transparent, colourless crystalline form of carbon. One important reason for its economic value is its extreme hardness, and it is used in tools for cutting hard substances. Because of its comparative rarity, it is extremely expensive.

Lampblack
Lampblack is an artifical form of carbon prepared by burning tar, resin or turpentine and condensing the products of combustion. The carbon thus collected is impure. It is a densely black, opaque substance which takes the form of a very fine, soft powder. Its most important property is that it does not reflect light from any angle, and it is therefore in demand as a black colouring agent, especially as a constituent of printer's ink. It is very cheap and easy to produce.

Two forms of carbon
Diamond is a natural form of carbon, whereas lampblack . . . .
. . . .
Diamond . . . .
whereas lampblack is a very impure form of carbon.
Diamond . . . .
whereas lampblack is black and opaque.
Diamond . . . .
whereas lampblack is extremely soft to the touch.

Diamond is used in the manufacture of cutting tools, whereas lampblack
....

Diamond is extremely valuable whereas lampblack...............
....

Comment: there is of course a wide range of exercises where something has to be supplied by the student. This one is fairly difficult. It does not require previous factual knowledge about the two forms of carbon, but it does require quite high reading ability. Some work with the dictionary, and/or some oral preparation under the teacher's guidance, may be needed before the students are ready to write. Then it is basically a fairly simple problem in constructing, for each given clause, a clause which is contrasted in meaning but parallel in structure. Thus the given clauses are used as models.

7 Addition. Level: intermediate to advanced.

Instructions to students: write the given sentence, add *because*, then think of a reason and add it. The reasons can be as crazy or as sensible as you wish.

– A jar of jam was lying on the floor of an empty concert hall. Why?
– A large dog was running along with a whisky bottle in its mouth. Why?
– Some girls were skipping in the street when an old woman came out of her house and joined in. Why?

Comment: the function being practised is that of explanation. This can of course employ a variety of linguistic forms, and the exercise might be set in alternative ways. What is asked for here is simply completion of the sentences, which will not give scope for elaborate explanation. Possibly the answers might give rise to further *why* questions and these to further explanations. It is hoped that the nature of the examples will stimulate some crazy and far-fetched answers.

8 Using a model. Level: elementary to intermediate.

Instructions to students: read the account of Tom's shopping trip. Then describe a shopping trip you made, visiting different places from Tom. Use *to* + verb.

Model:

Tom went to the post office first, to buy some stamps and post some letters. Then he went to buy some toothpaste and soap from the chemist. On the way home he called in at the library to return some books.

Comment: this type of exercise is useful when you wish to give practice on a particular grammatical form – in this case the infinitive of purpose. The model sentences are somewhat varied in their word-order, including the placing of the infinitive of purpose, and it is hoped that the students will pick up something of this variety – but not by slavishly imitating each sentence in turn.

151

9 Situational composition.   Level: advanced – the exercise was intended for upper secondary school students in Africa.

Instructions to students: you are Secretary of your school Swimming Club. Recently you met a swimming instructor, Mr Ziai, and recorded on tape your conversation with him, which is given below. You now decide to write a short article, to be duplicated and given to every student in the school, explaining, in a clear and orderly way, how to avoid dangers connected with swimming. Using information from the conversation, write the article.

Secretary: Mr Ziai, many people are scared of water. Do you think we should be?

Ziai: Not *scared* – I think we should be *careful*.

Secretary: Well, what are the dangers we should look out for?

Ziai: It's partly what's *in* water, and partly the way water *behaves*.

Secretary: Well, of course crocodiles and sharks are dangerous.

Ziai: Yes, but so are much smaller creatures, like the snail that carries bilharzia. And chemicals can be dangerous too, especially if you swallow polluted water.

Secretary: So we really ought not to swim at any place unless the water has been medically checked.

Ziai: That would be best. Mind you, swiftly flowing water is usually free from bilharzia, and clear enough for swimming – though not always for drinking – it may contain heavy quantities of minerals such as mica.

Secretary: What did you mean just now when you mentioned the way water *behaves*.

Ziai: Well, for one thing, we should avoid rough water, in rivers, lakes or the sea.

Secretary: So would you say that still water is generally safe, if it's clean.

Ziai: Well, the water near a dam *looks* still, but in fact it is sometimes being sucked down towards the outlet pipes.

Secretary: Are we safe then if we keep to fairly shallow water?

Ziai: On the whole, yes. But in rivers and lakes we can get entangled in weeds. And on beaches we may get swept off our feet by big waves.

Your answer might begin as follows:

Safety First for Swimmers

Are you a good swimmer? Even if you are, there are dangers you should always consider before you go swimming, and simple rules for avoiding them. I want to pass on to you some advice I recently received from an experienced swimming instructor.

Writing

Your article should be approximately 350 words – about 30–40 lines of *ordinary sized* handwriting.

Comment: this is a much more advanced and less linguistically controlled type of exercise than the previous ones. It is particularly appropriate in ESL situations at a fairly advanced level. In this type of exercise most of the material needed by the writer is provided, together with very precise instructions about the communication to be written. The student is told the purpose of the piece of writing in detail, the circumstances in which it is being written, and the addressee or addressees. He is usually given clear specifications regarding the length, and the form it should take. The content is spelt out, and the style that will be appropriate is either stated or implied.

Thus the student does not have to create his subject-matter from scratch. Mostly he will select, arrange and re-express from what is given. But he will have some scope, if he wishes, to add material and to amplify. In other words, he will have some scope for self-expression, but will not be forced into self-expression against his will. All this is not too far from the kind of situation in which most real-life writing is done by everyone except the professional creative writer.

Part 3: Writing as a goal of FL learning

A 'External' and 'internal' goals

As has already been suggested, we cannot rigidly separate W as a channel or means of FL learning from W as a goal. There is much talk these days of 'communicative' teaching and the use of 'authentic' texts, the implication being that students should learn to write those types of communication which they need or will shortly need to write, and that the models they should follow should be actual texts used in real-life communication for the particular purposes in view.

This is all very well in the case of ESP. Here we may have clear targets for written communication: operating instructions for a piece of equipment; laboratory notes on an experiment; a digest of information from a book or article; etc. Even if the students' English language level is far below their subject-matter level, we can begin relevant exercises. The language and format may have to be simplified at first, and we should not be frightened off doing this by the demands of certain theorists for absolute authenticity. Taken literally, the latter would mean starting with the finished product of instruction. If this were feasible there would be no need to pay us to teach English to such students. At the same time, there is no need to avoid technical language even with those whose English is very weak, provided their subject-matter studies make that technical language easy to understand.

The idea of communicative need is also valid in English-medium

153

school situations. For these the kind of approach advocated by Widdowson (1978) is particularly suitable. They can practise the kinds of written communication needed in their school subjects.

But in many English classes there is no question of the students having a real need to communicate in written English in the present or near future. In such TENOR situations (see Chapter 1) there is in fact no definite external goal for W apart from its use in external examinations. This may be a necessary goal for our students, but we cannot regard it as a truly 'external' goal, as it simply raises the question of why particular W tasks should be included in the examination.

In these circumstances we as teachers or examiners can try to set up goals which we can plausibly connect with W activities which students *may perhaps* have to carry out in English in their later studies, careers or personal lives. They *may* have to take notes in English at a seminar, a business meeting, etc., so we may decide to teach them, at an appropriate stage, to take notes from the spoken word. They *may* have to make an English abstract of a chapter, a conference paper, a plan for a housing project, etc., so we may decide to teach them to summarise and extract required information from written texts. They *may* have to write in English when negotiating with a customer, or advising a friend about travel arrangements, or applying for a visa extension, etc., so we may decide to teach them to write letters of various kinds.

These are long-term 'exterior' goals which may or may not provide a sense of reality for the students, depending on their situation and prospects. But even if they do have validity in the students' eyes, they are not sufficient as goals to maintain motivation through several years of a course. We need also short-term 'interior' goals for teaching and testing; that is, W tasks which the students find valid because of the interest of the subject-matter or problem being tackled. This means a problem to solve, some interesting information to collect and convey, some advice or instructions to give, etc.

For instance, suppose students have become interested in how you can identify a person from a description, how the police use such information to build up an 'Identikit' picture of a suspect, etc. This suggests, as an exercise, the writing of descriptions of real people known to the students, who then try to guess the names of the people. To make the game challenging, description could initially be limited to physical appearance. If this does not lead to correct identification, description could be continued to include personal habits, etc. Immediate 'give-away' details will be avoided for the sake of the game.

B Organising the work

The previous example is of course just one of many that could be given to illustrate the idea of 'interior' motivation for written work. But I should like to pursue it further in briefly considering ways of organising such work. While W may be seen as the goal of the exercise, it could be organised so as to give practice in L, S and R, and in writing in note form as well as in continuous prose. A possible sequence of events, with students working in pairs, is as follows:

1 Note-making stage. Each student chooses the person he wishes to describe and writes his description in brief note form. (10 minutes?)

2 Speaking stage. Each student in turn speaks his description to his neighbour and tries to guess the name of the person the other has described. If he cannot guess it, he can ask questions to elicit further information. (10 minutes?)

3 Writing stage. Each student writes out his description in full, including any extra information elicited by his partner's questions. (20 minutes?)

4 Reading stage. This time each student is paired with a student sitting at a distance from him. The written descriptions are exchanged and read silently. Each student tries to guess the name of the person described. If he wishes, he may write one question and send the paper back for an answer before guessing. (10 minutes?)

C Work in larger groups

In situations reasonably favourable to group discussion (such as many ESL secondary school classes) this work can be organised in larger groups. With not more than 6 or 7 students to a group, and with one member acting as group leader and another as group secretary, the sequence of events might be roughly as follows:

1 Decision-making stage. The group decide who they are going to describe, and a few of the points to be included. (5 minutes?)

2 Description-making stage. Each student in turn gets a chance to suggest a sentence to form part of the description – students could be given a few minutes first to draft their proposed sentence in writing. If their first idea is used by someone else, they will have to quickly think of another. As each sentence is spoken by its originator, other group members may suggest corrections or improvements. The sentence is written down by the group secretary in the form agreed by the group. When all have contributed, the secretary reads out the description, and further suggestions may be made to improve individual sentences or their arrangement. (20 minutes?)

3 Guessing stage. This could be conducted in various ways. Each group secretary could read out his group's description to the whole class, each group then discussing privately the guess they wish to make. Or fair copies could be made and pinned on the notice-board to be studied and guessed before the next lesson. Alternatively, fair copies could be shown on an overhead projector, etc.

I am not suggesting that the kind of group work just described is possible in all circumstances. It presupposes a high standard of discipline and organisation, and students who have some degree of fluency in English, with good motivation towards speaking in English, or a multilingual class who can only communicate with each other in English. If these conditions are not met, group work may lead to chaos or to the widespread use of the MT. Even if the conditions are favourable, there is the danger referred to in Chapter 5, that the more students are eager to communicate, the less they will worry about correctness. But this is less likely to be a problem where written work is concerned, and the students know that their object is to produce a short piece of a high standard of correctness. Problems of organisation can only be tackled by training the class over a period of weeks or months so that they adopt well-established routines for moving into and out of their groups and for conducting group sessions. These should be kept very short initially – the time should never be more than the minimum for the work assigned. A group should cover the whole ability range of the class, so that all groups are roughly equal in ability. The group leadership and secretaryship must be rotated frequently, as the holders of those offices get by far the most practice. Students must be trained to speak only as loudly as is necessary to be heard by the rest of the group, otherwise the 'cocktail-party syndrome' develops, with an ever-growing volume of sound which masks non-work talk and non-English talk and eventually leads to protests from neighbouring classrooms. This may seem a formidable catalogue of problems, but the potential benefits are such that it may be worth quite a lot of effort and experiment to try to overcome the problems. Experience has shown that it is sometimes possible to do so even in apparently rather unpromising circumstances.

D   More controlled work

We have been looking at some possible types of classroom procedure that can be adopted, and have not yet considered the actual language content of the descriptions. This would obviously vary with the students' level of English. At lower levels the teacher would need to impose tight control on the subject-matter and ordering of the descriptions, and to work through one or more model descriptions with the class before letting students try their hand individually. A possible procedure would be as follows:

(i) Class-work using BB table:

Name	Address	Favourite colour	Brothers and sisters	Best school subject	Favourite hobby/ sport
Ann	Grove Road	Pink	None	PE	Tennis
Betty	Brown Street	Blue	2S	English	Swimming

Carol	George Street	Red	1B, 1S	Science	Bird-watching
Denise	....	....	....	....	....
....	....	....	....	....	....

The names in the table are those of members of the class. The T gets students to give sentences orally describing Ann. This is done by giving prompts such as 'Tell me about her address', or just 'Address?' or by merely pointing to the appropriate column, rather than by asking a series of *wh-* questions, which is cumbersome and tends to lead to verb errors. As each sentence is produced the T, or the student producing the sentence, writes it on the BB. The words in the columns could be provided as shown, or could be filled in through oral discussion as the exercise proceeds. The following model description might emerge:

> Ann lives in Grove Road and has no brothers and sisters. Her best school subject is Physical Education. Her favourite sport is tennis and her favourite colour is pink.

Note that the ordering can be different from that of the table. It is suggested that the T ask the PP to suggest a good order. Another point is that five clauses have been combined in three sentences, using the cohesive possibilities of *and* and subject omission in the first sentence, *her* in the second, and the parallelism of *her favourite . . .* and *her favourite . . .* in the last sentence. All this is perhaps obvious but it is an important and often neglected part of teaching W at an elementary level. Perhaps with another class things might have been simplified still further, the desired order being given from the start and five points being covered in five sentences without conjunctions.

(ii) Similar work might follow on *Betty*, to give further practice.

(iii) The students now individually write the description of *Carol* from the information in the table. This should give no serious difficulty and the T should be able to concentrate help on the minutiae of correct writing, at this stage and during the two following stages.

(iv) When students have finished describing *Carol*, they go on to describe *Denise*, also an actual classmate. In this case they have to provide the information, guessing if they do not know a particular point.

(v) When they have finished with *Denise*, they go on to describe an imaginary girl who might join the class in the future, beginning by thinking of a name for her. Students who finish early are encouraged to write further sentences giving additional information about the imaginary girl.

(vi) Reading aloud of some of the descriptions of *Denise*, and checking with Denise herself to see who was right about her.

(vii) Reading aloud of some of the descriptions of the imaginary girl, including some with information additional to that required by the columns of the table.

E   Information transfer

The exercise just outlined makes a very simple use of *information transfer*. It was suggested that a table might be given with information supplied, or filled in orally by asking the class to suggest information. In either case information in tabular form is used in creating a text in continuous language. We have already seen, in Chapters 3, 4 and 5, how various types of information transfer can be used to practise L, S and R. You are recommended to refer to the exercises suggested there and to consider how these or similar ideas can be adapted for use in practising W. As well as tables, we can employ pictures, diagrams, maps, graphs and flow-charts.

For example, here is a diagram suitable for the five steps described in **EXAMPLE 1** at the beginning of this chapter:

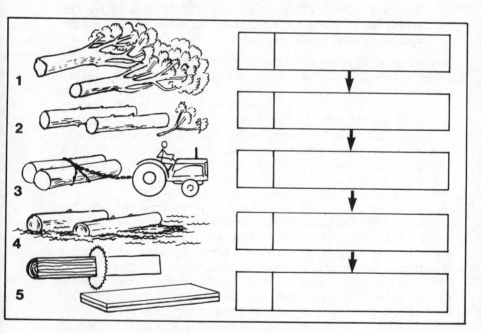

The possibilities are almost unlimited and there is plenty of scope for the T's ingenuity. Nevertheless, two notes of caution are necessary. One is against excessive complexity in the graphic information. Having a real problem to solve is a help to motivation, but information presented graphically can be confusing if there is too much of it, if it is culturally or intellectually unfamiliar, if it is not presented with absolute clarity, or if the mode of presentation used is unfamiliar to the students. The second caution is against using, in the graphic presentation, language forms which will be incorrect if transferred to the target text. For example, in the table given on pp. 156–7, the use of *None* would be unwise if there was any danger of it leading to sentences like:

    *Ann has none brothers and sisters.

    *Ann's brothers and sisters are none.

White (1980) gives more examples of these dangers of information transfer as well as examples of its effective use.

F Subject-matter

The examples so far discussed in this part of the chapter have been largely confined to personal descriptions. English course-books, especially those of an audio-lingual type, often lack ideas for written practice. One possibility is to take a situation described in the textbook and get students to describe their own situation in a parallel way. Often, however, written work is concentrated too heavily at the personal level, and this can quickly become boring. It is essential to widen the range. Look for material in any field which you know students are interested in, whether it is pop music, sport, travel, aspects of school or college subjects they are currently studying, current affairs, technology, etc., etc. This does not apply only to advanced students. It is possible to discuss many topics at a variety of levels, including a very simple level.

An example of a 'sub-technological' topic which may arouse interest because of the problem involved in trying to distinguish between similar things is the following:

Trains and trams

How are they alike or partly alike? And how are they different?

Alike or partly alike		Different	
Trains	*Trams*	*Trains*	*Trams*
Run on rails	Run on rails	Longer	Shorter
Electric, diesel or steam	Electric	Normally on special tracks	Normally on public roads
Normally several carriages	One or two carriages	Have specially built stations	Do not normally have specially built stations
Long or short routes	Normally fairly short routes		
In towns or between towns	Normally in towns		

This is material for a fairly advanced class. Presumably one would begin with oral discussion and BB summarising which might lead to the building up of a BB table along the lines of that given on p. 159 (though there are points which might lead to argument and views different from those given in the table). It might then be helpful to look at each column in turn to find one or more effective ways of expressing items in a sentence.

For example:

Alike: Both trams and trains . . .

Partly alike: Trams are electric, whereas trains may be . . .

Different (with comparative): Trains are normally much longer than trams.

Different (with contrast): Trams normally run on public roads, but trains do not.

One would then need to consider the best arrangement for a connected comparison. Should it be organised somewhat like the table? Or rather according to subject-matter?

A possible solution:

Paragraph 1: Location
 – What they run on (rails)
 – Where they operate (town/country)
 – Where they run (road/special track)
 – Where they stop (station/no station)
 – How far they run (short/long route)

Paragraph 2: Nature
 – How powered (electric/diesel/steam)
 – How long (short/long)
 – How many carriages (one/several)

Finally we should want to look at ways of linking the items. We might arrive at a text on the BB by joint class effort; or at a certain point we might want to turn over the completion of the task to individual written work.

A possible text:

Both trams and trains run on rails. Trams normally run on public roads, but trains run on special tracks. Trams operate in towns, so their routes are short. Trains operate in and between towns, so their routes may be long or short. Trains only stop at specially built stations, but this does not generally apply to trams. Trams are driven by electricity, whereas trains may be driven by electricity, diesel oil or steam. Trains are much longer than trams and normally have several carriages, whereas trams usually have just one or two.

Other possibilities for comparison will come to mind: the difference between rugby and association football, with expression of preference and reasons for this; differences between transistors and micro-chip processors, with reasons why the latter are displacing the former; etc, etc.

Part 4: Writing with cohesion

Cohesive features of language are *those which* are characteristic of texts, spoken or written, *and* would not be present in a series of disconnected sentences *or* clauses. A *text* means any continuous example of language in use; *that is*, language employed for some purpose. Cohesion consists in the relations of meaning *which* exist between different parts of a text. *It* is expressed *partly through* grammatical features *and partly through* features of the vocabulary used, *as well as* in *other* features *such as* punctuation and intonation.

This rough definition is based on the much *more* careful *one* in Halliday and Hasan (1976). *Cohesion* is a subject *whose* importance for the teacher of English is obvious. Taking as *we do* a communicative attitude to *the* job, *our* aim is clearly to help students to understand *and* produce texts of various kinds. *The present* chapter is concerned with written *texts, and* cohesion seems particularly important in the teaching of *writing, since* cohesive devices are used in a *more* controlled *and* deliberate way in written texts *than* in speaking – *or, rather, than* in conversation, *for* formal spoken texts *such as* lectures *and* speeches *also* have very controlled *and* deliberate *ways* of achieving cohesion.

Any reader who has not, by this point, a pretty clear idea of the area of language I am talking about is recommended, before going further, to read quickly through Chapter 10 of Quirk and Greenbaum (1973). Space does not permit a full outline in this volume, so we shall have to be satisfied here with reference to just a few examples of cohesive relations and devices. To highlight the subject I have italicised a certain number of the cohesive devices used in the first two paragraphs above. Only certain examples can be shown in this way, of course. Many others cannot – for example, omissions, or examples consisting of several words, or examples made up of two discontinuous parts of the text.

Cohesion is concerned with relationships both within and beyond the sentence. In many courses, practice is restricted to the sentence level. Cohesive devices cover such a wide range that they should be practised at every stage of an English course.

Cohesive categories are *functional* categories, though of course realised in grammatical, lexical or other forms. For any one cohesive function there are usually several or many different forms that could be used. Thus they clearly involve problems of selection and grading and cyclic teaching. That is, if we take a given function, there is a need to select the most useful form and train students first to use that in speech and/or writing. The most useful will generally, but not always, be the

F

simplest and/or the most frequent form. For example, as a means of signalling a relationship of *contrast* between what is expressed in two sentences, clauses or other elements, *but* is simpler, more frequent and usable in a wider variety of contexts than *although*. At an elementary level it is enough if we can teach students to recognise and use *but*. Reasonably soon, however, students will have to learn to recognise *although*, and probably other forms such as *yet* and *however*. We should not rush, however, to teach them to *produce* all these. If we do, we run into serious problems. The items are not freely interchangeable. Even their meanings are not always *exactly* the same. And there are differences of word-order, punctuation, etc. according to which is chosen. These differences tend to be ignored by the student if he is taught such items in an ungraded way, or simply assimilates them from his reading without special instruction. He may use *although* in place of *but*, without the necessary changes of order, or he may use both together, thinking in this way to reinforce the contrast: **Although the sea was rough but no-one was sea-sick.* Or he may use *however* as equivalent to *but*, not realising that it implies a stronger contrast. Compare:

> She was poor but she was honest. (One 'unfavourable' item plus one 'favourable'.)

> She was poor. However, she was honest. (There seems to be an implication that honesty is *surprising* in the circumstances.)

Then there is the movability of *however*, as with many cohesive devices signalling logical relationship of one kind or another. *But* is not movable. *Although*, together with its accompanying clause, can either precede or follow the main clause. *However* has at least three positions. For example:

> Echo-sounding was a very crude way of measuring the depth of water. { *However*, this device was not superseded for fifty years. / This device, *however*, was not superseded for fifty years. / This device was not superseded for fifty years, *however*.

There may perhaps be minor differences of meaning, emphasis or style here. If there are, they seem small enough to make it unnecessary to teach students to use all three of the above word-orders. The first seems adequate for all their productive purposes. However, students who have to read academic or argumentative English need to be able to easily recognise all three. The first word-order is the same as for *but*. However, students learning to use it should learn that it is normally followed by a comma, whereas *but* is not. Even if this comma is sometimes omitted by native speakers of English, we ought to teach it, because it points up the stronger contrasting value of *however* compared with *but*. It also indicates the contrasting use of *however* as distinct from the 'no matter how' use of *however*. Compare for example:

> However much English is learned, there is always more to learn.
> However, much English is learned.

We may conclude that an ESL or EAP student needs to learn to use *however* to express strong contrast in his writing. Probably, however, he does not need to learn to use *nevertheless* or *notwithstanding*, whose meanings are similar enough to that of *however* to make it unnecessary for him to use these two words. Many educated native speakers probably never or hardly ever use them. But their receptive use is necessary if the learner has a lot of serious reading to do in English.

With the example of *however* in mind, it is easy to see that punctuation is to quite a large extent a matter of cohesion: whether to use a comma or a full stop; when to start a new paragraph; the use of a colon, a series of semi-colons and a full stop to indicate the beginning, progress and end of a series of examples; etc. Punctuation should be taught as an aid to comprehension and a means of making clear the structure of the argument or other form of discourse.

Quite often in reading we have to infer the logical structure without the benefit of a cohesive device, because no explicit device is given. For example:

> The coastal peoples of what is now British Columbia developed large-scale building techniques. They had access to unlimited supplies of timber.

There seems to be an implication here that the second sentence states a cause of which the first sentence states an effect. However, the implication is not a certain one. It would be possible to have the following text:

> The coastal peoples of what is now British Columbia developed large-scale building techniques. They had access to unlimited supplies of timber. But this was not the fact which actually motivated them. Peoples living in hot climates and having access to unlimited supplies of timber often did not develop large-scale building techniques.

In view of such uncertainties, there seems every reason to train learners of English always to use an explicit marker to indicate such a cohesive relationship. Rather than the first of the two examples above, we should teach them to write, for example:

> The coastal peoples of what is now British Columbia developed large-scale building techniques $\left\{ \begin{array}{l} \text{, since} \\ \text{, as} \\ \text{, because} \\ \text{. This was because} \end{array} \right\}$ they had access to unlimited supplies of timber.

Whether taking notes for their own use, or writing a report, etc. for someone else's use, they will most easily make their meaning clear if they always use a marker. A useful exercise, in an EAP or advanced

ESL class, would be to give them a passage containing examples of implicit cohesive marking to rewrite using explicit markers.

It has been naively argued that certain types of 'defective rhetorical development' said to be found in the English writings of some non-native speakers are culturally conditioned. For example, it has been suggested that Arabic speakers have a tendency towards a kind of 'parallelism' of style, giving emphasis by juxtaposition of similar statements. I have arranged the following slightly edited example in lines to bring out this feature:

> The contemporary Bedouins,
> who live in the deserts of Saudi Arabia,
> are the successors of the old Bedouin tribes,
> who were fascinated with Mohammed's message.
> I have lived among those Bedouins
> for a short period of time,
> and I have learned many things about them.

Parallelism there may be here, but it does not seem particularly inappropriate to the writer's purpose on the occasion, presumably some kind of discursive essay. The logical structure is clear. The style is perhaps rather leisurely, and we might encourage the writer to see what he can remove to express it more concisely. But the notion that the rhetorical development is 'inadequate' in some way can hardly be sustained.

A more extreme example is the following, by a student from a rural background in a tropical developing country:

> We started by digging for about three hours. *After digging*, we went home to take tea. *As soon as we finished taking tea* we went back again to the garden to pick coffee. *We picked coffee* from one o'clock to three o'clock and went home to have lunch. *As soon as we finished lunch*, . . .

The 'defective rhetorical development' theorist might suggest that this was influenced by the leisurely pace of rural life, or by the repetitive structure of an oral narrative tradition. Less romantically, an English teacher might put it down to too much recent pattern practice on *after* + verb + *-ing* and *as soon as* + clause; or perhaps to the writer's fear of being penalised for mistakes, leading him to craftily spin out his material through repetition of phrases and structures he is pretty sure are correct English. The point is that we should not be too hasty or dogmatic in assigning causes; but we can give such a student useful practice in first identifying and then eliminating unnecessary repetition, through the use of appropriate cohesive devices. Herein may lie the major cause of the defects of the last example – inadequate teaching of cohesion.

The following is an example of valuable exercise material for practising the use of logical connectors:
Source: ALLEN, J. and WIDDOWSON, H. *English in Social Studies*
English in Focus series, page 24. Oxford University Press, 1978.

Link the following groups of statements together, where possible, by using *whereas, on the other hand* and *for example.*

1 (a) In a class system there is social mobility.
   (b) In a caste system an individual cannot move from one social level to another.
   (c) A member of the working class may, if he has the opportunity, become middle class in the course of his life.

2 (a) Some people who would be regarded as middle class earn less than some people who would be regarded as working class.
   (b) A school teacher sometimes earns less than an electrician.
   (c) A coal miner sometimes earns more than a bank clerk.

3 (a) Brothers-in-law and sisters-in-law are affinal relatives.
   (b) Consanguineal relatives are people who are related by birth.
   (c) Affinal relatives are related by marriage.

4 (a) There is only one wife and one husband in a monogamous family.
   (b) In a polyandrous family there is more than one husband and in a polygynous family there is more than one wife.
   (c) In a polygamous family there are more than two spouses.

If the use of such material is to be teaching rather than testing, it might be best to start by asking the students first to go through all the sentences marking general statements with a G and example statements with an E. Check this straight away and discuss any disagreements. The next step is to find out which G statement each E statement is an example of. We now have an arrangement of sentences in each set:

1 (a)=G+(c)=E   (b)=G
2 (a)=G+[(b)=E but (c)=E]
3 (b)=G   (c)=G+(a)=E
4 (a)=G   (c)=G+(b)=subordinate G

There are in fact numerous ways of embodying these elements in sentences, even given the restricted instructions at the head of the exercise. It seems wise to try to teach a standard procedure, if possible, provided it is an intelligent one, not merely a mechanical one.

By helping students analyse problems of cohesion (see table on p. 166), and by selecting from the multifarious possibilities existing in the language, we help them, it is hoped, to sort out for themselves future

165

Suggested solution:	*Teaching points:*

Suggested solution:

1 In a class system there is social mobility⊙ for example⊙ a member of the working class may, if he has the opportunity, become middle class in the course of his life⊙ In a caste system⊙ on the other hand⊙an individual cannot move from one social level to another.

Teaching points:

Wherever possible, attach the example to the general statement in this way. Use a separate sentence for the contrasting general statement. Use *on the other hand*, between commas, after the first phrase – note how this points the contrast.

2 Some people who would be regarded as middle class earn less than some people who would be regarded as working class⊙ for example⊙a school teacher sometimes earns less than an electrician○whereas○a coal miner sometimes earns more than a bank clerk.

Even though we get a very long sentence, it is quite acceptable, and we can thus follow exactly the same procedure as in 1 above. The two examples are contrasting and parallel and can thus be joined with *whereas*. No commas are required.

3 Consanguineal relatives are people who are related by birth⊙ Affinal relatives⊙ on the other hand⊙are related by marriage⊙ for example⊙ brothers-in-law and sisters-in-law are affinal relatives.

Exactly the same rules as in 1 above.

4 There is only one wife and one husband in a monogamous family○In a polygamous family⊙ on the other hand⊙ there are more than two spouses⊙ in a polyandrous family there is more than one husband○whereas○in a polygynous family there is more than one wife.

Exactly the same rules as in 2 above. Although the last part does not consist of examples as in 2, but of a pair of general statements, these are subsidiary to the second main general statement, and a semi-colon is the best way to make this clear.

cases they will meet of this very frequent type of sequence.

A danger to be guarded against is that of talking too much about cohesion rather than practising it. The following example may look like a caricature, but is in fact from a printed source, which it would be unkind to identify:

'Such words as *and* and *but* are important cohesive ties. *And* acts as a kind of plus signal. *Furthermore* introduces an additional important point or argument. *But* signals that a contrastive counter-statement is about to follow. *However* introduces a qualification or counter-statement to the one previously made. *For instance* signals that a particular example is to follow. *As a result* introduces a conclusion. *Next* and *finally* signal some kind of sequence. *Or* indicates an alternative.'

The above was intended for students. But a student who can understand it certainly does not need to be told it – he knows it already. A student who cannot understand it will profit little by reading it. Of course quite small children who speak English use *but* correctly, which suggests that they understand the meaning of the sentence beginning *But* in the quotation above. But no small child could understand the statement in the form given there. In other words, the above passage, and all similar talk to students, is useless because it explains what is linguistically simple in language that is more difficult; what is linguistically difficult is described in language that is even more difficult! An obvious but often-neglected truth in the world of teaching.

These remarks on cohesion have not, I hope, been incoherent. The subject is too large to deal with fully here, but too important to leave out. My intention has been to emphasise how important it is at every level of teaching writing, and to give a few pointers as to how it can be tackled. Good materials for teaching it are still fairly rare, and it is an area where teachers need to be watchful and inventive.

Part 5: Conclusion

We have looked in this chapter at some important aspects of the teaching of written English. In closing I would like to re-emphasise the aspect of appropriateness. It is vital for the learner to ask such questions as: 'Who am I writing for? What is the purpose of the communication? Why is it being made in writing rather than orally? What are the circumstances? What should I include and what should I leave out? How can I make this communication successful?'

Finally, a word about 'creativity'. The word has been used in two quite different ways by English teachers. Teachers of English as a MT often use it in discussing their aims and methods. Many of them feel that the English lesson is one of the few times in the school day when pupils have any freedom to express their own interests and feelings. They believe it is an important part of education for the pupils to have such opportunities. Thus creative self-expression, from this point of view, becomes an important aim in the teaching of the MT. Opinions tend to polarise between those who think like this and those who emphasise rather the importance of teaching pupils to communicate acceptably in the standard form of the written language. 'Creativity' advocates are accused of ignoring matters such as grammar, spelling and punctuation, and of having as a result produced a half-illiterate generation. 'Correctness' advocates, on the other hand, are accused of making their subject an arid wasteland of rules and formal exercises, leading to boredom and alienation on the part of the pupils, with no better results in terms of literacy. There are obvious dangers in both these extremes, and probably most MT teachers try to find a middle path between them.

The other sense of the word 'creativity' is that employed by Chomsky. He points out that every child, in learning and using his MT, creates sentences he has never heard or seen before. In this sense, 'creativity' is part of the capacity for language which all humans have – a part which cannot be explained on a merely behaviouristic theory of learning.

Teachers of ESL and EFL have taken up this second use of the word, and have argued that we have in some way to try and match in the ESL or EFL class the 'creativity' exercised by children in learning their MT. Simple repetition of forms and patterns will not achieve this. They have to be combined and re-combined in the course of using the language to some purpose. In this sense we can claim 'creativity' for the kinds of exercise that have been suggested in this chapter. The claim is justified even if many of these writing exercises involve mainly some kind of reproduction – the retelling in different form of information fully provided, where the students are merely required to re-arrange, to select and omit, to alter the form of the material. Such activity clearly comes within the realm of 'creativity' as defined by Chomsky.

But of course it does not come within the realm of 'creativity' as defined by the 'creative writing' school of MT teachers. I have suggested previously (page 146) that free creative writing is rarely appropriate in teaching ESL or EFL. I would stand by that. But at the same time, we have to admit the danger of boredom and frustration if students feel that they never have any substantial freedom of choice as to what they are going to write. Merely the freedom to re-arrange, select and omit will not always satisfy them. Thus we have to look for ways of setting up exercises, even at intermediate and lower levels, which give the learner some sense of being able to express his own view and his own personality. The type of exercise using a model (see page 151) offers some scope in this direction. As was said on page 146, we have to strike a balance between too much predictability, which leads to boredom, and too much unpredictability, which leads to error and confusion. But in the last analysis, the greater of the two evils is boredom.

Note (see page 142) The letter *c* represents the sound /k/ when followed by *a* or *o* or *u*. When *e* or *i* follows, the letter *k* is used. The main exceptions to this rule are loan-words such as *kangaroo* which have entered the language in the past 250 years or so.

Further reading

BRIGHT, J. and PIGGOTT, R. *Handwriting: a workbook.* Cambridge University Press, 1976.
> This provides excellent training for the learner coming to English without prior training in the Roman alphabet. There is an accompanying Teacher's Book by John Bright which gives clear and succinct guidance.

MOORHOUSE, C. *Helping adults to spell.* London: Adult Literacy Resource Agency, 1977.
> A small practical booklet. Though intended for teachers of English as a first language its numerous teaching and learning techniques will prove useful to the ESL/EFL teacher.

HILL, L. *Writing for a purpose.* Oxford University Press, 1978.
> One of the very few useful writing courses at elementary level.

JUPP, T. and MILNE, J. *Guided course in English composition.* Heinemann Educational Books, 1969.
> Though preceding the 'communicative' movement, this is still useful in that it trains students through carefully graded exercises which gradually reduce the amount of guidance.

ARNOLD, J. and HARMER, J. *Advanced writing skills.* Longman, 1978.
> A course which aims to develop written communication ability within a functional framework.

JORDAN, R. *Academic writing course.* Collins, 1980.
> A basic course in English academic writing for the non-native speaker embarking on an English-medium university-level course in any field of study.

MCELDOWNEY, P. *The test in English (overseas): the position after ten years.* Manchester: Northern Universities Joint Matriculation Board, 1976.
> This booklet, though mainly about examining, contains much material useful for teaching written skills at intermediate and advanced levels.

WHITE, R. *Teaching written English* (Practical language teaching series). Allen and Unwin, 1980.
> A short and practical guide written from a functional, communicative viewpoint and dealing with all levels.

WIDDOWSON, H. *Teaching language as communication.* Oxford University Press, 1978.
> This book is of particular interest to ESL and ESP teachers. Mainly theoretical, it is also a source of practical ideas for teaching written English using material from students' other academic subjects.

169

LAWRENCE, M. *Writing as a thinking process.* University of Michigan Press, 1972.

This book approaches writing as it should be approached – as a means of recording connected thought. As well as being theoretically sound it is very practical and contains many thought-provoking exercises at different levels.

HALLIDAY, M. and HASAN, R. *Cohesion in English.* Longman, 1976.

The standard text and reference work for anyone wishing to go at all deeply into this subject.

QUIRK, R. and GREENBAUM, S. *A university grammar of English.* Longman, 1973.

Perhaps the English teacher's most useful reasonably brief guide to English grammar. Chapter 10 gives a clear outline of cohesive devices in English.

Chapter 7: Assessment

by Peter Wingard

EXAMPLE 1

> Mr Das has just given his class a ten-item written test on last night's homework. He gets the students to exchange papers and uncovers a prepared BB with the correct answers for them to mark from. He goes over the items one by one, asking: 'How many got Number 1 (etc.) right?' Each student who has a correct answer on the paper he is marking raises his hand. Mr Das notes the approximate number of correct answers. At the end he has a good idea which items need further work and which do not. He does *not* ask 'Who got ten right? . . . Nine? . . .' etc, because he did not give the test to congratulate the good students or to blame the weak ones. The whole process from starting the test has taken just ten minutes, so he still has thirty minutes to get on with some teaching.

EXAMPLE 2

> At Lanchingham University, there are three terms in the academic year. The following table shows the number of weeks spent in different activities.
>
> | Term | Registration | Teaching | Examination | Total |
> |------|--------------|----------|-------------|-------|
> | A | 1 | 10 | 0 | 11 |
> | B | 0 | 10 | 0 | 10 |
> | C | 0 | 4 | 4 | 8 |
> | Total | 1 | 24 | 4 | 29 |
>
> A Commission of Inquiry asks the University to explain two things. First, why is the academic year such a small part of the calendar year (56%)? Second, why is the examination period such a large part of the academic year (14%)? The University's answers are not recorded, but the figures do seem to suggest an excessive emphasis on examinations.

Part 1: What is assessment?

Readers of this book may have been expecting to find a chapter headed 'Testing'. We have chosen the title 'Assessment' instead in order to take a wider view. For English teachers, 'assessment' includes any means of checking what students can do with the language. It also includes checking what they *cannot* do, but proper assessment gives due weight to the positive side of their achievement. Assessment may be carried out before, during or after a course, or it may not even be connected with a course. Assessment may be of individual students, or it may be to check the capabilities of a whole class. This means that assessment is concerned with the quality of teaching as well as the quality of learning.

Assessment includes a whole range of activities from the informal short test on last night's homework to the formal external examination which crowns several years of study. It includes regular marked coursework assignments forming part of a course, as well as periodic testing. It would be pointless to get involved in lengthy argument as to the difference between 'tests' and 'examinations'. The word 'examination' is most often used for a formal, extended measuring instrument covering a wide range of material. Examinations are things which, fortunately, do not come too often – at the most two or three times a year. They may of course be set and marked internally or externally. Everyone knows they are important and nearly everyone fears them. The word 'test' is used in two different ways. A teacher-made test is generally a short, informal measure covering a definite limited area of work. An 'expert'-made test may be of any length, but it has been subjected to a process of very careful planning, try-out, statistical analysis and refinement, to the point where it can be used and re-used with confidence in the results it yields – provided it can be kept confidential, that is.

For teachers, the distinction between teaching and testing is vital. Before you set your students a task, ask yourself: Is my prime purpose to *give practice* or to *check learning*? Too frequent testing is like constantly digging up a plant to see how its roots are growing. An exercise is a task designed to bring about learning through practice of reasonably high quality, and it is a failure as an exercise if it does not do so. A lot of test material is therefore inappropriate for teaching and even harmful when used for teaching.

In some countries where multiple-choice items have become a staple method of testing, they have come to be grossly misused by being employed as teaching material. Little books of multiple-choice vocabulary items have been published, for example, and used on a wide scale. For teaching vocabulary they are extremely bad. Words are studied in isolated sentences when they ought to be studied in the wider context of a conversation or a passage. The student meets two or three wrong answers for every correct one, which is hardly the best way to learn the correct one. These criticisms apply equally to multiple-choice grammar items used as teaching material. Some people think multiple-choice items on a reading passage are useful in teaching reading comprehension. They argue that, by discussing which choices are right and which are wrong, and by being required to give reasons why a choice is right or wrong, students are getting good training in comprehension. This may be true in a very good class but, in my opinion, more often students' time is wasted and they are confused and distracted by having to consider so many 'distractors' – that is, wrong answers designed to mislead. These criticisms are addressed to the use of multiple-choice items for *teaching*. For testing they have their uses, though they also have their drawbacks, as we shall see.

This chapter will not deal with 'marking' in the sense of what actual physical marks a teacher should put on a piece of written work for the student to see and, it is hoped, learn from.

Part 2: Why assess?

There is no universally good way of assessing. What and how you assess should obviously depend on your purpose. We can distinguish at least six important purposes of assessment, though there is some overlap between them. A single test may have more than one purpose, but the more multi-purpose it is, the less satisfactory it is likely to be. Before planning a test or other means of assessment, we need to see clearly its purpose or purposes.

A   Placement

One purpose is to place a student on a suitable course. Assuming that we have a range of classes with different levels of command of English, which should we place the student in? See John (1980), in Further Reading at the end of this chapter, for an example of a set of tests which can be used for placing incoming students in this way. Of course such tests may also be used as *progress* tests. (See Section E.) Suppose we have a student wishing to study engineering in the UK, or in any English-medium university or faculty. A *proficiency* test (see Section D) will give us some idea of whether his English is generally adequate. If it is not, how long an English course does he need before he can start his engineering course? A full-time six-month course? A three-month course? If such courses are available or planned, the question is one of placement. Placement is normally in relation to some defined standard.

B   Diagnosis

If we go further and try to specify the student's particular strengths and weaknesses, we are into diagnosis. For instance, the engineering student might be quite good at academic writing but very weak at listening to lectures. There is no fixed borderline here between placement and diagnosis. At Manchester University, for example, the above student would be advised to join a class in listening and note-taking. Another student might be advised to join a class in academic writing. A third student might be advised to join both. This would be placement. But it would also be diagnosis. If we had only one general course for all three of these students, it would be just diagnosis. Diagnosis is usually carried out by an individual teacher with reference to a particular class. It is carried out at the beginning of a course, or when taking over a class with inadequate information about them. The aim is to find out the strong and weak points of the class as a whole, and of individual students. The results will affect the teacher's planning for the course as a whole and for the special needs of individuals or groups. Diagnosis is usually carried out in relation to what you *expect* at a given time. If you are taking over a class which is supposed to have reached a certain level, and to have mastered certain topics, notions, structures, skills, etc., then the diagnostic testing can be retrospective – that is, checking to see how far they have in fact achieved what is expected. But diagnostic testing can also look forwards, sampling various elements of the syllabus you are about to begin on. There is no point in wasting time teaching things that everybody, or nearly everybody, already knows. Diagnosis is also needed from time to time *during* a course, as Mr Das recognised in **EXAMPLE 1**, to check what specific teaching points may need extra attention for all or some of the students. Some weaknesses discovered may indicate a need for remedial work. But if they are very serious and wide-ranging, they may indicate a need for revision of the syllabus. In diagnostic testing we are usually looking at specific sensitive areas where we expect problems. In diagnosis we are not normally conducting an overall assessment or trying to test *everything* in the syllabus. This would be too time-consuming as well as intimidating for the students. We are picking areas where we have reason to believe there may be difficulty. Our suspicions may arise from experience of previous classes, from knowledge of the students' MT and expectations of MT interference, and from any other source of information available.

C Selection

Here the aim is to select as fairly as possible the best candidates for a *limited* number of places or jobs. This is *competitive* assessment. What counts is the rank-order of the candidates. Unfortunately many teachers seem to treat *all* assessment as if it were a competitive business and to treat high ranking as the only criterion of success. It must be emphasised that, in reality, selection is the only one of the six purposes of assessment dealt with here for which competitive ranking is paramount. In many countries entrance to secondary or tertiary education is selective. Often the selection process is outside the control of the classroom teacher, but the assessment methods used are likely to have a very powerful influence for good or evil on his work. (See Part 3, Section D, Backwash.) If only a small proportion of those tested are to be selected, then maximum fairness will be achieved by making the test very difficult indeed. In this way it will tend to rank pretty fairly the students in the upper range of ability. But such a test will be deeply discouraging to the majority of students, and it will not be a fair measure as a *proficiency* test (see Section D) because even students with a quite good level of proficiency may not reach a qualifying standard. The practice which exists in some countries of using the same examination for secondary school leaving certification and also for selection for higher education can thus in some circumstances be a very unsatisfactory one. A selection measure is also unsatisfactory if it does not reflect closely the purpose for which testees are to be selected. An example would be a bank needing employees able to speak English, but selecting on the basis of a school-leaving examination which included only written English. (See Part 3, Section B, Validity.)

D Proficiency

Here the object is to assess the student's fitness for some stated purpose. An example of a proficiency test is the University Entrance Test in English (Overseas) run by the Northern Universities Joint Matriculation Board. (See McEldowney, 1976, in Further Reading.) The question this test sets out to answer is whether the candidate's general command of English is adequate for study in a UK university or polytechnic. The answer is of necessity a very rough-and-ready one. The English language needs of a student of physics are not the same as those of a student of economics or a student of English literature. Attempts are currently being made (see Carroll, 1980, in Further Reading) to refine such measurement by differentiating between the needs of broad academic fields such as Business Studies, Humanities, Life Sciences, Medicine, Physical Sciences, Social Sciences and Technology. A proficiency test, like a selection test, should obviously be related to specific tasks which the person is expected to be able to carry out in English. A selection test, as we have seen, is designed to identify those candidates who perform best in the abilities being measured. The same number would be selected even if some of them did not perform very well; they would still be the best of the group. A proficiency test tries to identify *all* those who have the required ability. Since proficiency tests are somewhat rough-and-ready in their predictions, we generally have to set a fairly low cut-off point if we want to avoid excluding a large number of candidates without adequate justification for doing so. Thus in a proficiency test the candidate ought to get the benefit of any doubt that exists – and usually a good deal of doubt does exist.

E Progress

This is the kind of test which the class teacher commonly has to make up and give. Here you are trying to assess what the students have learned of the specific syllabus you have been following, and what progress they have made since you last tested them. Assessment of progress should be fairly frequent but not too obtrusive. Very often it can be done, not by setting tests which are obviously tests, but by assessed pieces of work which require application of classroom learning. There is obviously a diagnostic element and a proficiency element in progress testing, but the assessment is focused on the actual course of study that has been followed. In the other kinds of testing you may test things you have not taught. In progress testing you will test only what you have taught or what the students are expected to have covered on their own. The danger with testing what you have taught is of course that you may encourage rote-learning. So it will not be adequate to test on the very passages and exercises the students have covered. What we require is the ability to *apply* what has been taught rather than to regurgitate what has been taught. Thus in reading comprehension, for example, we must find material which is of comparable difficulty to what has been studied and which makes similar demands on the student's skills. If the class have been practising scanning for particular detail, they must be tested on that activity. Likewise in testing command of grammatical structure, we require similar rather than identical contexts to those of the teaching material. This business of 'comparable' or 'similar' is a tricky one, of course – how similar is 'similar'? But this is what we must try to do.

F Aptitude

Attempts have been made to measure foreign language learning aptitude. It might be convenient if we could select those most likely to succeed, and excuse the rest from the pains of foreign language study. But it is difficult to make a test which can do this effectively. There are so many factors affecting success or failure. One is the type of course the students are going to take. An aptitude test which predicted quite accurately their success in a grammar-translation type of course might be wildly inaccurate in predicting their success in a course with strong emphasis on spoken skill; and vice versa. Then there are personal factors, such as the learner's attitude to the language, relations with the teacher, etc. So far research has not produced an aptitude test which can predict the relative success of members of a group of students in foreign language learning any better than you can do by just adding up their marks in all school subjects and ranking them according to the total.

Part 3: Good and bad assessment

A Anxiety

Good assessment is, as far as possible, *non-threatening* to teachers and students. External examinations, and sometimes internal school examinations, are often felt by the teachers themselves to be a threat to their reputation. If their students do not do as well as those of another school or another class, they fear that they will be blamed. One way of combating this is to associate teachers more in the examining process. This has been a particular feature of the work of some Certificate of Secondary Education (CSE) examining boards in the United Kingdom. A school can even propose its own syllabus. The board then provides moderators, who discuss the proposals with the teachers who have made them. When the proposals have been approved, the teachers carry out much of the actual assessment. This often includes, not just the traditional unseen examination paper, but various other means of assessment, including the submission by each pupil of a file of work done over a whole year. Moderators check a sample of the work to ensure that the marking is sufficiently *reliable* (see Section C, Reliability) and that the standard for a given grade is comparable to that for other schools. The teachers will feel less threatened by a system of this kind, where they have a responsible part to play in the assessment rather than feeling themselves put on trial alongside their students. But such a system is in no way a 'soft option' for teachers or students. For students it is at least as demanding as the traditional examination system. For teachers it is much more demanding, but also much more satisfying.

At school examinations, where there are unstreamed parallel classes taught by different teachers, there should likewise be collaboration among the teachers rather than competition which, in its most extreme forms, leads in some countries to outright cheating by teachers on behalf of their students. The examination paper as a whole should be jointly planned. Then different sections should be drafted by different teachers, the drafts being passed round, and considered in detail at a meeting, before being approved. The teacher in charge of a particular section of the paper should mark the work of all the parallel classes in that section. Any temptation to favour one's own students is likely to be suppressed, as the marking would of course be open to scrutiny in case of challenge or doubt. Openness and collaboration tend to bring out the best in people professionally, just as secrecy and fear tend to bring out the worst in them.

Assessment which is felt by the *pupils* as threatening often leads to lowered achievement. This can happen in two ways. Firstly, the actual test results may not give an accurate reflection of what the pupil could have done, because of the pupil's excessive anxiety. Secondly, a few experiences of this kind quickly reduce the pupil's motivation for further learning.

An instance of test results suggesting lower ability than that really possessed by the testees occurred in some of the research carried out in the USA in the 1960s into the English language use of members of ethnic minority groups. Language was tested in an individual interview. The interviewer was a professional person, nearly always of the majority ethnic group. The person being interviewed frequently found the situation intimidating and, as a result, under-performed. Generalis-ations about so-called 'language deprivation', made on the basis of such interviews, were later shown to be untenable when the same people were interviewed in less threatening circumstances.

Look for ways of reducing the anxiety associated with assessment. In a good class with a fairly narrow ability range, to be near or at the bottom is not necessarily to be inadequate. In such circumstances there is no point in publishing information about rank order and little point in even keeping such information. Give students specific feedback on the strong and weak points of their work. For the more frequent 'progress' testing, the standard demanded should be such as most students who have made reasonable efforts can satisfy. Formal assessment should not be too frequent. When an examination is coming, do not spend too long revising in preparation for it. When you give any formal test or examination, include at least a few easy items that everyone can do. Place these at the beginning of the test to build up confidence. If a test or examination is important to the students, you obviously should not include any question the format of which is unfamiliar to them. Research has shown that previous practice in the techniques of answering types of question found in the test can bring as much as 15% improvement in the score of a student. On the other hand, once students have had a small amount of practice with any new type of item, so that they are thoroughly familiar with the mechanics of it, they do not go on getting better simply by doing more items of that type. Thus there are strict limits to the amount of time that you can profitably spend on test techniques. A little time is beneficial. A lot of time may even be counter-productive, if it causes tension or boredom, or wastes valuable teaching-time. It must be admitted, though, that some adults certainly prepare for, and perform in, exams rather better when there is some tension (not too much!) than when there is none.

B Validity

A test cannot be a good one unless it is valid. The essence of validity is that the test measures what it claims to measure. This is in fact quite a complex matter, and you are recommended, for further guidance, to read Chapter 2, by Elizabeth Ingram, of Allen and Davies (1977) in Further Reading.

Many things can prevent measurement from being valid. As far as the classroom teacher is concerned, the first requirement for validity is that you should have a clear idea of exactly what it is about the students' English you are trying to assess. The best way of getting a clear idea is to make a brief written statement. This is worth while, even if the test or other assessment you are about to make concerns only your class and you. If possible – it usually is – state in *operational* terms what you want to measure; that is, 'the students' ability to . . .'. For example:

(i) the ability to use a dictionary to check spelling;
(ii) the ability to write a very short account (about 6 sentences) of a simple industrial or agricultural process, given the necessary information; or
(iii) the ability to ask questions and understand answers needed to find one's way in a strange town.

Having stated as clearly as possible what you want to measure, you are in a better position to judge any test item or means of assessment for its fitness to carry out this measurement. For example, if your objective is to test (ii) above, how would you judge a test item consisting of six sentences in jumbled order which, when correctly ordered, constitute an account of how hydro-electricity is produced? The subject-matter is right, but would you be testing ability to *produce* such an account, or just ability to *comprehend* such an account? On the face of it, only the latter. This is what we call *face validity*; that is, the task required should appear to an intelligent observer to have a very close relationship to the ability to be tested.

This is obvious as soon as it is stated. But you can easily forget or neglect it in the process of assessment. You may be drawn to a certain type of item because it is traditional or because it is easy to set or easy to mark. But is it valid, as a test of whatever you want to test? To get really firm evidence on this question might take more time and resources than you, as a busy teacher, can afford. You might have to ask the opinions of quite a large number of well-qualified judges. You might have to seek an independent criterion – that is, some other well-proven measure of the thing you want to measure, which could be put alongside your proposed measure to see if yours operates more or less as the established measure does. These and other aspects of validity may be beyond your everyday resources. But face validity, at least, you must consider. Without it a test, however efficient and practical it may appear, is worthless.

C Reliability

This topic too is a matter of some technicality, and you are again referred to Chapter 2 of Allen and Davies (1977) for a fuller account than can be given here. The essence of the matter is *consistency* of measurement. If two teachers mark the same test, or if one teacher marks it late at night and again early the next morning, or if the same teacher marks it again after a three-month interval, how closely do the results tally? If it is a Yes/No reading comprehension test of ten items, with no doubtful items, agreement should be 100% except for accidents and cases where a student has indicated his choice ambiguously.

On the other hand, consider a taped pronunciation test of ten items, on each of which the tester has to make a judgement, by listening to the tape, as to whether the pronunciation is 'adequate' or 'inadequate'; his judgement is likely to be rather unreliable unless vigorous measures are taken to increase its reliability. If a test is at all important, ways must be found of estimating its reliability and of ensuring that it is reasonably high.

A motor-cycle may be a perfectly valid means of transport from A to B for a healthy person. If the motor-cycle is unreliable, however, you never know how long the journey is going to take or whether you are going to arrive at all. Perhaps it goes very well in dry weather but stops immediately there is a shower of rain. Or a night journey may be impossible if the lights are not working. In a roughly similar way, a test that is valid but unreliable is unfit for its purpose.

On the other hand, a certain lawn-mower might be 100% reliable and never break down; but it would not be a valid means of transport to and from work in rush-hour traffic. Similarly you might have a listening test with 99% reliability – that is, the results would be virtually the same on all occasions – which would be invalid as a measurement of ability to understand lectures in English because it only involved listening to informal conversation.

D Backwash

Though less impressively technical-sounding than validity and reliability, backwash is just as important. As a comparison here we might imagine a speedboat travelling on a canal. This too might be a perfectly valid means of getting from A to B, considered in isolation. Its mechanism might be thoroughly reliable. But its speed makes it a danger to other boat traffic. Its noise and fumes make it a nuisance to human beings and a threat to bird life. The wash it creates will quickly cause the canal banks to crumble. Similarly, we may have to reject a test, however valid and reliable it might be, because it leaves in its wake undesirable 'side-effects' on teaching. One example is a multiple-choice vocabulary test. This has been found to be a very good measure of general proficiency in English. That is, it is valid – at least, for a very general, non-specific measure (though that in itself is of only limited usefulness). A multiple-choice vocabulary test is relatively easy to set and extremely easy to mark, and can be taken in a short time. That is, it is highly convenient. It can be marked by a computer, or by a relatively unskilled person – possibly even by a trained chimpanzee – and the results are always the same. That is, it is highly reliable. Why then should we not displace existing methods of measuring general proficiency in English in favour of such a test?

Where such an approach has been tried, it has unfortunately been often assumed by teachers, students and others that the best way to prepare for such a test is to do as many items of this type as possible in class. Numerous horrible collections of multiple-choice items have come on the market in various parts of the world as teaching books. But this is terrible teaching material. The vocabulary or other language material is presented in isolated sentences lacking context, and with distractors to assist confusion and cross-association. Surely this is the worst way of trying to improve your vocabulary; and it is useless as a way of trying to improve your general English proficiency.

One might argue that the fault here is not with the test, but with teachers, students and others who assume that the best way of preparing for such a test is an exclusive diet of items of the type of which the test is made up. Possibly they are to blame for being so naive. But the assignment of blame is beside the point. The point is that a kind of Gresham's Law operates here as in the realm of economics – bad currency tends to drive out good. Tests of this kind, carelessly used, have had a dangerous backwash effect and are likely to lead to a lowering of standards of teaching and learning. In such circumstances the offending type of test should be abandoned.

Backwash should not be seen only in terms of bad effects, but also in terms of possible good effects. That is, if we want to encourage particular types of work and practice in classes, we have to include very similar types of task in examinations. If we wish considerable attention to be given to the spoken language, for example, we have to give it a prominent place in assessment, despite the logistical problems involved. If we attach importance to particular types of continuous writing as objectives, we have to test these, and find ways of overcoming problems of marker reliability.

Part 4: Fun with figures

Many English teachers are unnecessarily afraid of the statistical side of assessment. The knowledge required by the ordinary class teacher, as distinct from the testing 'expert', is not difficult to acquire. This section deals with a few basic operations.

A   Range

Everyone is familiar with the concept of the average or *mean*. Am I overweight for my height, sex and age? Or undersexed for my age, height and weight? We are constantly asking, and being asked, such questions. We expect every parent to understand when we say that little Johnny's results are below average for the class.

Looking at the whole class, however, we need to know not just the *mean* of any set of scores but how wide the *range* of scores is. One occasion when this is important is when we want to combine two or more sets of scores. It frequently happens, for example, that we get a wider range of scores in reading comprehension than in written composition. In Reading there will probably be a larger number of items, and the decision on each item will be more clear-cut. This tends to give a wider range of marks than in Writing, where marks are probably given on a small number of criteria, or on just one general impression, and where the decisions are more subjective. Thus the marks might look something like this:

Reading (out of 100): Top mark 94; Bottom mark 22;
Range 94 − 22 = 72; Average of all marks 55.
Writing (out of 100): Top mark 74; Bottom mark 38;
Range 74 − 38 = 36; Average of all marks 55.

The figures are of course artificial, but their general trend is not unusual.

In the vast majority of schools and colleges, I regret to say, these two sets of figures would simply be added together in determining each student's final English mark, without paying any attention to the difference in range. The undesired, often unsuspected result would be that differences in Reading ability would have much greater weight than differences in Writing ability in determining the final results. Take, for example, an imaginary Student A who is outstanding in Reading but only average in Writing, and Student B who is outstanding in Writing but only average in Reading. Their results might be:

	Student A	Student B
Reading	94	55
Writing	55	74
Total	149	129

This again is a rather over-dramatised picture, because usually those good at Reading will also be good at Writing. But the inequity of measurement revealed is still a serious one, and should not just be ignored.

Of course someone might argue that this difference in range reflects a *genuine* difference in the range of abilities in the two fields – that there '*really is*' a much bigger difference between the best and the weakest pupil in Reading than in Writing. When you reflect on this '*really is*', however, can you give a clear meaning to it? How can we compare the 'real' range of abilities in these two activities? Only by some kind of 'general impression', which it is very difficult to be certain about. Thus we should need to be very sure of our ground before accepting that the 'true' range of performance in Reading is much wider than that in Writing. Unless the evidence for this is very strong indeed, we had better assume that the range in the two fields is about the same. In that case we should *equalise* the range of the two sets of marks before we can sensibly combine them.

Actually it is not all that sensible to combine them anyway. A much more meaningful way of expressing each student's ability would be a *profile* – a separate statement of his ability in each area, using a similar five-, six- or seven-point scale for each. But let us assume that, as is often the case, we have no choice but to combine the figures into an overall English score. How then can we equalise the range of the two sets of scores?

For the figures quoted above, where the range in Reading is exactly twice that in Writing, we could roughly put this right by either doubling the Writing range or halving the Reading range. Suppose we decide on the former. The following would be the calculation for Student B:

Writing: raw score	74
Less: Writing: mean score	55
Divergence	19
Divergence × 2	38
Add: Writing: mean score	55
Scaled score	93

Doing this for all the pupils' scores would, for this example, where one range is twice the other, be a rough-and-ready way of equalising the ranges. Actually this is not the exact technique that would be used in a normal case, though it gives a simple idea of the operation. What we should in fact do is to equalise the *standard deviations* (SD) of the two sets of figures. This is a little more complicated, though still very simple really. We will not go into the details here, but refer you to Chapter 3 of Allen and Davies (see Further Reading) or any simple manual on educational statistics.

We have of course been assuming that we do *want* to give equal weighting to Reading and Writing when combining the results. This might not be the case. For a particular class with particular needs we might decide that Reading was, say, twice as important as Writing. In such a case it would still be a good idea to equalise the ranges as we have suggested. But we should then go on to modify the *ratio* between the two sets of figures. If Reading is to have twice as much weight as Writing, we should double each pupil's Reading score before adding it to his Writing score.

B   Item analysis

Looking at particular items in a test, how do we know whether they are operating satisfactorily or not in terms of what we want them to do? To find out will require statistical analysis of the results item by item, which will often be too time-consuming for the ordinary teacher. But it must be said that without item analysis, testing – especially multiple-choice testing – is 'shooting in the dark'. Certainly anyone preparing a test for wide use, for important selection or other purposes, cannot manage without an item analysis. For this to be done properly, there has to be a preliminary pilot stage when the test is tried out before being put into service. The pilot version should include more items than you need for the final version, so that you can throw out any items which prove unsatisfactory while still having enough tried and tested items for the final version.

Coming now to actual item analysis, we should first like to know the *difficulty index* of each item. This simply means what proportion of the target population gets the item right. It can be expressed as a percentage, giving us a clear idea of the difficulty of the item in comparison with the difficulty of the other items, for that particular target population. How we interpret the difficulty index depends on the purpose of the test. If it is a *placement* test we shall probably wish to include a wide range of items, from easy to difficult. In a *diagnostic* test we may exclude items which are so easy that nearly everyone gets them right, since we are trying to pinpoint areas of difficulty that need treatment. In a *selection* test we may exclude easy items if only a small proportion of testees is to be selected. In a *proficiency* test we may exclude very difficult items since, as was suggested above, such a test should give the candidate the benefit of the doubt which usually exists. In a *progress* test we may exclude very difficult items since our aim is to find out what the class as a whole has learned during the course.

The difficulty index will also enable us to place items, as far as convenient, in approximate order of difficulty, in the test as a whole or in particular sections. This helps reduce student anxiety, at least in the earlier stages.

We may also wish to calculate the *discrimination index* of each item – that is, how well it sorts out the better students from the weaker ones. This will probably only be important when we require to place the students in a fairly accurate rank order over a fairly wide range of ability – for example, in an examination with several grades of Pass and the possibility of a Fail.

There are several ways of calculating the discrimination index of a test item. A simple way begins by ranking all the testees on the entire test, then dividing them into four *quartiles* – that is, the top 25% of them, the bottom 25% and the two middle 25%s. Then, to find the discrimination index of an item, we see how many of the top quartile got it right, and how many of the bottom quartile. The ratio between these two numbers is the discrimination index.

For example (choosing figures that will make explanation easy), if 100 people take the test, we pick out the 25 highest-scorers and the 25 lowest-scorers on the test as a whole. Then we can look at any item. Suppose we find that, on item 1 of the test:

23 of the top quartile got it right and
4 of the bottom quartile got it right.

The discrimination index is $\frac{23}{4} = 5.75$, which is high.

Suppose that on item 2
    21 of the top quartile got it right and
    18 of the bottom quartile got it right.
The discrimination index is $\frac{21}{18}=1.2$ which is not very high. Obviously on this item the difficulty index is very low – nearly everyone gets it right. Suppose that on item 3
    5 of the top quartile got it right and
    4 of the bottom quartile got it right.
The discrimination index is $\frac{5}{4}=1.25$ – again not very high, this time because it is so difficult that nearly everyone gets it wrong. Suppose, finally, that on item 4
    15 of the top quartile got it right and
    20 of the bottom quartile got it right.
The discrimination index is $\frac{15}{20}=0.75$ – a danger signal, since it is less than 1.

It may seem surprising to find an item which the weaker students tend to get right more often than the better students, but this does happen. It is frequently a sign that some of the better students are smarter than the teacher who made the test. They have probably seen something in the wording which the test-maker has not noticed, and have chosen an answer which, because of this, is really correct, though the test-maker has decreed that it is 'wrong'. Any item which produces a result of this kind is strongly suspect, and should be thrown out of the test. Sometimes, too, an item is so insultingly easy that the best students suspect a trap and do *not* choose the obvious answer.

There is of course one big, often unspoken, assumption about the discrimination index. Being based on the students' overall performance on the test as a whole, it assumes that the test as a whole is a sound measuring instrument, even if a small number of items in it may be unsound. But suppose a *large* number of items are unsound. Then the overall results cease to be a sound criterion against which to look at the results on any one item, and the whole idea of a discrimination index falls to the ground.

In the case of multiple-choice items, as well as looking at the numbers of right and wrong answers, it may be useful to know how many students chose each of the wrong answers – the so-called 'distractors'. For example, suppose that on item 5
    20 students marked choice A (wrong);
    50 students marked choice B (right);
    0 students marked choice C (wrong);
    30 students marked choice D (wrong).

We can see that, of the wrong choices, A and D were quite convincing whereas C deceived nobody. In an ordinary classroom test it does not much matter if you have a weak distractor which nobody or hardly anybody chooses. But if the test is an important one, the weak distractor

185

should be replaced or the item thrown out. It is, however, one of the defects of multiple-choice testing as a technique that you cannot always find a sufficient number of convincing wrong answers. Sometimes questions which we really need to ask have to be omitted for this reason.

This whole numerical business of item analysis belongs to what is known as the *norm-referencing* approach to testing, in which the performance of students is measured in relation to the performance of other students on the same measure. This is the traditional approach to testing, but it may not always be the most appropriate. For many purposes – for example, in proficiency testing – a *criterion-referencing* approach may be more appropriate. Here students' performance is measured in relation to clearly-stated criteria, and a judgement is made as to whether they are able to perform successfully in the specified tasks and conditions. (See Carroll, 1980, in Further Reading.) Criterion-referencing may in fact be more relevant than norm-referencing for much of the assessment carried out by the ordinary teacher. But you need to be informed about some of the statistical 'tricks of the trade' of norm-referencing testing. Sometimes you will be practically involved in using them. At other times you will require knowledge of them in evaluating the external assessment procedures to which your students are submitted.

C Correlation

Here is another statistical concept that English teachers need at least a nodding acquaintance with. In fact these days, in order to understand current debates about the effects of smoking, radioactivity, poly-unsaturated fats and other hazards of modern life, everyone needs to understand the concept.

Correlation is a measure of the extent to which two sets of measurements, made on the same population, agree in the way they rank or classify that population. If they agree totally, we have a perfect positive correlation of $+1.0$. Most positive correlations will of course be lower than this. Not *all* cigarette smokers develop lung cancer, for example, but a *significant* proportion do. The *level* of significance can be stated, and we can say: such a correlation would only occur by chance 5 times in 100, or once in 100 times, etc. We can also have a negative correlation. For example if, of 100 sailors, the 5 tallest do not work in submarines, whereas a good number of the rest do, we have a perfect negative correlation, in this group, between the two categories 'height' and 'working in submarines'.

I do not intend to go into details of calculation of correlations and their degrees of significance. The important matter for teachers to consider is the meaning of a correlation. It is often assumed that a high correlation between two factors can be taken to imply a causal relationship between them. For example, if there was shown to be a high correlation between hyper-tension and TV-watching, some people would immediately conclude that TV-watching caused hyper-tension. But there are other possibilities. Maybe it is the other way round: perhaps hyper-tension causes people to increase their TV-watching. Or maybe neither is the cause of the other, but they both have some common cause. For example, perhaps both hyper-tension and TV-watching increase with unhappiness in the home. Finally, the correlation might be coincidental, and without causal connection.

How does all this affect the assessment of English learning? It comes into the measurement of validity and reliability. For example, a high correlation between the scores awarded by two markers of a spoken interview test may indicate high reliability. On the other hand, the fact that a test of foreign language learning aptitude does not correlate with language-learning success any better than does the sum of students' grades in all academic subjects may be taken as a sign of poor validity of the test. Again, suppose two English tests, given to the same students as measures of general English proficiency – say a cloze reading test (see Part 6, Section B, 3) and a vocabulary test – give results that correlate very highly, we may perhaps conclude that we could save time by giving only one of the two tests to future groups. These are a few examples of ways in which correlations could be relevant. But use them with extreme caution, guarding particularly against the fallacy that, because B follows A and is highly correlated with A, it necessarily *results* from A.

D Correction for guessing

It is sometimes thought that successful guessing, in the absence of knowledge, can have a substantial effect on multiple-choice test results. This is not the case, in a test of reasonable length, provided a correction is made to allow for such guessing. The students must of course, in fairness, be told beforehand that wrong answers will be penalised, not simply ignored, in arriving at a student's score, and that they should therefore leave a blank where they are not reasonably sure. On a 4-choice test of 100 items, pure guesswork would give an average raw score of about 25 – an individual figure might be rather higher or lower, but would be most unlikely to be very much higher or lower. The correction to be applied must therefore be such that a raw score of 25 or less would come out as a score of zero. The formula to be applied is:

$$\text{Total right answers} - \frac{\text{Total wrong answers}}{\text{Number of choices} - 1}$$

In the case we are looking at, Number of choices is 4, so Number of choices minus 1 is 3. Thus if Total right answers is 25, which could be achieved by pure guesswork, then

$$\text{Total right answers (25)} - \frac{\text{Total wrong answers (75)}}{3}$$

works out at 25 minus 25, that is 0%.

We will look at two other possibilities, one where the total of right answers is 55, and one where it is 97.

$$\text{Total right answers (55)} - \frac{\text{Total wrong answers (45)}}{3}$$

works out at 55 minus 15, that is, 40%.

$$\text{Total right answers (97)} - \frac{\text{Total wrong answers (3)}}{3}$$

works out at 97 minus 1, that is 96%.

On a True/False test, of course, Number of choices minus 1 is 1, so the full total of wrong answers is subtracted from Total right answers.

Part 5: Subjective and objective testing

The two terms *subjective* and *objective* tend to be used very loosely. I wish to use them with reference to marking. By *objective* I mean 'capable of being marked with 100% reliability'. This is a pretty definite fixed point. Anything which does not approach it is called *subjective*, though obviously there are widely differing degrees of subjectivity.

Traditional English language testing, both MT and FL, was of course highly subjective, with a preponderance of essay-type items. Objections began to be raised in the 1920s and 1930s, when research revealed very great unreliability in this kind of MT testing, when comparing results of different markers and those of a single marker on separate occasions. Dissatisfaction with this kind of testing was obviously linked with the growth during this period of psychometrics generally – the attempt to measure objectively mental factors such as intelligence, memory, etc. While standardised tests of reading, vocabulary, etc. became available to MT teachers during these years, it was not until the 1950s that psychometrics began to filter through to the EFL and ESL worlds.

When the pendulum did begin to swing, it swung with a vengeance. Essay-type tests were rejected in many quarters not only on grounds of unreliability, but because the 'creative writing' types of task customarily set were considered invalid. Objective testing was now embraced by many as a panacea, as being not only more reliable, but more specific, more appropriate, easier to administer, etc. The 1960s may be regarded as the heyday of this movement in our field – though it is dangerous to generalise about dates of educational developments, since there can be a time-lag of 20 years or more between the dates at which changes affect different parts of the world or different parts of the same education system!

This development was linked to the dominance of behaviourist attitudes to FL learning and the related views of structural linguists on language. FL learning tended to be atomised into the learning of a long series of linguistic items of pronunciation, grammar and lexis. This view lent itself perfectly to the growth of objective testing. The multiple-choice item flourished mightily.

The area of grammar was a particularly fertile field. Here are three examples – not caricatures, since they are taken from a highly reputed test of this kind, which it would be unkind to identify.

1 Who $\begin{cases} \text{(a) does have} \\ \text{(b) is having} \\ \text{(c) has} \end{cases}$ the right time?

The 'correct' answer is (c). But surely (a) could also be correct, given a suitable context?

2 The committee has nearly finished $\begin{cases} \text{(a) their} \\ \text{(b) its} \\ \text{(c) his} \end{cases}$ business.

The 'correct' answer is (b). But many people would consider (a) correct, and (c) is certainly correct.

3 The sheep on the farm up the road $\begin{cases} \text{(a) are having} \\ \text{(b) have} \\ \text{(c) has} \end{cases}$ its wool clipped twice a year.

The 'correct' answer is (c). But we can only convince ourselves of this by ignoring common sense. Whoever heard of a farm with only one sheep?

If such faults were rare aberrations they would not be important. Unfortunately, they are extremely frequent, so that, rather than attributing them to oversight or incompetence on the part of the tester, one is more and more forced to the conclusion that the nature of the test leads one almost inevitably into such problems.

It is clear that the '100% reliability' of marking of such items is spurious. More fundamental, however, is the question of their validity. This can only be judged in relation to what we expect the test to do. Certainly items of this type test basic grammatical knowledge of some kind. But they do not seem to bear any close relation to the ability to use the grammatical items concerned in continuous writing or speaking, or indeed to comprehend them when they are met in continuous context. If, on the other hand, the aim is to diagnose particular areas of grammatical common error, such a test may do so validly if it is well made.

The attempt to measure reading comprehension objectively by multiple-choice items is, if anything, even more beset by problems. We have space here only for brief illustration of this.

---

1 Research and experience showed that

(a) penicillin could not be used to combat human disease.
(b) only small amounts of penicillin could be produced.
(c) penicillin could become ineffective if over-used.

Probably the testees could exclude (a) and (b) on the basis of their general knowledge. Any questions which can be answered without reading the passage are invalid as tests of comprehension of the passage. This is obvious, yet many such items occur. Giving a friend the questions without the passage is one obvious precaution to take in order to weed them out.

---

2 A *subservient* wife is one who gives her husband

(a) too much respect.
(b) too little respect.
(c) the right amount of respect.

It may depend on the student's background whether he or she regards (a) or (c) as correct. This problem can be overcome by inserting 'According to the passage', provided the passage does give a clear view of the matter. There is also a grammatical hurdle in that the student cannot respond correctly if he equates *too* with *very*, as many EFL learners do. The fact that we are testing understanding of the question as well as understanding of the passage is a particular problem with multiple-choice reading, because it forces us into rather lengthy wording of questions, and it is difficult always to ensure that the wording of the question is, as it should be, easier to understand than the wording of the passage under test.

---

3 The name of William Caxton is famous as that of

(a) a rich merchant.
(b) a man of prodigious industry.
(c) a contributor to the easy communication of information and literature.

A common fault is to make the correct choice, as here, easily recognisable by its much greater length.

A more general problem commonly occurs: a passage which is highly relevant to the comprehension needs of a given group of students may be unusable for multiple-choice testing because it does not lend itself to the production of the right number of items, each with the right number of distractors.

Multiple-choice testing can of course be used in numerous other areas besides grammar and reading comprehension. I am not declaring total war on it here. Some of the faults I have mentioned may of course be found in other types of test too. Heaton (1975) is a persuasive advocate of multiple-choice English testing and an excellent guide to the techniques and pitfalls involved. But in my view we should always look at any multiple-choice test with a suspicious, critical if not jaundiced eye. Certainly no teacher should rely on his own judgement alone in making one, even for a routine school examination. A draft should be made and submitted to careful critical inspection by at least two fellow-teachers. There should be advance try-out of questions on comparable students if this can be done without loss of secrecy.

The 1970s saw a return swing of the pendulum towards subjective testing. Among the manifold problems of objective testing, some of which we have touched on, the most serious of all were perhaps bad backwash effects and low validity, in terms of the actual abilities we wish to teach and measure. Attempts were therefore made to rehabilitate subjective testing by making it more valid and reliable.

One attempt at increased reliability which should be dismissed as a false trail is *error counting*. Its drawbacks as a way of assessing continuous writing ability may seem so obvious as to make it hardly worth mentioning. But it seems to be quite firmly entrenched in many countries, so it may be worth brief consideration.

It gives very low inter-marker reliability. Teachers vary in what they consider acceptable, and in their assiduity in noting errors. Often it is impossible to say with certainty how many errors a defective passage contains, since several are compounded together. Nor does error counting give a reliable picture of pupils' standard of correctness, since this varies enormously with the topic and task set. Errors obviously differ in seriousness, but any system of scaling errors according to their seriousness is bound to be cumbersome and difficult to apply reliably. Again, one would presumably regard the same error occurring four times as less serious than four different errors, other things being equal. But any attempt to allow for this is fraught with difficulty.

In addition to all these reliability problems, the process is not even efficient – on the contrary, it is extremely time-consuming. More serious still is the problem of validity. Error counting measures only negative aspects and gives no credit for positive aspects such as success in communicating. Perhaps most damning of all is the backwash effect. Error counting encourages students to be unadventurous, repetitive and over-simple in their choice of language.

What methods, then, have proved effective in judging students' performance in the necessarily subjective areas of continuous writing and spoken interaction? Actually a considerable amount of research has been done, and a firm consensus of opinion has been built up.

First, if the work can be marked by two markers (or better still, three, but this is unlikely to be practicable in everyday circumstances) the pooling of their results will obviously increase reliability. The use of two markers will of course double the time taken. But the extra time can be compensated by adopting a 'quick impression' method of marking.

To operate in this way we need a scale with a fairly small number of grades. Five, six or seven seem workable numbers of grades. Teachers often assume that they can make much finer distinctions than this. For example, we find a piece of written work being marked subjectively out of 20, with the teacher giving one script 14, another 15 and another 16 marks. But research has shown that we cannot reliably distinguish more than seven categories in carrying out such an operation in normal circumstances. So the differences between grades of 14, 15 and 16 are not likely to reflect any consistent difference of quality in the scripts – unless, of course, the whole range of marks covers no more than seven points – say from 12 to 18. Carroll (1980) uses a 9-point scale, but the top and bottom points are rarely used so, as he points out, it is in effect a 7-point scale. (See Further Reading.)

Each point or grade needs to be clearly described in terms of what the student can do. The following is an example of a set of descriptions which could be used at the level of English proficiency needed for university study in the UK:

Impression scale for rating continuous writing

Grade	Description
5	*Excellent:* virtually indistinguishable from a well-educated native speaker in use of standard written English, range of language, organisation of content, relevance and appropriateness.
4	*Good:* clearly a non-native speaker, but reaches a standard of expression that would amply satisfy UK university teachers in his subject field. Exhibits some or all of the following: —grammatical errors few and not affecting communication; —varied, flexible, appropriate use of grammatical, lexical and cohesive elements;

	—subject-matter well organised and appropriate to purpose.
3	*Adequate:* satisfies minimum standard for UK university study. Exhibits some or all of the following: —moderate number of grammatical errors but rarely impairing communication; —reasonable range of grammatical pattern in clause and sentence; —reasonable command of cohesive devices though with some defects; —reasonable appropriateness and range of lexis, though with some defects; —reasonable ability to organise subject-matter in relation to purpose, though with some defects.
2	*Below par:* falls noticeably short of minimum adequate standard for UK university study. Exhibits some or all of the following: —excessive frequency of grammatical errors, some of which threaten communication; —inadequate range of grammatical pattern; too sparse use of modifiers and complex sentences; —inadequate command of cohesive devices; —excessive frequency of unacceptable lexical use and/or inadequate range of lexis, either or both of which threaten communication at times; —inadequate ability to organise subject-matter in relation to purpose.
1	*Inadequate:* falls very far short of minimum adequate standard for UK university study. Exhibits some or all of the following: —very weak command of grammatical structure with errors frequently threatening communication; —very limited range of grammatical pattern; practically all simple sentences with little use of modifiers; —very poor command of cohesive devices, leading to a bald, disjointed text; —very poor command of lexis; —poor organisation of subject-matter in relation to purpose.
0	*Non-communicating:* shows little or no ability to communicate in continuous writing at the level of UK university study. Language command and/or organisation of subject-matter merely rudimentary.

G

In addition to such a set of descriptions, we need for each point on the scale an *example* of a script which, the markers can agree, typifies that grade. All the markers need to get together to discuss all this and to have a practice session in which they all mark the same scripts separately and then discuss any differences of opinion until they reach a common mind. Given a procedure along these lines, and given markers of reasonable competence, a very high level of reliability has been found to result, both in the marking of continuous writing and in the marking of taped spoken performance.

It has been found that, once a marker has a clear idea of a suitable range of grades for a given piece of work, he can mark more reliably by quick impression than by slow, painstaking scrutiny of each piece of work. Unpalatable as this may be for the over-conscientious, it is a fact. It may be that it is easier to keep steady standards in mind if you see a large number of cases in quick succession. It is also difficult to mark reliably if you are trying to mark on several different criteria at the same time. Thus a quick impression of one criterion at a time is generally better than trying to mark on several criteria at once. But time is usually limited, and it has proved perfectly satisfactory to use a quick *overall* impression – that is, not judging consciously on separate criteria at all. Of course, to work effectively in this way, you must have gone through the process of discussing and considering separate criteria beforehand.

If two markers follow this method they will of course differ on a certain number of scripts. Where they differ by just one grade, their marks can generally just be added together or averaged. Where they differ by more than one grade (probably not on more than 5% of cases if they have been well prepared for their work) the script ought to be re-checked by both of them or by a third marker. While occasionally the discrepancy will prove due to a lapse of attention by one marker, it will usually turn out to be due to some unusual feature of the script. For example, the *language* may be very much better or very much worse than the *content*, as compared with most other scripts in the group.

Subjective testing of this kind, then, can be reliable and reasonably economical. Still more important, it can be valid and have a healthy backwash effect. Emphasis on practice in writing and speaking will result from inclusion of direct tests in these activities. The needs of communicative language teaching are served if assessment includes tasks involving the closest possible approach to real communication.

Part 6: Taking it apart and getting it together

We now face perhaps the most difficult question regarding assessment; exactly what is it about the learner's knowledge and command of English that we wish to assess? Broadly speaking we may distinguish two contrasted approaches to this question, with the rather forbidding names of *discrete-point* and *integrative* assessment. Discrete-point assessment attempts to measure separately the learner's knowledge and/or command of individual items in such areas as grammar, vocabulary, pronunciation, the writing system, functional and notional usage – in fact, any area where learning units can be listed in such a way that they can be individually tested. Integrative assessment, on the other hand, attempts to measure the learner's ability to bring all this knowledge and command to bear in tackling 'work-samples' related as closely as possible to the forms of real-life communication we expect him to be able to take part in.

A Discrete-point assessment

Merely taking an area such as grammar for separate assessment does not constitute discrete-point assessment. You could, for example, set a piece of continuous writing and give it separate general impression ratings for grammar and vocabulary, using for each a scale from very good to very weak, without testing specific points of grammar or vocabulary. This would not be discrete-point assessment as intended here. A discrete-point grammar test, then, is one which aims to test knowledge and/or command of specific points of grammar. For example, look back at the three items on page 189 and consider what each of them aims to test.

To get item 1 right you have to choose from *does have, is having* and *has*. This actually involves choices in two dimensions. You can begin by choosing the appropriate *tense*, which is the Present Simple. The tester then expects you to choose between 'regular interrogative' *does have* and 'irregular interrogative' *has*, the latter being correct because the verb *to have* as used here is irregular. (The tester ignores the fact that 'emphatic' *does have* might be correct, given a suitable context, but that is not the point under discussion here.) We may now wonder whether the tester really intended to test both tense and interrogative form in the same item. To do so seems a dubious proceeding, which was perhaps forced on him by the multiple-choice format. In other words, this item is not as 'discrete-point' as it should be – it tests two grammatical points, not one. The same is true of item 3, where you have to choose between *are having, have* and *has*, which involves a choice of tense (Present Simple *have/has* versus Present Continuous *are having*) and a choice for Subject-Verb concord between *have* and *has*. Even item 2, where you have to choose between *their, its* and *his*, involves two points: Number (singular *its/his* versus plural *their*) and Animate/Inanimate reference (animate *his* versus inanimate *its* versus animate/inanimate *their*).

These examples illustrate, then, that discrete-point testing sometimes fails to achieve its aim of testing a single point at a time. The same is true, in the area of vocabulary, of item 2 on page 190. Aimed at the vocabulary point *subservient*, it tests, or at least requires knowledge of, the distinction between the two grammatical words *too* and *very*. This is a common problem of discrete-point testing. Because language largely has to be tested by means of language, it is often difficult to isolate a particular linguistic point and test just that.

A way of minimising this difficulty is to have *several* items to test a single linguistic point. Suppose, for example, we had *three* items testing Subject-Verb concord in the Present Simple tense. It is possible that *any one* of these might be 'contaminated' in the way we have seen. But unless *all three* were contaminated in the same way, they would together provide good evidence of the student's mastery or lack of mastery of the grammatical point. To have three items per point would of course make a test longer, or the number of points tested in it smaller, but it may be necessary if the test is to achieve validity.

Apart from the question of how to measure discrete points validly, there is the more fundamental question of *why* we should wish to do so. We have already voiced doubts as to whether command of discrete points of grammar, vocabulary, etc. can be equated with ability to use them communicatively. The answer to this question is that, insofar as we consider it useful to teach discrete points of grammar, vocabulary, etc. specifically and individually, we may legitimately want to test them specifically and individually, particularly in diagnostic and progress testing, to see if previous teaching has been successful.

It is also important when planning a discrete-point test to be clear whether we are trying to test ability to *produce* each point, or merely to *understand* it when it is met. To answer a multiple-choice item we have merely to recognise the correct form among those given. But to produce an item in context we have to recall it to memory (and, if in doubt, recall possible alternatives and then make a correct choice). Thus a multiple-choice item may test ability to *recognise*, but certainly does not test ability to *produce*.

An *open-ended* item goes a bit further towards testing the ability to produce. For example:

I go to the cinema regularly, but I .... to the theatre for months.

This is supposed to elicit the Present Perfect tense *haven't been*, triggered by *for*. It is, however, very difficult to make a context which really *forces* the use of a given grammatical point. In the present case, any of the following would be acceptable:

> *sometimes don't go*   (habitual)
> *may not go*   (modal possibility)
> *am not going*   (planned future)
> *lived in Stratford-on-Avon for ten years and didn't go*   (past).

You may be able to think of other possibilities. For any student who makes any of these correct completions not using the Present Perfect, the item cannot be said to test that tense.

A constant problem with single-sentence items, both multiple-choice and open-ended, is the lack of any wider context. This tends to make the task a mechanical one, quite unlike the processing of continuous text. It also makes it difficult, as we have just seen, to narrow down the choice to the point it is desired to test. Things are improved in this respect, both for multiple-choice and for open-ended items, by inclusion in a longer text. For example:

The interest of botanists in the history of corn is largely practical. They (1) _____ the genetics of corn in order to produce hybrids. The search for the wild ancestors of corn narrowed to two tassel-bearing New World grasses that had features (2) _____ the domesticated plant. The wild ancestor of corn (3) _____ previously been sought for nearly a century.

(1) (a) studied   (b) study   (c) studying
(2) (a) resembling   (b) to resemble   (c) resemble
(3) (a) have   (b) had   (c) has

Item (1) seems dubious. We could say *study* in view of *is* in the previous sentence. Or we might say *studied* in view of *narrowed* in the following sentence. However, a student doing item (1) can first eliminate *studying* on the grounds that a finite form is required, and then choose either the present tense *study* or the past *studied* according to his judgement of the context. In item (2) he can first eliminate *resemble*, since *had* + nominal phrase + verb stem, as in *The teacher had the children scrub the room*, is inappropriate. The choice of *resembling* will then probably be fairly straightforward if the student is familiar with the 'reduced relative' structure noun + verb stem + *-ing*.

Such a test is very much more valid than a single-sentence test, provided the text chosen is one which represents a realistic reading task for the students, in line with the objectives of their course. As far as backwash effects are concerned, contextualised discrete-point testing has a great advantage, in that good test material is also good practice material, which, as we have seen, is frequently not the case with isolated-sentence test items.

The same type of test can be set in open-ended format:

Three one-word verb forms are missing in the following. Write each word near the place where it should go, and mark the place where it should go with a⌞.
Example: His father⌞an engineer.   is

Basket-making is one of the oldest crafts. During the time that it is known to developed, different races have basketwork to make the walls and roofs of houses. It has used for rafts and sails, traps and nets.

Here the student should be able to identify spots where a verb word is missing:

(i) *to* cannot be followed by the *-ed* form verb *developed* unless this is adjectival, as in a phrase such as *developed countries*. Thus clearly a stem-form verb must be inserted. This can only be *have* or *be*, and only the former fits the context.

(ii) *different races have basketwork:* Taking the clause in isolation, it contains no error. But in the context clearly a Present Perfect tense, formed by inserting *used/employed/*etc., makes better sense.

(iii) *has used* is a possible verb form, taken in isolation. Using context, *it has* first to be related to *basketwork* before we see that a passive *has been used* is needed.

We might have certain doubts about validity in that the kind of behaviour needed to solve this is somewhat different from normal text-processing behaviour. But it is not *entirely* different. Another possible criticism of this series, or of any series of multiple-choice or open-ended items employing continuous text, is that the items are to some extent *inter-dependent*. That is, if you fail to get (i) right, your chances of getting (ii) right are greatly reduced, and so on. This is a valid criticism in terms of the testing of discrete linguistic points. On the other hand, there is no doubt that such inter-dependence is a natural feature of the processing of text. In real-life reading or listening, as well as in a test of this kind, if you fail to understand one bit, your chances of understanding the next bit are likely to be reduced. Such inter-dependence means that this type of test is to some extent integrative as well as testing particular items.

Another point which raises a doubt about the validity of the above kind of item is that, the better you are at reading, the more likely you are in reading to 'supply' a missing structure word, perhaps without even noticing that it is missing. This objection could be met, however, by showing a blank where a word has been omitted.

Our examples so far have been restricted to grammar and vocabulary. They have also been restricted to the processing of *written* language. It is in fact very rarely that we find grammar or vocabulary specifically tested in a listening/speaking situation. It is obviously so much easier to test them in a reading/writing situation. But it is important to remember that ability to handle a given point in reading/writing is no guarantee of ability to handle it in listening/speaking, and the converse is also true.

Discrete-point testing of pronunciation, however, can only be carried out validly through listening/speaking. Attempts to do it by means of 'paper and pencil' tests alone are dubious. For example:

Mark the syllable with the strongest stress:
im   poss   i   ble

A student who has learned the correct answer from a teacher or a dictionary may mark this correctly even though his ear cannot recognise the strongest syllable and he cannot speak the word with correct stress. Conversely, some people who *can* say it correctly may be unable to make their knowledge conscious to the extent of being able to mark it correctly. These drawbacks may still be present if the 'paper and pencil' work is accompanied by actually hearing the word spoken. Ability to hear phonemic distinctions can be quite easily tested. For example:

Listen, and mark	AAA	if the sentences are all the same,
	ABC	if the sentences are all different,
	AAB	if the first two sentences are the same and the last is different,
	ABB	if the last two sentences are the same and the first is different, and
	ABA	if the first and last sentences are the same and the second is different.

(Heard) He hurt his finger with the pen.
         He hurt his finger with the pin.
         He hurt his finger with the pen.
(Correct answer: ABA)

This is useful as far as it goes, but is of course no guarantee that the student can make the distinction in speaking or, even if he can, that he will regularly do so.

Sentence stress and intonation can be tested receptively in somewhat similar ways, but one feels some doubts about the validity of such tests, given the present state of research on these features of the English language.

The testing of discrete points of pronunciation in *speaking* usually involves asking students to read aloud a passage containing key points which the tester is instructed to grade as satisfactory/unsatisfactory. For example:

(Passage)	(Points to be marked)
The speaker, bowing ironically to his opponents, said that their speeches amounted to little more than a protest. It was easy to urge people to take up emotional attitudes.	*bowing:* correct diphthong *protest:* stress on 1st syllable *urge:* correct vowel

There are problems here. A passage specially written for such a purpose tends, like this one, to be stilted. In any case, reading aloud is not a valid test of speaking ability for most students. Although marking here is

199

itemised on discrete points, the judgement to be made on each point is subjective, whether it is made live or from a tape.

In addition to grammar, vocabulary and pronunciation, discrete points of the writing system of English can be tested. This includes spelling and punctuation, and will not be illustrated here.

In recent years, attempts have been made to test discrete points of functional and notional usage. In principle, these should be tests of what the student can *do* with the language rather than what he *knows* of or about the language. A sample of spoken or written language is provided. Usually this consists of a single 'move' or 'exchange' in an interaction, or a short portion of a communicative text of some kind. The student is often required to identify the context of situation, or the purpose, the topic or level of formality of the communication, or the role, status or mood of a participant, etc., etc. For further discussion see Morrow (1977) in Further Reading. As Morrow is at pains to point out, this type of testing is in an early stage of development, and problems of validity and technique remain to be solved.

In mentioning so many problems that can arise in discrete-point testing it is not my intention to discredit it or to discourage teachers from using it. We should keep the problems in mind, however, so as not to give discrete-point testing too much emphasis, so as to beware of pitfalls in constructing test items, and so as to avoid jumping to unwarranted conclusions from the results of such tests. The advantage of discrete-point testing, to be set against all these problems, is the potential ability of checking a wide range of learning items, in detail, quickly, accurately and objectively.

B Integrative assessment

It will be clear from the foregoing section that there is not an absolute distinction between discrete-point and integrative assessment. We have seen that complete texts may be used in discrete-point assessment. In functional discrete-point assessment in particular, the task the student is asked to perform may be very closely related to a real-life communication task. On the other hand, a general impression rating on a piece of writing for its command of grammar would in a sense be integrative, particularly if it tried to judge the adequacy of the grammar for a given kind of communication.

Again, we cannot make an absolute distinction between continuous-text grammar tests, which we have called discrete-point tests, and reading comprehension tests, which might include items testing vocabulary and perhaps grammar, as well as items testing broad reading skills (such as ability to distinguish main points from examples, to scan for particular information, to skim for a general idea of the content, etc) and items testing more specific skills serving these broader skills (such as ability to make use of graphic features including sub-headings, italics, etc). Clearly such reading tests may contain both discrete-point and integrative assessment. We shall, however, consider them under the heading of integrative assessment, since we shall assume that their main purpose is to measure the student's ability to integrate all his knowledge and skill in tackling a task closely related to real communication, receptive and/or productive.

'Receptive and/or productive' should remind us of a point emphasised in Chapter 6: real-life communication rarely consists of *one* of the 'four skills' of L, S, R and W acting in isolation. For example, Carroll (1980) has suggested that, in academic English, the commonest modes of activity are, in this order:

Reading (when studying);
Reading + Writing (when making notes from written sources);
Listening + Speaking (when conversing);
Listening + Writing (when making notes at lectures).

Only the first of these involves a single one of the 'four skills', and even here we are really concerned with a very wide and complex variety of activities and abilities as well as the ability to integrate these.

A 'pure' test of Reading is possible in the sense that we can set up a Reading test such that the student does not have to do any L, S or W. For Listening tests we can rarely exclude S, R and W entirely except in the kind of test where the student is instructed to carry out actions, mark pictures, draw diagrams, etc. But usually a Listening test involves a certain amount of R, if not W or S. A Speaking test without L is hardly conceivable, and most Writing tests involve some R. We may be justified in trying to test the 'four skills' separately to this extent: that in any one part of the test we may *emphasise* one of them and minimise the amount and difficulty of any of the other three required as part of the testing process. The advantage of trying to deal separately with each of the four to this extent, even though we cannot separate them wholly, is that we may get a clearer profile in this way of the differential abilities of our students, which could be useful for placement, diagnostic or progress testing purposes.

But we clearly also need the *most* integrative type of test, where we set up something closely approximating to a real communication task, regardless of whether it needs one, two, three or all four of the 'four skills', and whether these are used in alternation or simultaneously. For example, to prepare and deliver a short talk, giving it from only brief notes, and to reply to questions and comments on the talk by the student's peers: to do this may involve R; will involve at least a small amount of W; L will be important; but the most important 'skill' being judged will be S.

Where ESP is concerned, the idea of a model for communicative test design (see Carroll, 1980) is highly relevant. The full process to be followed using such a model is lengthy and highly technical. First the testee is described and his communicative purposes outlined. This leads to a detailed specification of the major events he is to participate in, the main activities required for each, the spoken and/or written media to be used, whether productively and/or receptively, the role relationships and dialects needed, the performance levels for each medium, the topic areas for each event, the language skills for each activity, the functions and attitudinal tones for each interaction. Only then can we begin to select types of test item for each activity.

Without going into further explanation here of the above categories, it is clear that this sequence, logical as it is, is an extremely tall order even for the most favourable circumstances. For most teachers it may be a rather distant ideal which in practice will be more honoured in the breach than in the observance.

The 'communicative model' and the 'work-sample' approach, while suited to ESP, do of course present problems when we are involved in a *general* English course for students who have no very definite use of the language in mind. Attempts to solve the problems for assessment, in this situation, must harmonise with attempts to solve the problems for the course as a whole.

The rest of this chapter will consist of a brief discussion of integrative testing centring on L, S, R and W respectively. I shall not give many examples, because I consider that, generally speaking, the nature of good integrative tests of L, S, R and W does not differ fundamentally from the nature of good training exercises in integrative skills of L, S, R and W. You are therefore advised to turn to the chapters on L, S, R and W respectively for further ideas on testing these 'skills'. Adaptation will often be needed to turn a good practice exercise into a good test or vice versa, but the basic 'skills' being tested or practised are the same.

1   Listening.   Integrative tests in L comprehension should be used much more widely than they are at present. This would do a great deal to encourage increased emphasis on the spoken language where it is neglected. L comprehension tests are not difficult to construct – no more so than R comprehension tests, once you have had a bit of practice. They can be made thoroughly valid and reliable, and are not difficult to administer.

It is important, as for L exercises, that valid samples of spoken language be used. Simply reading aloud a piece of written English will not do. Even lecture-type material (apart from the very worst lecturers) does differ from written material, both in the choice of language and in the organisation of content. Spoken text needs more repetition. The commonest fault of bad L tests is excessive density of information. Even if we are experienced in testing L comprehension we need to be on our guard against it, remembering that *we* have the script, and have therefore seen the information in written form. Even with an effort of imagination it is difficult to put ourselves in the position of the student, who has *not* seen the information in written form. The fault of too dense information can be overcome by letting the students hear the passage several times. But this makes the task too unlike real-life L to be valid in *assessment*, though in *teaching* there is much to be gained from giving several hearings, with a different task set each time.

Material for L comprehension tests includes not only short talks or stretches of lecture-like text, but also conversation. All texts for L comprehension tests should be fairly short, and it is better to have several short pieces of different types than a single long one.

For an important external examination, presentation on tape has the advantage of standardising the test as between different centres. But it has problems. L to tape is more difficult and tiring than L to live speech, and for classroom tests or internal school examinations live presentation may be preferable. For tape presentation a single high quality loudspeaker in a room containing not more than about 40 people may be adequate, given good acoustics. But some research suggests that students placed in Section A in Diagram 1 below do significantly better than students placed in Section B, while those at X and Y in Diagram 2 do better than those at W and Z.

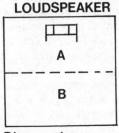

Diagram 1

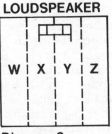

Diagram 2

The difference may not be very large but, ideally, in an important external examination, it should be calculated and allowed for. This can easily be done provided the students are seated randomly in respect of ability – alphabetical placing should normally achieve this. These difficulties can perhaps be avoided by holding the test in a high-quality language laboratory, which also cuts out possible aural and visual distractions.

Great care is needed in the way tasks or questions are set in a L comprehension test. If the test is an important one, they will probably be given in written form as well as being read orally to the students. Information transfer of many kinds is extremely useful, but needs very great care so that the test does not become one of special visual or spatial skills rather than of L comprehension.

Finally a word about cloze L tests. Cloze tests generally are more fully discussed under R below. A cloze L test is a tape-recorded discourse in which the tape has been edited after recording so as to obliterate one word at regular intervals – every tenth word, for example. The gaps are usually identified by being filled with what telephone engineers call 'white noise'. The student has to guess and write down the missing words while the tape is played – it will need to be played at least twice. For methods of marking see under R below. Cloze has been shown convincingly to be a valid way of testing L comprehension (though there are still some doubters regarding cloze testing in general). It takes a skilled technician quite a long time to produce the edited tape, and this may put cloze L testing outside many teachers' resources. But, where it *can* be done, it is worth considering.

2 Speaking.   It is understandable that testing of S has been so widely neglected. It is time-consuming and administratively awkward. Problems of validity and reliability have also loomed large. But unless S is tested, it will continue to be under-emphasised in teaching.

Let us look at the logistical problems. Take for example a class in their first year of English. A well-planned S test could be conducted in 5 minutes per pupil. Depending on the size of the class, it might take 4 class periods to test them all. For a single teacher working alone, this seems impracticable. Who is going to look after the class while he tests each individual? In any case, the nature of the test would be known to those pupils tested later. However, a co-ordinated team of 5 teachers (including one to 'feed' the pupils to the other four) could manage the test in a single class period. This might be feasible, particularly at examination time, when such co-operation might be possible without disrupting normal classes. Surely, in view of the importance of the spoken skills, and the strong backwash effect of testing, it would be worth trying to conduct a test of this kind at least as part of the half-yearly or thrice-yearly examination programme.

At this beginning level the test might have to be a discrete-point one. At an intermediate or advanced level it can be integrative, and can involve some definite communication task such as giving instructions, describing something, giving opinions, telling a story, etc. Pictures or other visual stimuli can be used to guide the student.

However, the stilted and unnatural conversation with the examiner (often starting with questions on a picture) which has been so much used in FL examining in the UK is not a satisfactory test. Far better are situational tasks such as the following from an Institute of Linguists examination (1975) – the example is part of the material handed to the candidate 15 minutes before he is tested:

> You go to a bookshop to buy a book, which you find is not in stock. Arrange to order the book and find out how much it will cost and how long it will take to get. (The examiner will act as shop assistant.)

This will take only about two or three minutes, so probably time could be afforded for two or three test items of this length.

Role-playing of this kind, where the examiner also has to play a part rather than merely acting as inquisitor, may reduce the anxiety which can be a problem with S testing. Two more ways of reducing tension are: first, letting the examiner, even in an external examination, be the student's own class teacher; and second, having a short unmarked 'warming-up' period at the start of the test. Research has shown that (as with tests of continuous W) high reliability can be achieved by team-work and training of assessors. High correlations have been found between assessment by the student's own teacher and by other teachers, both experienced and inexperienced, both native and non-native speakers of English.

As with W tests, pooling of marks by two assessors improves reliability. It has been shown that assessment can be carried out equally reliably whether it is done live or from a tape recording. Thus if testing by the student's own teacher would not have enough local credibility, students could be tested by their own teacher but marked by someone else listening to the tape. In fact a good way of establishing credibility for assessment by the class teacher would be to have double marking – live by the class teacher and from the tape by another teacher. As with W tests, it has been found that general impression marking is as effective as analytical marking on a number of criteria – and far quicker, of course.

Another method, group testing, is particularly suited to more advanced students who are capable of interacting fairly freely and fluently in English. About 8 students are tested at a time, and they should preferably know each other well. Each student is given a choice of about 3 topics for a talk lasting a few minutes, and has time to think it out and prepare brief notes. Each student in turn then gives his talk to the group of his peers. After each talk, the hearers may ask questions or make comments, to which the speaker briefly replies. In grading the students, these questions, comments and replies are taken into account as well as the talks. The examiner sits a little apart and takes no part in discussion but merely acts as informal chairman. This leaves him free to evaluate, unlike the traditional interview-type S test, where the examiner may do half the talking, and may become quite exhausted in the course of a day in which he may deal with 20 or more candidates in succession. It might be thought that having the examiner observing and making notes would cause anxiety, but candidates do not seem to find this type of test threatening. Many find it positively enjoyable. Depending on the level and the duration of the talks, a group of 8 can be tested in 1 to $1\frac{1}{2}$ hours.

For integrative S testing, as for W testing, the examiner needs a scale describing in detail performances at about 5 to 7 different grades, with a typical tape-recorded example for each grade. This marking scale needs to be very carefully worked out by a team, and all examiners must attend a standardising session at which they practise its use with 'guinea-pig' candidates, before they begin actual examining.

3 Reading. The problems of multiple-choice testing of R have already been discussed. Cloze testing of R is a practical and effective alternative for certain purposes. To make a cloze R test, you simply remove one word from the text at regular intervals – for example, every 8th, 10th or 12th word. The frequency of omission must not be too high, or the test becomes too much of a puzzle. Blanks of standard length (often indicated by dots) are shown in the text. A short example follows:

> Majorca is one of .... loveliest islands in the Mediterranean. Because of this and .... of its proximity to the countries of western and .... Europe, it has become exceptionally popular as a holiday .... and tourism has been developed accordingly. Yet in spite .... the transformation of remote harbours and bays into summer .... and in spite of the ever-increasing number of hotels .... blocks of flats, the island has not yet been .... spoilt and is unlikely to be so for many ...., if ever.

Filling the blanks in such a passage has been convincingly shown to be a valid test of comprehension. It involves a grasp of the grammatical structure, an ability to follow the structure of the discourse and a good command of vocabulary. It correlates well with other measures of comprehension.

Questions have been raised as to exactly what is measured by a cloze test, and the relationship between that and normal reading behaviour. One well-supported view is that multiple-choice and cloze measure different aspects of R ability and should therefore be regarded as complementary rather than in competition. According to this view, multiple-choice measures the *product* of R – ability to interpret the information obtained, whereas cloze measures the *process* of R – ability to extract information or meaning from the text. Whether or not this is true, there seems little doubt that cloze is a useful means of testing R, though it has its critics.

From the teacher's point of view it has great advantages. Once you have ensured that passages chosen are suited to the needs and level of your students, and decided the word-omission rate, you have no further problems of test construction. You will never have to reject suitable passages because of difficulties of question construction. You will not waste time in the search for effective distractors.

There are two methods of marking cloze tests. One is to give a mark only where the student has inserted the *precise word* which was in the original text. This has the advantage of 100% objectivity. The other way is to give a mark for *any word* which is *acceptable* in the context. This sounds much fairer, and is certainly preferable in any situation where the answers are to be gone over with the students. It does, however, reduce the objectivity of the test slightly. For external examining it is likely to increase costs because it means that the test must be marked by English teachers. Research comparing the two ways suggests that, provided the test is reasonably long, the ranking of students is likely to differ hardly at all. Therefore the first method can confidently be chosen for an external selection test, for example.

In addition to cloze in its pure form, various modifications of cloze may be used. For example:
(i) You can close up the gaps so that the student is not shown *where* there is an omission. You could give an instruction such as the following:

'In the following passage of 12 lines there are *eight* words missing. No line has more than one word missing. Insert the missing words, showing clearly *where* each word should go.'

(ii) Rather than simply omitting every 10th word or so, you can omit *particular types* of word – for example, verb words, or articles, etc. The test then becomes more a discrete-point grammar test. An example has already been given on page 197.
(iii) You can combine cloze with multiple-choice. At each gap, instead of a blank, you can provide three or four choices, only one of which will suitably fill the gap. An example has already been given on page 197.

There are many integrative skills of R which a cloze test can at best sample, and cannot test systematically. For example:
(i) the ability to draw inferences – conclusions implied by the text but not actually stated;
(ii) the ability to scan rapidly to get a general idea of the content of a text;
(iii) the ability to state the overall significance of the text – to summarise it in a title, a sentence or a paragraph, etc.;
(iv) the ability to evaluate a text – to judge its effectiveness, trustworthiness, cogency, relevance, etc.;
(v) the ability to grasp the structure of a discourse and thus to distinguish main points, illustrations, digressions, contrasts, etc.; and
(vi) the ability to restate such major constituents of a discourse as those in (v) above, in the form of clearly-structured notes.

To measure abilities such as these, as well as to test knowledge of particular language forms and functions occurring in a text, we still need specific multiple-choice or open-ended items. Pure cloze testing, in other words, while useful, cannot solve all our problems of testing R.

4 Writing. The integrative testing of W has already been discussed in some detail in the present chapter. Examples of exercises of the 'situational' and 'information transfer' types were given in Chapter 6, and such exercises readily lend themselves to use for testing. We will conclude with an example of a W test using information transfer:

Processing coffee berries in Brazil
From the following chart write a continuous account explaining and
briefly comparing the two methods shown. Your account should be
suitable for inclusion in a small booklet to be handed out to students
and visitors attending an exhibition in your school or college.

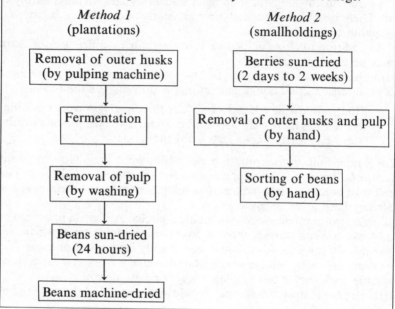

A number of sub-skills are involved in carrying out these instructions,
including:
(i) ability to produce a sentence containing a suitable verb form when
only a heading is given:

(Given)	(Possible text)
Method 1 (plantations)	The following method is used on plantations, where machinery is available.

(ii) ability to modify the grammatical form in which information is
given:

(Given)	(Possible text)
Removal of pulp (by washing)	The pulp is removed by washing.

(iii) ability to use sequence signals and other markers of cohesion to
form a continuous text:

(Given)	(Possible text)
Beans sun-dried (24 hours) Beans machine-dried	The beans are then sun-dried for 24 hours and afterwards machine-dried.

(iv) ability to use appropriate forms to show comparison:
    (Given)   (Possible text)
    (Whole given texts)   The method used on smallhold-
                                 ings is much simpler than that
                                 used on plantations.

Of course each of the above given examples could be realised in a variety of different possible texts. In teaching one would undoubtedly wish to look separately at each of the above four abilities (among others). In testing, we may sometimes wish to look at them separately, and sometimes just to make an overall assessment of the success of the whole communication. Which we choose will depend on whether we are assessing for placement, diagnosis, selection, proficiency or progress – a final reminder that, in assessment as in all other aspects of English teaching, there is no single road to success, but a wide range of paths to choose from according to our purposes and our circumstances.

Further reading

ALLEN, J. and DAVIES, A. (Eds.) *Edinburgh course in applied linguistics, Volume 4: Testing and experimental methods.* (Chapter 2 by Ingram, E. and Chapter 3 by Davies, A.) Oxford University Press, 1977.
    A useful reference source for the technical aspects of testing and related statistical analysis.

HEATON, B. *Writing English language tests.* Longman, 1975.
    A practical guide by a convinced advocate of multiple-choice tests, giving full coverage to ways of avoiding or minimising their pitfalls.

OLLER, J. *Language tests at school.* Longman, 1979.
    A thoughtful survey emphasising the value of communicative and integrative testing.

CARROLL, B. *Testing communicative performance.* Pergamon Press, 1980.
    An interim study of the most recent lines of development in the assessment of communicative skills. Of particular value for teachers of ESP.

MCELDOWNEY, P. *The test in English (overseas): the position after ten years.* Manchester: Northern Universities Joint Matriculation Board, 1976.
    This short pamphlet compares discrete-point testing of linguistic areas with largely integrative testing of communicative skills, for university-level study in the United Kingdom. The numerous examples make it extremely useful.

MORROW, K. *Techniques of evaluation for a notional syllabus.* Royal Society of Arts, London, 1977.

> Necessarily a rather speculative study. It remains to be seen whether the sort of multiple-choice methods suggested will prove suited to the purpose.

ROYAL SOCIETY OF ARTS EXAMINATIONS BOARD. *Examinations in the communicative use of English as a foreign language: specifications and specimen papers.* Royal Society of Arts, London, 1980.

> The Board will begin limited examining on this syllabus in 1981, but emphasises that it is still at an experimental stage.

PERREN, G. and TRIM, J. (Eds.) *Applications of linguistics.* Cambridge University Press, 1971.

> This symposium contains useful articles on testing by Burstall, Chaplen, Davies, Spolsky and Upshur.

MCCLAFFERTY, J. *A guide to examinations in English for foreign students.* Hamish Hamilton, 1975.

> A useful guide to offerings of various public examining bodies in the United Kingdom.

JOHN, R. *Collins graded English tests, books 1–6.* Collins, 1980.

> A useful set of tests for placement or diagnostic use, at a variety of levels from elementary up to Cambridge First Certificate.

Chapter 8: Error analysis

by Douglas McKeating

ERROR

> *I saw him opened the window.*

REACTION 1

> Senior police officer to a colleague, in a country where English is used
> as an official language in government departments:
> 'My God, look at this report! What do they teach them at school
> these days? I thought they all had to have a pass in English before
> we'd consider them – this fellow's illiterate!'

REACTION 2

> Research worker in applied linguistics to worried teacher, in the same
> country as Reaction 1:
> 'Very interesting. He's obviously working on the hypothesis that
> all actions in past time must be referred to by a verb marked for past
> tense. He's just over-generalised – it's a typical developmental error.
> Well, not an error at all really – you could call it an essential stage in
> the learning process.'

REACTION 3

> Worried teacher: 'But they have an exam next week!'

Part 1: Attitudes towards errors

Attitudes towards the errors made by language learners vary enormously. To the researcher in applied linguistics they are of great interest
and usefulness. To the native speaker who comes into informal contact
with foreigners, e.g. with tourists asking the way to the nearest 'Buses
stop', errors are often a matter for amused tolerance, though this will

depend to a great extent on his attitude to foreigners in general. Unfortunately, some native speakers appear to make no effort at all to understand people who 'just can't speak the language'. (Note the assumption behind their use of the definite article.)

To employers (potential and actual) and to senior colleagues, errors are often a source of intense, even irrational, irritation. A few 'glaring mistakes' can easily mean no job or no promotion, especially if they include examples of mistakes which, though fairly trivial in themselves, are particularly prevalent in local second language usage and therefore particularly despised by 'people who know better'.

A similar attitude can be detected in some examiners for whom errors are things to be pounced on, counted and held against their perpetrators. Some examiners consider that errors which are very common are particularly serious and though they might not actually deduct more marks in an objective count, they will certainly look less favourably on candidates who make them when it comes to subjective assessment.

The attitude of learners themselves to their own mistakes will depend to a great extent on personality factors and on what they know to be the attitude of other 'people who matter' (e.g. employers, teachers and examiners).

Some learners seem to prize fluency more highly than accuracy and will carry on happily making countless errors provided they appear to be getting their meaning across. Other learners seem so worried about the possibility of making mistakes that they are extremely reluctant to produce anything at all in the FL, apart from a few one-word utterances or essential written work, which is produced with great caution and anxiety. In view of all this, what should the attitude of the teacher be towards the errors made by his students?

My own view is that a knowledge of the difficulties in learning a FL and a consideration of the possible causes of error should lead a teacher to develop an attitude which is sympathetic and helpful but non-permissive. Sympathetic and helpful, because if students know that their teacher has such an attitude they should not be so worried about error avoidance that their fluency is unduly impaired. Non-permissive, because it *is* an important part of a teacher's job to help students to eliminate errors, and they cannot eliminate errors which they do not know they are making.

Whatever your own opinion may be about the seriousness or otherwise of certain errors, if you know that they are stigmatised by 'people who matter' it is your job to help your students to get rid of them or avoid them. (See next chapter.)

Part 2: Aims and uses of error analysis

Error analysis involves collecting errors, studying them, classifying them in various ways and suggesting possible causes. Language teachers have been doing this for years but recently, partly as a result of increased interest in psycholinguistic research, attempts have been made to make more systematic and formal analyses of errors. Much useful discussion about learning processes and strategies has resulted from this research but there have also been a few less desirable by-products which are discussed below. We need to distinguish the aims of the researcher from those of the teacher.

A   Aims of research workers

Errors are studied in order to find out something about the learning process and about the strategies employed by human beings learning another language. (See Chapter 1.) By studying samples of language produced by the FL learner the researcher can discover, or at least make informed guesses about, what he thinks the rules of the foreign language are. For example, if a learner often produces sentences like:
    * *I saw him opened the window,*
it is reasonable to suppose that he does think that in English all past actions must be referred to by verbs in the past tense. If the researcher wants to know *why* the learner has arrived at this hypothesis about English he will have to examine other factors such as the structure of the learner's MT and the kinds of material and teaching to which he has been exposed. A study of other samples from the same learner at different stages throughout the course will give us some insight into how his ideas about the rules of English change.

The aims of such research are important and laudable but there have been a few undesirable side-effects on teachers, and some are listed below.

(i) For the purposes of research it is necessary to examine the learner's version of the FL (sometimes referred to as his 'inter-language' or 'idiosyncratic dialect'), and to work out the rules he appears to be following, e.g., 'the plural of nouns in English is formed by adding /s/ or /z/ to the singular as in:
    *cats, dogs, *mans, *sheeps, *foots, etc.'*
This has led some researchers to say that as long as he is following his own rules the learner is not making an 'error' at all. *In terms of his own system*, his utterances are not 'ungrammatical', they are merely 'different' from the utterances of native speakers because they are based on a different grammatical system.

In a sense, of course, this is perfectly correct and such a view of learners' errors should help us to develop a similarly sympathetic attitude. Unfortunately, an ill-digested version of this theory has led to the view that there are no such things as errors. Some people have abandoned all notions of correctness and others take the view that all mistakes are 'developmental' and will go away eventually.

213

There may be a little truth in this last point. Many errors would just disappear as learners found out more about the language; but I do think that, as teachers, we have a duty to help learners to recognise their mistakes as mistakes, and that an extremely permissive attitude towards errors is ultimately unhelpful. Whatever researchers may say, as far as languages are concerned a great many people set considerable store by getting things right.

(ii) A good deal of the research has been carried out within the framework of transformational-generative grammar (TG) and the impression is often given that people actually *use* TG rules to produce utterances; e.g. that in order to produce a question the speaker somehow starts with the statement form and applies to it the series of transformations necessary to turn it into a question.

Not all the research workers claim that this actually happens; but as they often discuss errors in terms of failure to *apply* various transformational rules, it is easy to see how other people get the idea that this is how sentences are assumed to be produced. TG has provided valuable insights into language structures, and transformational descriptions of languages are of considerable theoretical interest, but the psychological reality of TG rules has certainly not been proved. It is unfortunate if teachers get the impression that it has.

(iii) Whether couched in TG terms or not, the explanation of causes of error is often highly speculative. We simply do not know exactly why learners make many of the mistakes they do, yet some researchers are quite dogmatic in their assertions. This can have important practical consequences, as teachers may base remedial work and subsequent teaching on such explanations. Error analysis *can* be most instructive; but it should be remembered that much explanation is based on subjective judgement rather than hard facts. (See further in Part 5.)

(iv) A full-scale piece of research into the errors of a particular group is complex and time-consuming, but this should not discourage teachers from making their own less formal surveys, which can still be most illuminating. Unfortunately some researchers actually discourage teachers from doing this by referring to their efforts as 'mere collections of errors'. As long as the tentative, speculative nature of *all* error analysis is borne in mind there is, on the contrary, much to be learnt from small-scale informal surveys carried out by teachers.

B Aims of teachers, syllabus designers and materials writers

There are two main purposes in studying your students' errors:
(i) in order to give the most relevant help you can to your present groups of students; and
(ii) in order to plan programmes for future groups.

214

A study of their errors shows what problems your students are having now, and helps you to plan remedial work. This is often done very informally from week to week and is based on the common errors thrown up by various written tasks, e.g.: 'I see from this week's composition that 4C are still having problems with conditional clauses – I'd better do something about it'.

This is often based on a general impression rather than any objective count and many teachers do not have much time to do very much else. However, for class teaching purposes, it is sometimes a good idea to check just how many students actually did make a particular error and how many used that language item correctly. This often reveals that there is only a small group of students involved and saves you from having to bore the whole class unnecessarily.

In the same way a rather more careful study might reveal that it is not 'conditional clauses' in general that 4C are having problems with but only a particular type of conditional clause. Again, the implications for remedial work are obvious. (See the section below on the need for a variety of data.)

A survey of the errors of one group may help one to predict the likely problem areas of a future similar group. Of course one has to remember that each group is different and that plans may have to be modified accordingly; but students of the same age and with similar language and teaching backgrounds are *likely* to have similar problems.

An error analysis may indicate learning items which will require special attention and extra practice. This is also a major aim of contrastive analysis. (See Part 5.) An analysis may also suggest modifications in teaching techniques or order of presentation if one has reasons for suspecting that some of the students' problems may have been caused or added to by the way in which a particular item was presented. Some teaching techniques, for example, seem to encourage cross-association. (See Chapter 1, and Part 5.)

Part 3: Data for error analysis

A   Both correct and incorrect instances should be included

The label '*Error* Analysis' is misleading in suggesting that the data to be studied should consist exclusively of errors. Both for research into the learning process and for pedagogic purposes, we need to consider the learners' overall performance; it is for this reason that some writers prefer the term 'Performance Analysis'. Such data will include errors, but will also include examples of *correct* usage. These may be of equal interest for the following reasons:

(i) because they reveal what learners *have* learnt, or appear to have learnt, as well as what they have not; and

(ii) because they indicate areas where there is still instability or uncertainty.

One of the outstanding characteristics of many a learner's performance is that it is erratic and unstable: he gets things right in one paragraph and wrong in the next. Many people put this down to 'carelessness' but there are often other reasons. If he is genuinely *unsure* of what to do, he will frequently try out first one 'rule' and then another perhaps on the assumption that in this way he is more likely to be right *some* of the time, whereas if he chooses incorrectly the first time and goes on following the same rule he will always be wrong. A student of mine once offered this as an explanation of why she had written *angry on me, *angry to me and *angry with me* all through the same composition. Finally, looking at correct as well as incorrect samples of learners' language could be useful

(iii) because they may show the extent of the damage, i.e., whether there is misunderstanding of a whole linguistic system or whether the ignorance or uncertainty is confined to a small part of that system or even one item. For example, a student may go on producing sentences like – * *I have a lot of works to do*, * *When I had finished these works* . . ., even when he appears to be able to handle the countable/uncountable distinction in many other nouns. He understands how the general system works but he is still wrongly classifying this particular noun.

Similarly on the phonological level. I once had a group of students who, I thought, could not pronounce /w/. This was because they said, /'ʊmən/ and /'ʊd/ for 'woman', 'wood', and 'would'. Further investigation showed that they *could* say /w/ (or something very like it) in words like 'we', 'wet', 'with', 'way', 'were' and 'what'. Their real difficulty was pronouncing /w/ before the closely rounded vowel /ʊ/. So all my exercises about 'Wee Willy Winkie' etc. were largely a waste of time!

B Data from individuals or groups

For research into learning processes, data from individuals at various stages of learning is needed. Such data can be used for making 'longitudinal studies' of an individual's progress.

For pedagogic purposes, teachers and others are more likely to be concerned with the performance of whole groups and especially with the problems they have in common. For these purposes we need to ensure that the data comes from a fairly homogeneous group as regards mother tongue, age, previous teaching and, if possible, intelligence. Perhaps the most important of these factors is the mother tongue, particularly if phonological errors are being studied. In a class which has groups of students with different MTs a separate analysis should be made for each group. It should be remembered, however, that not all syntactic and lexical errors are caused by the influence of the MT, though perhaps the majority of phonological errors – and spelling errors influenced by phonological factors – *are* caused by such interference.

It is interesting and instructive to note which problems are common to the various groups as these may be the very errors we can do most to prevent in the future by changing our teaching methods.

C Variety of data

It is best to examine samples from as wide a variety of sources as possible. For example, it is usually necessary to consider errors of pronunciation and speech perception as well as written samples. Many spelling errors and some errors of syntax, e.g. non-use of regular past tense endings, may have their origin in the faulty perception of speech, which in turn is often reflected in pronunciation. Conversely, some teachers only become aware of their students' problems in perception and pronunciation through a study of their written work. This may be because written errors are more obvious; we tend to be much more tolerant, or much less aware, of variations in pronunciation than we are of mistakes in written work.

For a reasonably thorough analysis, it is also necessary to consider a variety of data from one mode. An analysis based on one writing task, or one set of compositions on a particular topic, is bound to be very limited. A narrative composition topic, for example, may require the use of only one tense throughout and will not reveal whether or not the students can handle a greater range. A topic like 'What I would do if I won £1,000' will almost certainly reveal any problems they have with one type of conditional clause; but it may not show whether or not they can use the other two basic types.

For this reason a really useful analysis would have to be based on work produced over, say, a whole term during which a wide variety of writing tasks had been attempted. Examination scripts are a particularly useful additional source of data as these reflect the students' unaided efforts, whereas work done at other times is, one hopes, often guided or controlled.

D Data obtained by using elicitation techniques

Even data collected from a wide variety of exercises will not always reveal many of the things learners just do not know or the areas which they are *avoiding* because of uncertainty and confusion. Normal production, e.g. in a composition, is often an error-avoiding activity; learners tend to 'play it safe' and use only the language they feel confident about. Unless we are careful, we can easily overlook the resulting poverty of expression.

To overcome this and to build up a more complete picture of the learners' overall ability, some investigators use elicitation techniques. The aim is to put the learner in a position where he *has to* use a particular language item and thus reveal his true ability in that particular area.

This is, of course, very similar to testing though it is for a different purpose, and the same techniques are used, e.g. exercises calling for completion, substitution or transformation. (See Chapter 7 for further details of techniques of assessment. On the collection of data in general, see the recommended article by Etherton.)

Part 4: The process of error analysis

Most writers on EA divide the process into 5 stages: (i) recognition, (ii) interpretation, (iii) reconstruction, (iv) classification, (v) explanation. These stages are, in fact, interdependent, as an examination of the following sentence shows.

I used to clean my teeth every night.

Looked at in isolation this is an error-free sentence. But let us look at it in context. Recognition of an error depends on interpretation, i.e. on what you know (or assume) the student meant. Usually the stages of interpretation and reconstruction take place simultaneously. If the context suggests that the student is talking about the present, we may provisionally interpret what the student meant and reconstruct the sentence as:

I usually clean my teeth every night.

In view of this, we may now want to classify the original sentence as containing an error of substitution: *used to* for the correct *usually*. We may now make a tentative explanation that the similarity of the two forms and the fact that they share an element of meaning (habitual) has led to cross-association. (See Chapter 1.)

We may be right. On the other hand our interpretation and reconstruction may be wrong; perhaps the student meant:

I always clean my teeth every night.

This is just as likely in view of the inclusion of 'every', and a request for a MT translation may prove that this *is* the correct interpretation. We now have a case for saying that substitution of *used to* for *always* has taken place, and the diagnosis becomes more complicated. Why does the student confuse *used to* and *always*? They seem much less confusable than *used to* and *usually* (which is probably why *we* chose *usually* for our first reconstruction!). The answer may involve confusion about all three forms, i.e. the student is uncertain about the precise meaning of adverbs of frequency in English, and in particular of the difference between *usually* and *always*. In fact in ordinary usage there is often very little difference. However, because of the similarity of form and meaning he also confuses *usually* and *used to*, perhaps encouraged by contrastive exercises designed to establish the difference.

So because of a different interpretation and reconstruction, we now have a different explanation, which, incidentally, suggests a different approach to remedial work in this area.

I have worked through this example at the beginning of this section in an attempt to show how careful one has to be in examining students' errors. The immediately 'obvious' interpretation is not necessarily the right one.

I now want to consider each stage in more detail but it must be remembered that the process is not a simple linear one.

A Recognition

1 What is an error? Problems of acceptability. In many cases what is regarded as an error depends on what standard of performance is considered to be acceptable. This will obviously vary according to circumstances, and will take into account factors such as the standard being aimed at; the stage in the course; the age, ability, motivation, etc. of the students; the amount of time available; and a realistic assessment of the possibilities of improving performance in that time.

Consider, for example the likely attitudes towards variations in pronunciation of the following three teachers:

Teacher A has a group of highly motivated young business executives whose firms operate in London and who want to develop an accent which is as close as possible to British 'Received Pronunciation'.

Teacher B has a group of high school students, some of whom hope to visit Britain as tourists and be generally understood.

Teacher C is in a country where English is used as a second language. His students will be communicating almost exclusively with other users of the local form of English.

In the areas of syntax and vocabulary there may be more agreement about what is considered acceptable. But even here notions of acceptability may vary, especially in a country where English is fairly widely used and a local standard with its own special characteristics is developing. A local English teacher may find himself having to call some usage an error because it is considered to be so by examiners even though it is widely used among local educated speakers of English. For example, it is common in some countries to use the word 'pick' to mean 'collect', where standard British English would have 'pick up', as in **I'll pick you at six o'clock*. This usage is condemned by teachers and examiners in these countries but many of them use it themselves outside school and their friends would think they were trying to be 'superior' if they used the 'correct' form.

There is no clear-cut answer to the problem of when an error ceases to be an error and becomes an acceptable 'variation' but teachers, especially native speakers of English teaching overseas, need to be flexible and sensitive to the development of local standard forms.

2 Other problems of recognition. Apart from questions of acceptability, recognising errors is not particularly difficult, and most teachers have a highly developed sense of error detection. There are, however, cases like the one discussed at the beginning of this section, where the error is only apparent to someone who knows what the student 'really means'. It is in the detection of these 'covert' errors that the teacher of a particular group of students often has a considerable advantage over the research worker working from samples collected from students he does not know.

The teacher often recognises errors because he knows that his students are prone to that particular mistake, so even when the context makes an alternative, 'correct' interpretation possible, the teacher who knows his group may suspect the worst. For example, without a knowledge of the students concerned one may not suspect that the following contains a particularly common error:

There is one boy outside who wants to see you.

But if you know that all these students regularly use *one* in contexts where *a* would be much more usual you are less likely to accept it as correct here. If, in addition to that, you know that their MT predisposes them to confuse *a* and *one* you are even more likely to recognise it as an error. In such circumstances there is, of course, always the danger that a teacher may be too hasty in his judgement and may 'correct' errors where they do not exist.

Errors of this covert type are particularly difficult to deal with in examinations where, it is hoped, the examiner wishes to give candidates the benefit of any reasonable doubt. The teacher may also know that a possible correct interpretation is unlikely because his students just do not know that particular usage. For example,

I saw some boy in the field

is a possible sentence if *some* is stressed and the meaning is 'some boy or other'. But a teacher who is aware that his students do not know this use of *some* will recognise an error here.

Often the linguistic context helps you to determine whether an error has been made or not. Consider the following sentence:

*I used to clean my teeth every night before I go to bed.

If the general context employs the Present Simple tense, then *used to* is probably wrong; but if the context employs the Past Simple tense, then *go* is probably wrong. Context is all-important in recognising an error in the following:

* It was seriously injured in the accident.

The fact that 'it' refers back to 'car' and not to e.g. 'horse' makes the error clear. Similarly a sentence like:

My brother is too tall

may contain an incorrect use of 'too' if in the context it is clear that there is no implication of 'excess' and that 'very tall' would have been more appropriate.

Sometimes the wider, non-linguistic context has to be considered. This is most obvious in the case of 'situational' errors, such as using a style which is too formal or too familiar for the situation. For example, there is nothing inherently wrong with ending a letter:

Hope you are all well there. Give my love to all at home.

But if it is used to close a formal business letter it is surely an error. This type of mistake gets scant attention in the literature on error analysis but is often of considerable importance. The non-linguistic context may have to be considered in recognising syntactic errors too; e.g.:

We sat on the table and ate our lunch.

Without knowing the context we cannot tell whether this is correct or not. A more subtle example of the importance of non-linguistic context is:

We rested under a tree and made fire.

For several months, while teaching in the Solomon Islands, I treated this as an error, reconstructing it as 'made a fire'. I then went on a picnic with some of the students and began to have serious doubts about whether it was an error or not, because the students did 'make fire': using no matches or artificial devices, fire was made, then a cooking fire was lit from it.

Because of the importance of context for recognition and interpretation, records of errors for analysis later should be long enough to include relevant information or notes should be added to indicate the general context.

B Interpretation

As we have seen, interpretation is central to the whole process, because our interpretation of what we think the student meant may determine whether we recognise an error at all, and will certainly determine our reconstruction.

Clues to interpretation may be available from a combination of any of the following: (i) the general context, (ii) a knowledge of similar errors made by similar students, (iii) a knowledge of the students' MT and the possible results of phonological interference or of direct translation into English, (iv) direct questioning, perhaps in the MT, as to what the student meant.

Thus I can interpret the seemingly incomprehensible sentence:

*My teacher used to were sot pens.

(i) I know the general context. The student is describing his teacher, in particular his appearance and clothing, and I know what kind of clothes teachers wear in this country.

(ii) I know that this group of students has difficulties with 'used to', 'usually', and 'always'.

(iii) I know that the spelling of 'were' and 'where' is often confused, and guess that perhaps 'wear' can be added to the list. I also know that the

3rd person singular, present tense 's' is frequently omitted.

(iv) A knowledge of the phonology of the MT, of its actual effects on some words and of its likely effects on others tells me that there may be problems with the following pairs of sounds /ɒ-ɔ:/, /ʃ-s/, /æ-e/. I also know that in English /t/ and /d/ are frequently elided after /n/ in such words as *wants* and *hands* and that as a result students may not actually be aware of them in these words.

The sentence can now be interpreted and reconstructed as:

> *My teacher usually (or always) wears short pants.*

C Reconstruction

Many of the problems of reconstruction have already been discussed but I would like to highlight two points:

(i) It is sometimes necessary to differentiate between (a) what a native speaker would have produced in the same context and (b) what the learner was trying to produce, i.e. the English forms he was aiming at but getting wrong. An obvious and simple illustration of this is the example discussed above, which I reconstructed as: '. . . usually wears short pants'. In fact, most British native speakers would probably not say 'short pants' but 'shorts'. We therefore need to consider whether what the learner was aiming at was actually appropriate in the context. In other words we must not be so preoccupied with matters of spelling, pronunciation and syntax that we forget to consider the possibility of wider 'communicative' error. This is particularly important for a teacher making suggestions for the correction of errors. I once saw the following:

> **My father is a very kind man. On other hand he is very good to everyone.*

This had been 'corrected' to 'On *the* other hand' with no indication that 'on the other hand' is not appropriate here.

(ii) The most obvious reconstruction to the teacher, especially the native-English-speaking teacher, is not necessarily the version at which the student was aiming. We are often tempted to assume that the best reconstruction is the one which involves the least alteration.

> e.g. **He threw some mangoes with a stick*

can readily be changed to

> *He hit some mangoes with a stick.*

Yet further thought will show that although this seems straightforward there is actually a distinction between hitting something and throwing something at something, which it does not necessarily hit. In this case the student actually meant:

> *He threw a stick at some of the mangoes.*

One must also be careful that the language item one imagines the student to be aiming at is actually known to the student. This was also mentioned above as a factor in error recognition. I have seen: **we felt* *asleep* reconstructed as: *we felt sleepy* with the explanation that the student is confused between *asleep* and *sleepy*. In fact, it was unlikely that these students knew the word *sleepy*. They had heard *felt tired* and *fell asleep* and confused *fell* and *felt*. The context also indicated that the students were aiming at *fell asleep*.

Similarly, but less understandably, I have seen:
*We were working along the beach to our boat . . .
reconstructed as
We were working our way along the beach to our boat . . .
It was almost certain that the students had never heard the expression 'to work one's way along' and in any case it was quite inappropriate in the context. The solution was much simpler; the students had confused *working* and *walking* because the spelling 'o' + 'r' is more frequently pronounced /ɔ:/ as in *fork*.

D Linguistic classification

There are a great many ways in which errors can be assigned to classes and one should use whatever system or combination of systems is the most useful and enlightening according to the purposes of the analysis. Obviously, the linguistic classification of an error will depend largely on how the stretch of language in which it occurs has already been interpreted and reconstructed. Some people seem to omit the stage of linguistic classification altogether and classify errors immediately in terms of their assumed causes, e.g. errors of hypercorrection, cross-association, false analogy and so on. Yet in any analysis an explanation of causes of error is the most highly speculative part of the whole process and for most practical purposes, e.g. remedial teaching or syllabus planning, we certainly need a linguistic classification.

Superficially, errors can be classified as those of:

omission:	e.g. **Cow is a useful animal.*
addition:	e.g. **She came on last Monday.*
substitution:	e.g. **He was angry on me.*
mis-ordering:	e.g. **He asked her what time was it.*

Obviously such a classification is far from sufficient; to start with we need to know *what* was omitted, added, etc. and later we will want to assign these items to more general classes: prepositions, tense forms, questions, etc.

But even this preliminary stage of classification is far from being as straightforward as it may at first appear. We must be constantly on our guard against assigning an error to the first, 'most obvious' category that springs to mind and leaving it at that. Further consideration will often reveal an alternative classification and in such cases the error will have to be placed tentatively in both categories until further evidence is available.

Some of the problems of classification have already been discussed under 'interpretation' and 'reconstruction'; whether we regard an error as being one of e.g. omission or substitution, will depend on our reconstruction.

For example, I have classified *Cow is a useful animal* under omission of definite article on the basis of the reconstruction: *The cow is a useful animal* but an alternative reconstruction would mean classifying it as substitution of singular nouns for plural: *Cows are useful animals.* And what about *A cow is a useful animal*?

This brings us back to the question of whether we choose a reconstruction which reflects what the learner was aiming at or what the native speaker would be most likely to say and might therefore be the most appropriate version to teach the learner. In this case there is probably little to choose between the three versions, though the use of a plural countable noun for generalising seems to be more common in informal English than the use of *The/a* + singular. It is also instructive to consider *why* I first classified this as an error of omission. Could it be because when correcting, it is easier for me to add the single word *the* than to change three words? It could well be, and this is something we should also guard against.

Even an apparently simple example like:
She came on last Monday
could be classified as an error of mis-ordering on the basis of the reconstruction:
She came on Monday last.
This seems an unlikely reconstruction to me since students are unlikely to know this idiom, but it is certainly not impossible.

Similarly, consider how we might classify the errors in:
Not long we reached at the top of the hill.
Is the first error one of substitution of 'not long' for 'soon', or omission of 'afterwards', or even omission of 'It was . . . before'? Knowledge of the students' MT (Fijian) suggests the first. Is the second error addition of *at* or substitution of *reached* for *arrived*? This is not mere academic quibbling, as decisions in such cases are of practical importance, whether for researchers investigating the learners' hypotheses about the rules of the language or for teachers planning remedial teaching.

A linguistic classification of errors also involves assigning them to various levels of linguistic description, i.e. phonological (both speaking and listening), orthographic (spelling and punctuation), syntactic (grammatical), lexico-semantic (choice of vocabulary, which in turn affects meaning), situational or socio-linguistic (appropriacy).

Such classification is often quite straightforward but again alternative ways of classifying an error may be possible, depending on interpretation and reconstruction.
e.g. *Go to the shop and get a bread.*
Is this syntactic: substitution of *a* for *some*, or lexical: substitution of *bread* for *loaf*?

It is not always possible to assign an error to only one level of description. Errors involving prepositions, for example, sometimes involve both syntax and semantics; certainly the substitution of one preposition for another can have important semantic consequence as in:

He threw a coconut at his friend

where the context implies *to*.

An error like:

*She said that yes you can go

may be regarded as a combined error of syntax and punctuation; addition of *that* and omission of punctuation:

She said, 'Yes, you can go.'

or it may be regarded as an error of syntax alone, i.e. lack of knowledge of the rules of reported speech:

She said that I could go.

Again, how we treat it should depend on what we think the student was aiming at.

As has been mentioned above, errors at one level of linguistic description may cause related errors at another. This can be seen most clearly in the case of spelling errors which are related to phonological problems, e.g. the substitution of *leave* for *live*, or *sot* for *short*. These are still errors of spelling of course, but it may be useful to sub-classify them as 'phonologically related' errors, since remedial work on these may involve trying to improve perception and production of the sounds concerned.

It can happen that errors at one level are mistaken for errors at another. A well known example is the effect of the Japanese tendency to palatalise /ʃ/ before /iː/. This results in *she* being pronounced /çiː/ which may be misheard as *he* and wrongly classified as a syntactic error.

Classifying errors also involves assigning them to linguistic systems, e.g. if the error is one of syntax does it reveal a deficiency in knowledge of the verbal group, the nominal group, or the whole clause? If it is in the verbal group does it concern tense, the use of auxiliaries or voice? If it is in the nominal group does it involve number, the countable/uncountable distinction, use of articles and other determiners, or what? The exact terminology you use for all this will depend on the particular model of grammar which you find most suitable.

By studying further errors and instances of correct usage it should be possible to tell more precisely whether students are unsure of a whole system, find certain parts of a system difficult or have trouble only with a few isolated examples. An illustration may make this clearer:

The following errors were collected from a group of students; in most of the errors the past tense form of the verb should have been used, though it may not always be obvious from the context given here. Errors not involving verbs have been corrected.

1 Yesterday Samu and Epeli *miss* the bus so they *walk* to school and the headmaster *bit* them because they were late.

2 She *climb* the tree and *pick* that ripe fruit.

3 When she fell down her friends all *laugh* but Ana was crying because her arm *was broke*.

4 Then he cleaned his teeth and *wash* his face, then went to bed.

5 Last Saturday I *was helped* my father in our garden.

6 We *digged* some holes and *plant* the cassava.

7 When we went to the beach we *play* football, then we made a fire and *cook* the food for our picnic.

8 There I saw one of my friends and I said, 'Good morning' and we *talk* about our examinations.

9 He got out of bed, put on his clothes and *wash* his face. Then he *drinked* some tea and *go* to school.

10 He picked up rubbish round the school and *talk* to his friends, then the teacher *bit* the drum.

Obviously these students are having problems with the past tense but exactly what is it that they do not know or are uncertain of? Have they got no idea about when to *use* the past tense or is it the *forms* of the past tense which they are unsure of?

An analysis may reveal some sort of pattern. There are few problems here about interpretation or reconstruction, with one possible exception (Sentence 5). Any doubts one may have had about the headmaster in Sentence 1 should have been cleared up by Sentence 10 where *beat* is obviously intended.

First we can count the total number of verbal groups in the sample, correct as well as incorrect. (Results are given in the table below.) Then the number of correct and incorrect groups. We count the number of complex and simple verb groups and note that two out of the three complex groups are incorrect. We can divide the simple groups into those with verbs with the regular *-ed* past tense and those with irregular verbs, noting the numbers correct and incorrect.

When we look more closely at the incorrect complex groups we find that the *tense* is correct but the participle is not: **was broke* and **was*

	Verbal groups	
Incorrect		19
Correct		12
Total		31
Complex:		
Incorrect		2
Correct		1
Total		3

Simple:	
Regular verbs:	
Incorrect	12
Correct	2
Total	14
Irregular verbs:	
Incorrect	5
Correct	9
Total	14

helped. In fact we cannot be sure what the writer of Sentence 5 intended, as either *was helping* or *helped* would be correct. Perhaps the student meant *helped* but added *was* as an extra past tense marker. We just cannot tell. In any case it seems reasonable to include the *was* in these groups among the irregular verbs correctly marked for past tense.

An examination of the 5 incorrect irregular verbs in sentences 1, 6, 9 and 10 shows that two of them (**digged, *drinked*) are marked as past, though incorrectly. If the two occurrences of *bit* for *beat* are classed as *spelling* errors deriving from phonological causes they too can be regarded as being marked for tense. This means that out of the total of 31 verbal groups, 18 are actually marked in some way for past tense. Clearly, then, these students do have *some* idea about when to use the past tense, as they use it appropriately (though not always in its correct form) in over half the verbal groups in the sample. In all but two cases of appropriate usage, irregular verbs are involved.

One may speculate that these students think that there are two classes of verb in English, one which marks past tense and another which does not. One may speculate further that at least some of them have reached this conclusion because they have been taught English mainly through oral practice and have failed to hear the regular *-ed* ending, or have heard it and not thought it significant. The past tense ending is almost inaudible in many contexts especially before a following *the* as in *climbed the* or *to* as in *walked to.*

Whatever the reason for these errors, the analysis shows where most remedial teaching is needed and may suggest ways of approaching it. It is clear for example that it is not the *concept* of past tense that the students need to be taught again but that almost all past tense verbs in English are marked in some way. (Exceptions being *put, cut*, etc.)

This small sample reflects a tendency among many groups of learners, though I have simplified the data to make the point more obvious. In a class of 40 students it is likely that there would be a greater degree of variation and inconsistency.

227

Some errors are not associated with whole linguistic systems but with individual items which just have to be learned separately. Some of the uses of prepositions fall into this category and errors in this area are particularly difficult to remedy as there are no general rules which can be given or induced by the learner.

    e.g. *She was angry on me*

shows substitution of *on* for *with* but in all probability this occurs only after *angry*; there may be no confusion elsewhere between *on* and *with* so there may be many other contexts in which they are used correctly. Although we can classify such errors in terms such as 'preposition (incorrect substitution)' it should be remembered that such a category is something of a rag-bag of individual errors.

1 Multiple classification of errors. In view of all the difficulties in classifying errors outlined above, it is probably best for both teachers and researchers to use a system of multiple classification with cross-references. (This is discussed in the recommended article by Etherton.) Thus an error could be listed under individual lexical items, linguistic systems, semantic areas, etc. Here are some examples:

(i) *Cow is a useful animal* could be classed under

    (a)   Article usage (omission)
    (b)   Number system
    (c)   Generic reference

(ii) *She came on last Monday* under

    (a)   *on*
    (b)   *last*
    (c)   preposition (addition)
    (d)   time phrases

(iii) *She was angry on me* under

    (a)   *on*
    (b)   *with*
    (c)   *angry*
    (d)   preposition (substitution)

2 Other processes of analysis. Having recognised, interpreted, reconstructed and classified errors, what else can we do with them before trying to explain their causes? This will depend on our original aims but as teachers we can (i) count them and (ii) try to assess their seriousness. (i) Counting. Enough has already been said to show that it is not enough just to count the number of omissions, additions, etc.; we have to go into more detail as discussed in the analysis of past tense errors above, which included a comparison of instances of incorrect and correct usage. Assessing the comparative frequency of different types of error in this way is clearly an important preliminary to much remedial teaching.

(ii) An assessment of 'error gravity' would also be a useful preliminary to remedial teaching. The gravity of an error is the extent to which it interferes with communication. Knowing the relative gravities of errors would help to determine priorities. (See next chapter.) Unfortunately, this is a highly subjective matter. It raises the whole question of acceptability again and of the known attitudes of 'people who matter' and of others with whom the students will be communicating.

Attempts have been made to assess error gravity in terms of the number of linguistic rules broken but this again depends on what system of grammar you are using. Attempts to do it within the framework of TG, (e.g. by counting the number of transformational rules omitted or misapplied) beg the question of the psychological reality of such rules and in any case do not always match the subjective judgement of unprejudiced assessors.

Any attempt to assess error gravity in terms of the effect on the efficiency of communication is subjective and highly dependent on the attitudes and past experience of the person with whom the learner is communicating.

This topic will be discussed further in Chapter 9.

Part 5: Explanation of causes

Explanation of the causes of errors has not been included in the section on the process of analysis. This is because it is not strictly speaking part of the *analysis* at all. Apart from problems of interpretation, the analysis of errors is basically an objective procedure involving classifying, counting and tabulating; explanation on the other hand is much more speculative. As long as we bear this in mind, however, and are prepared to consider alternative explanations, there is much to be gained from a consideration of the possible causes of error.

A   Interlingual causes of error

This is also known as MT or external interference, and language transfer. (For an account of what this entails see Chapter 1.) On the face of it this would appear to be the most obvious cause of error and it was the belief that almost all errors had their origin in MT interference that gave rise to Contrastive Analysis (CA).

To understand some of the current attitudes towards error explanation we need to have a brief look at the history of CA.

In the late 1940s and early 50s CA was seen as the major contribution which the rapidly developing linguistic sciences could make to language teaching. Linguists could provide good structural descriptions of languages and these descriptions could be compared and contrasted.

Such analyses were seen as the key to the new 'scientific' approach to language teaching.

It seemed reasonable to suppose that wherever the structures of the MT and target language differed there would be problems in learning and difficulty in performance, and that the greater the differences were, the greater the difficulties would be. Thus CA sets out to *predict* where errors are likely to occur and to indicate likely problem areas on which teaching should be focused.

Unfortunately, fascinating though CA is, its predictive powers are limited, as experience has proved that

(i) errors occur even where CA predicts that because of similarities between the languages there should be no difficulty; in fact, as we have seen in Chapter 1, it is the partial similarities that often cause great difficulties.

(ii) errors often do not occur where there are big differences between the languages, e.g. many learners have no difficulty in remembering to use a totally different word order; perhaps big differences are easier to remember.

(A full discussion of the problems of CA can be found in the Wilkins reference.)

CA was found to work well on the phonological level but its failure to predict all the errors made in other areas led to a growing interest in Error Analysis (EA), which *starts* with the errors and then tries to find out their causes. It is perhaps only natural that writers trying to highlight the inadequacies of CA while pressing the claims of EA should have concerned themselves more with the type of errors which CA failed to predict; those *not* caused by MT interference. Certainly, for a time the literature on EA seemed to be preoccupied with trying to prove that there were many errors which could not be attributed to language transfer and this may have led some writers to overstate their case. Estimates as to the percentage of errors caused by MT interference vary from 33% to as low as 3%. This variation is itself a reminder of the speculative nature of error explanation, but considerable differences in such figures could also be due to the type of data selected or the expectations of the researcher. (See Abbott, 1980, in Further Reading.)

Perhaps the time has come for a more balanced and a less dogmatic approach. It seems highly likely that a great many errors *are* caused by MT interference; this is certainly where most teachers would look first for an explanation. Similarly, a CA may serve to alert us to probable trouble spots provided we are aware of its limitations. On the other hand, there are also many errors which cannot be satisfactorily explained in this way and it is those I would now like to consider.

B Intralingual causes of error

Studies show that speakers of a wide variety of languages produce similar errors which reflect not the structure of the MT but faulty generalisations about the rules of the target language. Various labels are used for different types of intralingual (or 'internal') causes of error but the distinctions between the categories are by no means clear-cut and in many cases it is quite possible that the error is caused by a combination of factors.

1 Cross-association.   This is fully explained in Chapter 1. Cross-association may be quite spontaneous and accidental but it is also very easy for teachers to encourage it by methods of presentation and practice. For example, presenting items with similar meaning but different structures together, or practising them by way of 'transforms' can easily lead to 'hybrid' structures. The following way of presenting *too* + adj. + *to* + verb is very common:

> *This tea is very hot. I can't drink it.*
> *This desk is very heavy. I can't lift it,* etc.
> We can join these sentences like this:
> *This tea is too hot to drink.*
> *This desk is too heavy to lift.*
> Now change these sentences in the same way:
> *This apple is very sour. I can't eat it,* etc.

Not surprisingly some students will produce sentences like:
> **This apple is very sour to eat.* or
> **This apple is too sour to eat it.*

Later, *so* + adj. + *that* may be introduced by a similar method:

> For: *The apple is too sour to eat*
> we can say: *The apple is so sour that I can't eat it.* etc.
> Now change these sentences in the same way:
> *The bag is too heavy to carry.*
> etc.

There are now even more chances of cross-association and if *for me to drink* etc. has also been introduced we should not be too surprised if our students produce, along with a few correct forms:
> **The bag is very heavy that I can't carry it.*
> **The bag is so heavy for me to carry it.*
> **The bag is very heavy for me to carry it.*
> **The bag is too heavy that I can't carry it.*

2 Wrong analogy and over-generalisation.   This is also fully explained in Chapter 1. The learner searches for patterns and regularity in the target language in an effort to reduce the learning load by formulating rules. But he may over-generalise his rules and fail to take exceptions into account because his exposure to the language is limited and he has insufficient data from which he can derive more complex rules. It is likely that this is the explanation of an error like:

She explained me how to mend it.

This may be based on sentences like:

She showed/told/taught me how to mend it

which contain verbs that the learner has met and used before he encounters the exceptional *explain*.

Another reason for over-generalising may be that having found a rule which appears to work well the learner is not inclined to go looking for exceptions which will only complicate matters. Or, in the interests of simplicity, he may just ignore counter-examples to his rules. This has the effect of simplifying or regularising the language and is a feature of the language of young children learning their MT, accounting for the familiar *goed, *buyed, *foots, *mans, etc.

Some writers suggest that this strategy of ignoring exceptions in the interests of simplification may account for the common omission of the third person singular, present tense -s. The learner notes that most verbs are not inflected for person in any other instance, that he can say:

I/you/we/they like ice-cream, and:

I/you/he/she/we/they liked the picture.

The occasional addition of -s is an unnecessary complication which can be ignored.

C   Other possible causes

1   Carelessness.   Several writers on EA point out that we should distinguish between errors and lapses. Errors result from the learner following rules which he believes, or at any rate hopes, are correct but which are actually wrong or inadequate in some way. The learner may find it difficult or impossible to correct an error of this type as he is following the only rule he knows.

Lapses ('careless' mistakes) result from failure to follow a known rule, usually because of haste and forgetfulness. Once his attention is drawn to the mistake the learner usually remembers the rule and can correct it.

This is, in fact, something of an over-simplification and should not be pressed too far. As pointed out above learners tend to be unstable and erratic and it may be very difficult to assess the point at which a student can be said to 'know' the correct rule. Many of the rules of language are so complex or prone to exception that a student may go on making genuine errors involving *partially* known rules for a very long time.

The possibility of self-correction will not always distinguish between errors and lapses either. As mentioned in Part 3, there are many cases when the student knows that one of two forms is correct but is uncertain which. Once the teacher tells him he has made an error, the student knows that the alternative is correct and produces it. This, of course, is useful for the learner and is one reason why teachers need to point out errors but it is not proof that the error was really a lapse.

2 Other errors 'encouraged' by teaching

a Hyper-correction. This sometimes results from over-emphasis on items that CA indicates may present difficulty or EA indicates do present difficulty. This gives learners a false impression of the importance of such items and they are so worried about not using them correctly that they over-use them. Over-emphasis on 3rd person-*s* is a common cause of hyper-correction. Its use may get so intensively drilled that we panic the learners into using it inappropriately as in:

> **I lives in a small village.*
> **She cans sings very well.*
> **They likes to eat bananas.*

Hyper-correction is common with difficult sounds too. For example, many Fijian students have difficulty with final voiceless consonants as words do not end with voiceless segments in Fijian. A common error is to

> pronounce *price* as *prize*
> and *ice* as *eyes*

However, once hyper-correction has been at work, you are quite likely to hear students say
*She won the first price, or **She has beautiful brown ice.*

b Faulty rules given by the teacher. Teachers sometimes give students rules which are far from adequate and when students follow them they make errors similar to those caused by the over-generalisation of their own rules. Particularly common is the rule:

> 'If the action is in the past, the verb must be in the past tense.'

This is obviously well intended, but it results in a form of hyper-correction and errors like:

> **Last night he wanted to played football but his father said he got to finished his homework*

and

> **I saw him opened the window*

at which our police officer at the beginning of this chapter quite rightly exclaimed:

> 'My God! What do they teach them at school these days?'

Further reading

The literature on EA (error analysis) is extensive and many useful small-scale surveys of the errors of particular groups of students will be found in the journals: e.g. *ELTJ*, *IRAL* and *Language Learning*. Other useful articles and texts include:

ETHERTON, A.   'Error analysis: problems and procedures'.   *ELTJ* 32, 1, 1977.

This very practical article gives sound advice to teachers wishing to catalogue and classify errors.

ABBOTT, G.   'Towards a more rigorous analysis of foreign language errors'.   *IRAL* 18, 2, 1980.

This article offers a step-by-step procedure for classifying a given set of errors. The procedure does not include the establishment of causes.

RICHARDS, J. (Ed.)   *Error analysis*.   Longman, 1974.

A collection of articles mainly of a theoretical nature. Essential reading for anyone really interested in this topic.

CORDER, S.   *Error analysis, interlanguage and second language acquisition*.   Cambridge University Press for the English-Teaching Information Centre, 1975.

A good survey article on current trends including Corder's own influential ideas.

WILKINS, D.   *Linguistics in language teaching*.   Edward Arnold, 1972.

Chapter 7 gives an account of contrastive analysis and the move from CA to EA.

LADO, R.   *Linguistics across cultures*.   University of Michigan Press, 1957.

This short and very clearly-written book is a classic expression of ideas on MT interference and CA.

Chapter 9: Remedial work

by Douglas McKeating

EXAMPLE 1

Miss Bain's beginners' class had learnt how to ask questions in the present tense. She decided to introduce past tense questions gradually. She read them very short stories in the past tense and then asked a few questions about them such as *Why did the old man smile?* and *When did he wake up?* The students answered well. Sometimes she wrote one or two questions on the board *before* reading the story, so the students became familiar with the written forms too.

Later she got them to ask *each other* questions about a story they had just heard. At first they produced a few questions like **Why did the old man smiled?* and **When did he woke up?* but she explained in their MT that *did* showed that the question was in the past tense so the main verb 'lost its tense'. She reminded them about what happens to the *s* in *likes* when you change *Sally likes ice-cream* to *Does Sally like ice-cream?* Soon the students became quite good at asking past tense questions.

EXAMPLE 2

Miss Bain's intermediate class was driving her crazy. First, they had decided that English verbs had no endings. She had at last succeeded in convincing them otherwise. Now they were using the past tense everywhere. Even the question-forms she thought she had taught them so well as beginners were affected, and every day she was subjected to horrors such as:

*When did Tom left the disco last night?
*What did you wore at the party?

She reminded them of the rule and then gave them some enjoyable practice. They played 'Alibi'. She explained to them:

'A jeweller's shop in Market Street was robbed at 2 p.m. yesterday. Bashir and Ali were suspected of the crime, but claim they were together all afternoon and were never in Market Street.

'Bashir and Ali, leave the room for a few minutes and agree on your story. You will come back one at a time and we will question you separately. If your answers do not agree we will accuse you of robbing the jeweller.' The game went well and most questions were correctly formed; but several people were still using a sound more like /v/ than /w/ in the question words. She would do some intensive practice on that separately, she thought. Meanwhile, let them enjoy the game . . .

Part 1: The need for remedial teaching

Learning a new language is such a complex process that it is hardly surprising that things sometimes go wrong. However careful the initial teaching of an item may be and however well the students perform in controlled practice sessions, errors are bound to occur: rules will be forgotten or only half remembered; similar forms and structures will be wrongly associated; the need to communicate may demand pieces of language for which no rules are known except those of the MT; the speech organs may revert to much longer established habits and produce sounds nearer to those of the MT than the FL. These and other possible causes of error have been discussed in Chapter 8.

Ideally, a great deal of 'remedial work' should be done incidentally, as soon as the need for it is apparent, in the form of frequent revision of problem areas. This can be done in the early stages of a course, when problem areas are likely to be few and fairly clearly defined; however, as time goes by and there are more and more things to remember, it becomes impossible to revise everything frequently enough for everyone, and more and more mistakes begin to creep in.

Perhaps in the best of all possible worlds this would not happen. Teachers would make absolutely sure that one point was so thoroughly learned by every student before moving on that it would never be forgotten; similarly, learners would be so strongly motivated that such an approach would not become tedious and uninteresting to them. As things are, however, we cannot achieve such a standard of perfection. It is difficult to keep track of everything and everyone. Most of us teach classes, not single individuals; and we tend to teach at a rate suited to the *average* student, moving on when most people (as far as we can tell in a large group) have got the general idea.

In such circumstances it is inevitable that, for those students who need more practice and revision than the rest, there will be more and more rules and relationships which are only dimly perceived, partly learned, or even completely misunderstood.

Another problem most teachers face is that even if they are convinced that *they* could have prevented many problems from arising in the earlier stages, they keep inheriting groups of students from other teachers who could not. We all tend to complain about the inadequacies of earlier teaching; but having done that, what can we do about helping our present group of intermediate or 'advanced' students?

If you often get the impression that a great deal of remedial work is constantly needed, perhaps you are forcing or encouraging your students to make errors by setting them tasks which are too difficult for them or by giving far too little help and guidance. This applies particularly to the use of 'free composition' at too early a stage in the course. (See Chapter 6.) Over-enthusiastic and ill-conceived examination preparation is a frequent cause of this tendency to set tasks beyond the students' resources. Students are often given exercises to do at exactly the same level of difficulty as the examination itself, a year or even two years before they are due to take the examination. If students are expected to cope reasonably well with these tasks at such an early stage, one wonders what it is they are supposed to learn in the intervening period.

In fact, of course, in such circumstances most students perform badly; the students become demoralised and the teacher becomes depressed and convinced of the necessity for a great deal of remedial work.

Much of this can be avoided by a more gradual approach to the target standard. Such an approach may in itself be a form of remediation, especially if the students have already been demoralised by past experience of exercises which were actually too difficult for them. By setting tasks which are interesting but which the students can cope with without making numerous errors, you can restore their confidence, give them a sense of achievement and convince them that the subject is not hopelessly difficult. Even such a simple thing as demanding much shorter pieces of written work on more straightforward topics can go a long way towards reducing errors and restoring confidence.

There is sometimes the problem of how to make such easier tasks interesting and worthwhile, though often the mere fact that work is returned without being covered in red marks is encouragement enough. Some ideas I have found useful for written tasks in ESL contexts are:

(i) short, simple accounts of events for a class or school newspaper or magazine;
(ii) similar accounts for a daily 'news board' read by the whole school;
(iii) short talks to be given either to the class or to junior classes;
(iv) short personal anecdotes, stories, etc. to be used for extensive reading by more junior classes.

A great advantage in asking for things to be written for the whole school or for junior classes is that it provides a clear reason for writing in a simple, direct style, which in itself often reduces the number of errors. Some students need to be reminded that they *can* do this effectively, as they may have got into the habit of trying to write in a style which is too complex for their command of the language. A compelling reason for ensuring that the language is correct is that it is going to be made public.

The two main points I have made are:

(i) that some remedial work is necessary and inevitable; but
(ii) that we can get a false impression about the *amount* of remedial work needed if we set our students unrealistic tasks.

Part 2: Selection of problem areas for remedial work

A   Errors for incidental correction

Some remedial work can be done by correcting mistakes more or less as they occur during the normal course of teaching. I am thinking here of incidental errors, not those involving the main teaching point of a controlled practice session, which would be corrected in any case.

In dealing with such errors, however, there is a need for caution, selection, and sensitivity. As I said in Chapter 8, Part 1, we must not make learners so worried about making mistakes that they lose all confidence and fluency. It follows that we should not pounce on every mistake as it is produced and demand immediate correction. This applies particularly to errors in speech, both of pronunciation and grammar. Such errors can be divided into four categories, according to whether they are to be

(i) dealt with immediately;
(ii) tackled at the next convenient point in the lesson;
(iii) left to a later lesson; or
(iv) ignored altogether at this stage.

In general, Category (i) should include only those mistakes which you are sure the student can correct with the minimum amount of interference to his fluency. Many of these will be 'lapses'. (See Chapter 8.) Such mistakes can often be indicated non-verbally (by raising the eyebrows, for example) or by saying a single sound, word or short phrase:

e.g. Student: *She didn't had any . . .
    Teacher: Have
    Student: She didn't have any money left.
or Student: *She won a price . . .
    Teacher: /z/
    Student: She won a prize in the competition.

In selecting mistakes for such treatment you need to be sensitive to the possible reactions of individual students. Some students will happily correct themselves in this way whereas others may become worried and confused.

The errors of students who may be worried by immediate correction will be included in Category (ii). They can be dealt with as soon as the student has finished speaking, e.g. 'That's right, but you said "*She didn't *had* any . . ." What should you have said?'

Also in Category (ii) are other errors which can be dealt with quickly but cannot be corrected 'in mid-flow', or which you have decided to ignore temporarily in order not to distract attention from something more important or in order not to spoil the fun. Miss Bain, in

EXAMPLE 2, may well have put the /w/ – /v/ confusion into this category and spent a few minutes on the problem at the end of the lesson as well as giving more time to it in later sessions.

Errors to be included in Category (iii) will be those requiring more intensive remedial work. These are considered in the next section. It is useful to keep a note-book for jotting down such errors when they occur. It is no use imagining you will remember without making a note: you rarely will.

B Selecting errors for more intensive remedial work

The elimination of many errors requires teaching that is concentrated and regularly revised. It is, for example, of little value merely to correct fifteen different errors in a piece of written work or write up on the blackboard corrected versions of twenty or thirty different errors made by the whole class, and then to assume that you have dealt with remedial work for the week and that the students will not repeat the mistakes. Such activities *partly* fulfil *one* of the requirements of remedial work: that learners should be aware of their errors; but they are unlikely to have very much effect on their future performance. This is because, with so many topics to deal with in one session, you cannot focus sufficient attention on any of them and, with so many isolated problem areas to think about in quick succession, students are likely to remember only a few of them in any case. It is more efficient, therefore, to select a few errors yourself and really concentrate on them.

The importance of some sort of Error Analysis as a preliminary to the selection of errors for remedial teaching was stressed in the previous chapter. The analysis need not be elaborate but the more thought you give to it, the more revealing and helpful it is likely to be. The following factors should be considered in selecting problem areas for attention:

1 Frequency of error. The frequency of errors in the performance of individuals and in the group as a whole is much easier to assess in written work than it is in speech. Without going to the extent of studying recorded samples of speech, you will have to rely on a subjective assessment of the frequency of pronunciation errors.

One difficulty, particularly in counting syntactic errors, is deciding what to count as 'the same' error. This will depend on the system of classification you use but care has to be taken both not to over-generalise (for example, by counting all incorrect uses of prepositions as the same error) and not to under-generalise (for example, by counting all incorrect irregular plurals as isolated errors, thus missing the point that your group is regularising *all* plurals).

You should also consider errors which may not be particularly frequent in the sample analysed but which may affect later performance considerably. So, for example, if your analysis is based mainly on written work it is likely that there will be few errors involving question forms. (Even in oral work, students may not be asking as many questions as they will need to later outside the classroom, although if this is the case the course is not really adequate.) It is easy to neglect errors of this type, which could be called 'potentially frequent'.

2 Overall effect on performance.   Some errors affect more than one linguistic level or more than one system, so that to remedy them is likely to improve several aspects of performance at once. This is particularly obvious in the case of aural perception and oral production, which in turn frequently affect spelling. For example, students who confuse the pronunciation of /ɪ/ as in 'live' with /iː/ as in 'leave' probably do not hear the difference and will almost certainly confuse the spelling of other words in which the sounds occur, e.g. bit/beat, ship/sheep, still/steal. Such confusion, both in speech and writing, may also appear to be a mistake in the choice of vocabulary, as in *The headmaster bit me.

It follows, then, that if we can get our students to discriminate between these two sounds in listening and speaking, their performance is likely to improve in the other areas too. In fact, it sometimes happens that work on aural/oral discrimination leads to quite dramatic improvements in *spelling* without having very much effect at all on speech. This, I think, fully justifies such work, as people tend to be much more tolerant of errors in speech than in writing. This is especially important, of course, if your students will be taking a written examination.

On the other hand it is probably not worthwhile making such great efforts to improve discrimination between the 'th' sounds, /θ/ as in 'thin' and /ð/ as in 'than'. If these sounds are confused there is no effect on spelling, as they are both spelt 'th'. Even in speech not many words are affected and there are hardly any 'minimal pairs' which may lead to one word being mistaken for another as in 'bit/beat'.

Another area in which aural perception, oral production, spelling and syntax are all involved is the recognition and production of the regular past tense marker, *-ed*. (This has been discussed in Chapter 8.)

3 Effect on intelligibility.   This is often considered to be crucial in trying to assess the relative 'seriousness' of errors. The limitations and ultimate subjectivity of the concept have been discussed in Chapter 8. In any discussion of intelligibility one must be realistic and remember that the listener or reader does not rely solely on discrete linguistic signals but on the whole context. In the context of a normal conversation, for example, nobody who says what sounds like *I saw a sheep in the bay* or *We'll have our spots next week* is likely to be misunderstood.

Much work on minimally paired words (e.g. *live, leave*) and sentences (e.g. *I don't want to live/leave all on my own*) implies that such misunderstandings occur frequently whereas, in fact, what is much more common is complete lack of comprehension. In speech this is more likely to result from incorrect stress patterns than discrete segments. (See Chapter 2.)

The degree of intelligibility is also highly dependent on the attitudes of the people with whom the student is trying to communicate, and on their experience of listening to non-native speakers of English. Some people find it very hard to adjust to variations in the way English is spoken; on the other hand, after a few weeks of contact, many people become so accustomed to differences in pronunciation that they hardly notice them at all.

The majority of grammatical errors, taken separately, do not seriously affect intelligibility, given a reasonable amount of good-will and intelligence on the part of the listener or reader. This of course cannot always be guaranteed, and in any case if a speaker makes a great number of such errors their effect becomes cumulative; the receiver is so busy re-formulating everything he hears or reads that his comprehension process is unable to function properly or he becomes impatient and stops trying. There is also the risk that if the speaker makes too many errors his opinions will not be treated very seriously.

There are some grammatical errors which do cause misunderstanding or confusion, however. For example, some learners have difficulty with the *he/she, his/her* distinction. As this can be very misleading most teachers would give high priority to eliminating such mistakes.

4 Effect on 'people who matter'. You may consider this to be an important criterion in choosing what to concentrate on. It has been discussed in Part 1 of Chapter 8.

5 Chances of success in eliminating an error. Most errors could be eliminated if sufficient time were spent on them and if the learners were sufficiently motivated to co-operate. In selecting errors for remedial work, however, you need to assess realistically how likely you are to succeed, how much time it is likely to take, how much time is actually available and how many other, possibly more important things your students could be doing in that time.

I have no wish to encourage defeatism here, but we must be realistic. For every group, there are some errors whose elimination would be so time-consuming that the students would learn very little else. I once came to this conclusion about the use of the invariable question-tag *isn't it?* among a group of Indian students (e.g. **You have lost your text-book, isn't it?*); others disagreed with this decision, but I did not notice that their students used the correct forms any more frequently than mine, and mine had more time to spend on other things, such as extending their knowledge of vocabulary and improving fluency.

6 Genuine error or frequent lapse? The problem of deciding whether a mistake is one of ignorance or of forgetfulness has been fully discussed in Chapter 8, Part 5. If you *can* be fairly sure that a widespread mistake is caused by forgetfulness or carelessness, the best way to deal with it is to draw attention to it but insist on self-correction. If what you think are 'careless mistakes' are very frequent, you may need to think again; it may be an area of uncertainty and confusion requiring more concentrated attention.

There is no general formula which can be given for establishing how much weighting should be given to each of the above factors when choosing problem areas for remedial teaching. Much will depend on the standard being aimed at, the purposes for which English is to be used and the degree to which students are motivated to improve their performance. For most practical purposes it is likely that the effect on 'people who matter' will be of considerable importance and this will often be influenced by frequency and effect on intelligibility.

The important thing is to be selective, to deal with a few problems thoroughly rather than try to deal superficially with everything at once.

Part 3: Methods of remedial teaching

A Similarity to initial teaching

There is very little difference between good remedial work and good initial teaching. There are three *essential* stages, plus a few optional, additional ones which will be discussed later.
You have to:
(i) define the problem area and decide on your 'teaching point';
(ii) give the students clear examples of appropriate correct substitutes for the incorrect language they have been using; and
(iii) give adequate opportunity for practising the correct usage, preferably in some meaningful context.

1 Defining the problem area.   This has been partly dealt with in Part 2 and in Chapter 8. You need to know precisely what it is the students are doing wrong and in what circumstances they are most likely to make the error. You may not know exactly *why* they are confused, though of course it certainly helps if you do.

You also need to consider whether you are going to make the topic of the remedial work explicit to the students. Some teachers favour doing all remedial work in the guise of practice in other activities (see following section 2) without revealing their true motives to the students. The argument is that remedying errors will be seen as boring and motivation will be reduced. On the other hand, there may be cases, especially with older students, when it is much more effective to go straight to the point and say something like: 'You still seem to be having difficulties with the tenses of verbs in *if*-sentences, so we're going to have another look at this problem.'

What you decide to do will depend largely on the age of your students and on their general motivation. If the work itself is not boring and dull there is much to be said for telling the students exactly what you intend to do and what you hope they will achieve.

2 Giving correct substitutes and practising correct usage. These are like initial presentation and practice, with the important difference that, whatever method you use, it should not be an exact repetition of the initial presentation to the same group of students. The reasons for this are that:

(i) it may be seen as boring and repetitive, so that the students will not pay full attention unless they are highly motivated to eliminate the particular error; and

(ii) if errors are still being made, it could well be that the initial presentation was not appropriate for the group of students concerned. However much we may personally like a technique, if it did not work adequately the first time we will need to think of another way.

It is sometimes possible to do remedial work in the guise of practice in other activities, such as the communication games, information gap exercises, etc. discussed in Chapter 5; even if you have made the topic explicit, these activities are an excellent way of *practising* the correct usage. This was Miss Bain's solution to her problem in the example at the beginning of this chapter when she decided to introduce the game 'Alibi'. Here the students had to produce correct question forms in order to play the game; all they needed was a few models as reminders and a plausible reason for practising the forms.

It is often easy to find new ideas for remedial practice by looking at some of the exercises associated with communicative approaches to teaching. If your students have been taught from a structural syllabus, many teaching items can be revised by reintroducing them under some communicative heading. For example, the *there is/are* distinction could be re-introduced and practised as part of the topic 'Complaining':

Sue and Sam have booked in at a hotel. They are shown to their rooms but a few minutes later they meet again at the reception desk:

Sam:　　　　　Hello, have you come to enquire about something?

Sue:　　　　　Not really. I've come to complain. There are no towels in my bathroom, there's a wet bath-mat on the floor and there aren't enough blankets on the bed.

Sam:　　　　　Well in my room there aren't enough coat-hangers in the wardrobe, there's a big hole in the pillow case, and there's no light-bulb in the bathroom.

Receptionist:　Good evening, madam, can I help you?

Sue:　　　　　Yes. There are no towels in my bathroom . . . etc.

Receptionist:　I'll attend to it at once, madam. Can I help you, sir?

Sam:　　　　　Yes. There aren't enough coat-hangers . . . etc.

Students practise the dialogues, then make up their own based either on the following tables or on pictures of rooms with similar defects.

Complain about the following items:

Missing or not enough	*Unwanted or damaged*
bedside lamp	wet towels
soap	broken light-switch
mirror	vacuum cleaner in the
toilet paper	wardrobe
bath plug	holes in the sheets
pillows	dirty tea-cups
blankets	dirty ashtray
drinking glasses	a pair of pyjamas
	broken window

B Additional stages in remedial work

The following additional stages are all to some extent controversial, in that you will meet teachers who think that one or more of them is essential and others who make it almost an act of faith to avoid and denounce them. Like many controversial issues in language teaching the real question is not 'Should I never do this?' or 'Should I always do that?' but 'In what circumstances and with what kind of students could this be helpful and effective?'

1 Explicit discussion of causes of errors.   Answers to questions like, 'Why do you think you often say **You will regret for it* instead of *You will regret it?*' can be very illuminating for both students and teachers. The answer tells the teacher something about how the student thinks the language works and may in itself alert the student to other possible danger areas. Explicit discussion of this kind often reveals long-standing misconceptions and confusions which are comparatively simple to clear up.

This is perhaps most helpful for older learners; it may also be particularly useful in helping you, if you do not know your students' MT, to understand some of their problems and likely areas of misunderstanding.

Even with younger students, a teacher who does know the MT can often help by saying things like: 'I know that in Hindi we say **I asked him that, what do you want?* but you can't do it like that in English.'

Similarly, with errors which appear to be caused by confusion within English (intra-lingual errors) it may be helpful to draw attention to the possible source of the confusion and point out the differences between the two potentially confusing items.

244

e.g.   'I know *few* and *a few* sound very similar but they have very different meanings. *Few* is used when we mean *not many* or *very few* and *a few* when we mean *some* as in: *'Few of my friends came to meet me. I was disappointed. A few of my friends came to meet me. That was nice of them.'*

Of course, all such explanation and discussion is of little use without practice and it is certainly *not* an adequate substitute for it. Explanation alone will not eliminate the error but it may help to speed up the process.

2   Giving practice in discriminating between contrasting items.
Contrastive initial presentation is very likely to lead to cross-association (see Chapter 1) and should in general be avoided; but at a later stage, once cross-association *has* occurred, learners may welcome clear examples of the correct use of the contrasting items and an opportunity to discriminate between them. This is one way of following up the explicit discussion of such items mentioned in the preceding section 1. Thus *in addition* to practising the use of *few* and *a few* separately, students may be given exercises like the following:

Decide which of the two endings is the more likely:

A few of my father's friends have cars so he
(i) often gets a lift to work.
(ii) usually has to walk to work.
Few people came to the party so it was
(i) a great success.
(ii) rather disappointing.

---

3   Giving grammatical rules and explanations.   Older learners often welcome this, indeed they may expect and demand it: 'Why can't I say ** We made him to do it*, when I can say *We forced him to do it*? Tell me the rule.' Unfortunately, the rules are often either too complex to be of practical use or, as in this case, not particularly satisfying: e.g. 'Well *make* is like *let* and a few other verbs. It is never followed by *to* + infinitive.'

If you are going to give explicit grammatical rules it is worthwhile bearing in mind the following points.
(i) The rules should work, without too many exceptions. They should not be gross over-simplifications such as 'if the action was in the past the verb must be in the past tense'.
On the other hand, a clear rule which applies to only part of a problem can be useful, e.g. students who confuse *used to, usually*, and *always* often welcome the information that the *I used to do* form can only refer to *past* habitual actions whereas the other two words are often used with the present tense.
(ii) The teaching of grammatical rules should not become an end in itself and it is certainly no substitute for practice.

245

4 Error avoidance. Sometimes a major aim is merely to *avoid* certain errors in written work, e.g. for examination purposes. If the students are reasonably well motivated this is not particularly difficult to achieve. It is useful to draw the students' attention to known areas of weakness and encourage them to check their work for specific points. For example, I once succeeded in helping a group of students to reduce their total number of errors significantly by getting them to proof-read their work three times: the first time looking at all the verb forms and checking the tense; the second time checking on subject-verb agreement; and the third time checking on the use of articles. Proof-reading in this way seems to be much more effective than more general checking, and the fact that the piece of writing is read over a given number of times helps to ensure that other careless mistakes get corrected in the process.

Proof-reading and self-correction can be encouraged by setting aside specific class time for it, and by *not* correcting errors which students should be able to spot for themselves. Some teachers use a phased withdrawal of help for this type of mistake. In the first stage the error is underlined and a symbol placed in the margin showing what type of error it is (e.g. Sp for Spelling, T for Tense, Ag for Agreement). In the second stage the error is underlined but an indication of the error type is not given. In the third stage the error is not underlined, but crosses are placed in the margin indicating the number of errors on a particular line. I have sometimes used a fourth stage, merely counting the number of errors and saying, 'There are five errors you should have spotted yourself when proof-reading. Find them and correct them.'

You can also help students with their proof-reading by giving them mnemonic devices to jog their memories. A good example of this to help with the 3rd person present tense -*s* has been given in Chapter 1.

In extreme cases, when passing the examination is of vital importance, it may help if you just ban certain expressions altogether and suggest suitable alternatives. This is often the easiest way to deal with the *few/a few* problem. I have never met a student who used *a few* where *few* would have been correct; the error is always the incorrect use of *few*. Consequently, I tell students that every time they see *few* in their own work it is almost certain to be wrong and they should change it to *a few*, *several* or *some*. This is rough-and-ready advice but such advice is often better than none.

Further reading

MORGAN, D. 'A discussion of remedial teaching'. *ELTJ* 10, 3, 1956.
Gives an account of attempts to improve the written English of a large number of students in Rangoon. The effectiveness of various remedial methods is lucidly discussed.

GEORGE, H. *Common errors in language learning.* Newbury House, 1972.
Contains a very sane and practical section on remedial work.

CORBLUTH, J. 'Remediation or development'. *ELTJ* 18, 2, 1974.
Discusses the attitudes of teachers to errors and the selection of errors for remediation.

JAMES, K. 'Judgements of error gravities'. *ELTJ* 31, 2, 1977.
Discusses the marking of written work and the different attitudes of native speakers and non-native speakers to different types of error.

ABBOTT, G. 'Intelligibility and acceptability in spoken and written communication'. *ELTJ* 33, 3, 1979.
Discusses pronunciation difficulties, their effect on spelling, and people's attitudes to both.

Chapter 10: Planning your teaching

by John Greenwood

EXAMPLE 1

'Well, I look at it this way. There's Book 1 for the first year and Book 2 for the second, in a course that's graded from simple to difficult. Of course the first year classes have got to finish Book 1, otherwise there's too great a jump in difficulty when they start Book 2. The yearly exams are based on the books too. Well, it's a bit of a rush, I admit, but I stick to the textbook and manage to get them through it.'

EXAMPLE 2

'Oh, I never bother with the teacher's book. I find it so restricting. Don't you? Especially when you are advised to give so many hours to this or that stage. And when the course-book writer tells me to spend five minutes here and ten minutes there on something, I give up. No, I like to have just the course-book itself, so that I can pick and choose as I like. And I don't think it matters whether I finish the book or not. After all, I'm teaching them general English, not course-book English; so I make up my lessons myself. I use the textbook in my own way.'

Part 1: Planning the use of time

Perhaps these seem extreme positions, but they reflect widely-held contrasting views among language teachers. In **EXAMPLE 1** the teacher expresses his anxiety to keep to a rigid syllabus, which could mean no more than following the textbook. He has probably drawn up a detailed year's programme to cover the book and he is reluctant to jeopardise it in any way. He no doubt feels he is fulfilling his duty both to his learners and to their parents by such careful planning. He is naturally also concerned about the results of the end-of-year examination based on the textbook. His self-esteem is at stake.

On the other hand, the teacher in **EXAMPLE 2** rejects the restrictions of a tightly-controlled syllabus and textbook, as well as detailed directives for each lesson in the teacher's book. Such an attitude does not necessarily mean the teacher is disorganised, relying solely on instant inspiration in the lessons. There are many excellent teachers who prefer

248

to plan their teaching independently of the textbook writer, some using the textbook substantially, others using it more sparingly.

Whatever our attitude, we surely agree that it is necessary to plan, though there will be much variation in the planning itself from teacher to teacher. There are many factors contributing to the actual performance by the teacher in the classroom, not least of which is the teacher's own personality. An observer might easily be deceived into thinking that an impression of spontaneity and creativity is thanks to a mere stroke of luck, completely unplanned. However, teachers are well advised to plan their teaching carefully, so that they have a clear idea of what they hope will take place in the classroom before they actually enter it. If there is a teacher's book, you would be wise to consider the suggestions of the writer when you plan your lessons.

Planning lessons entails answering certain questions:
(i)   Planning for whom? (the learners)
(ii) Planning for what? (the syllabus)
(iii) Planning for when? (the schedule)
By answering these three questions, we will at the same time be answering two other questions: why? and how?

A   The learners

Knowing who the learners are, the teacher is able to plan the course in the light of their ages, purposes in learning and levels of English. With such information available, the teacher is able to determine the material and the learning activities – the textbook, the audio-visual aids, etc. Of course, in many school situations the teacher has no choice; that is, the textbook has already been decided upon and bought in bulk, the school either has or has not got tape recorders, overhead projectors, a language lab, etc. Still, the teacher has to decide whether or not to use such material as is available, and also how to use it.

B   The syllabus

You may have come across such terms as 'the learner's needs', 'performance objectives' and the 'terminal behaviour' of the learners. Terminal behaviour is usually stated in such terms as:
(i) By the end of the course, our learners will be able to:
   (a) use the Present Simple, Past Simple and Present Progressive tenses;
   (b) use the article system;
   etc; or
(ii) By the end of the course, our learners will be able to:
   (a) give information about themselves – their names, ages, addresses, nationality, interests, etc.;
   (b) ask for information;
   (c) express agreement and disagreement;
   etc.

249

The type of items listed under (i) would make up a structure-based syllabus, the type listed under (ii) a function-based syllabus. Clearly defined functional needs and objectives appear for instance in the work of Van Ek (1975) and colleagues for the Council of Europe. (See Further Reading.) But they are dealing with a special type of learner: an adult with a definite purpose to his learning. A tailor-made syllabus can often be drawn up in such circumstances. The same is true of courses in English for Specific Purposes. See Holden in Further Reading.

The vast majority of teachers in schools do not have the luxury of these favourable conditions because:
(i) the school learner normally has no clearly defined needs for learning English (e.g. for higher education or a future job) but is learning a foreign language as a component of his general education; and
(ii) in effect, the syllabus often consists of the textbook plus whatever the teacher may supply as supplementary material. However, the teacher often has reasonable freedom within these general constraints.

C The schedule

Given a class to teach and a textbook to use, how do we go about planning our year's work? How do we turn the textbook into lessons? To begin with, we need to know how much time is available in the school year. Here is one example:

> The school year has three terms: September to December provides 13 weeks, January to March 12 weeks and April to June 8 weeks. There are 4 lessons a week for English, so that means $33 \times 4 = 132$ lessons. However, because of national and religious holidays, examinations and the school trip in May, about 12 lessons are lost, so 120 lessons are available for teaching, including revision.

The figures will obviously vary from school to school. I have avoided using the word 'hour' because, even where the timetable is divided into hourly blocks, rarely is there in practice more than 50 minutes' teaching per period. Also, even when publishers claim that a textbook is intended for so many hours' work, it is usually an unreliable figure because not all learners work at the same speed. I will therefore use the word 'lesson' to refer to the classroom period. Publishers sometimes use the term 'lesson' to refer to a chapter in the textbook, the teaching of which could cover much more than one period. For this I will use the word 'unit'.

To return to our example: the teacher knows he has roughly 120 lessons with a particular class to cover the syllabus/textbook. It would be useful at this stage for the teacher to ask himself:
(i) Can I rely on any help from an English language assistant? This might be the case in certain West European countries. The teacher would have to plan the lessons so that the assistant was used to best advantage. This could take various forms, such as joint teaching of a lesson or allocating a small number of learners to the assistant for oral work. (See Jordan and Mackay in Further Reading.)

(ii) Is it possible to liaise with other teachers of English and their classes? For example, if the timetable allows, it might be possible occasionally to have joint activities such as the viewing of a film or television lesson, or for one class to act as audience for an activity which another class had prepared. Such collaboration would have to be carefully planned.

(iii) Do I want to (or even have I got to) use the language lab regularly? If so, the teacher will have to think not only about the language lab lessons themselves, but also about any preparation and follow-up. Furthermore, it is normally not sensible for the learners to spend the whole lesson listening to taped exercises through headphones and responding into a microphone. They need some variety of activities – not always easy to provide if the class has to remain cramped in language lab booths for the whole lesson.

Returning again to our example: let us suppose that the textbook contains 24 units to be covered in our 120 lessons. It would be simplistic merely to decide on a straight division, so that 5 lessons are devoted to each unit, because it is most unlikely that all units are of equal difficulty and length. Some units might be covered adequately in one or two lessons, while others might take much longer. Of course, some textbooks have a suggested time-scale which you can follow if you think it is satisfactory. Others use the same format for each unit, so that roughly equal treatment may be attempted. However, a fairly close analysis of the textbook is normally necessary before you attempt to use it. After such an analysis (see Part 2 below) you ought to be in a position to draw up some kind of overall plan, a part of which might look like the following:

Timetable			Textbook	Supplementary activities
Week	Lesson	Unit	Language content	
1	1	1	Superlatives: *the biggest boy*, etc.	———
	2	1		Introduce class library; issue books
	3	2		———
	4	2		(Last 15 mins) Prepare for TV lesson
2	1	2	Present Simple Passive	TV lesson
	2	2		TV follow-up: role-playing
	3	2		One text from a science book illustrating use of Passive

Timetable			Textbook	Supplementary activities
Week	Lesson	Unit	Language content	
	4	3	Superlatives: *the most beautiful girl,* etc.	Check class library reading: change books

The amount of detail in the overall plan, and the degree of flexibility in using it, will depend on the teacher.

Part 2: Using and adapting the textbook

Any kind of adaptation will entail one or more of the following changes:
(i) *separation* – you deliberately present and practise separately items which the textbook lumps together;
(ii) *supplementation* – you deliberately supplement the textbook by providing extra teaching material;
(iii) *omission* – you deliberately ignore some textbook material that is unsuitable or superfluous – or even wrong!

A Separating language items

Chapter 1 dealt with the phenomenon of cross-association, and Chapter 8 considered errors arising in this way. What should the teacher do when the presentation in the textbook is likely to cause confusion in the learner's mind and thus encourage such errors? Some modification of the textbook presentation would seem advisable.

For example, although many textbooks present all types of relative clauses together, it would be better to space them over a series of lessons, not necessarily consecutive ones. Having sorted out the different patterns and relative pronouns, you can decide in which order to present them and how long a gap to leave between them. You may wish to have intervening material and consequently return to the textbook at times for something different. Having taught the different relative clauses separately, you may then want to see if the learners can cope with all of them together. It is only at this stage, when mixing of the different types occurs, that the textbook material can be used. But before this stage, you will want to find suitable material elsewhere. You may find it in another textbook or in materials such as the British Council English Language Units. (See Further Reading.) The plan for a series of lessons on the relative clauses might look something like the following:

252

Week	Lesson	Relative clause type introduced
3	2	(i) The man who shouted . . .
	3	(Other language items – not relative clauses)
	4	(Other language items – not relative clauses)
4	1	(ii) The train which left late . . .
	2	(Other language items – not relative clauses)
	3	(Other language items – not relative clauses)
	4	(iii) The boy I saw . . ./The chair I broke . . .
5	1	Revise (i), (ii) and (iii)
	2	(Other language items – not relative clauses)
	3	(Other language items – not relative clauses)
	4	(iv) The house that belongs to him . . ./ The teacher that lives . . .
6	1	Revise (iii)
	2	(v) The man we spoke to . . .
	3	Revise (i), (ii), (iii) and (iv)

This does not necessarily mean that the whole of each lesson which includes relative clauses will include nothing else. You may decide that about 20 minutes is enough for presentation and practice of a relative clause item, with say 10 minutes' consolidation in the next lesson, and so on. And of course, relative clauses will not cease to exist after Lesson 3 of Week 6!

Confusion of forms might be reduced if you were to use a cyclical approach. The first time you want your class to practise the function 'expressing preferences', for example, you could confine the practice to one form – say: *prefer* + Verb + *-ing*; e.g.

I prefer playing tennis to washing up.

Then after a few weeks you could return to the same function, but this time your learners would practise the form: *would rather* + Verb; e.g.

I would rather play tennis than wash up.

These two forms, if introduced together, could well produce cross-association leading to production of sentences such as:

*I would rather playing tennis than washing up.

Textbooks often present in close proximity items which would be better taught separately. The word *enough* may appear to the textbook writer to be just one item; so in one unit of his textbook he may unwittingly present two uses of the word without any indication of their difference: e.g.

The knife isn't sharp enough.
Have you got enough bread?

It is not surprising that errors are frequently encountered of the type
Is the knife enough sharp?
Your job in this case is to plan something like the following:

Lesson 1   Adj + *enough*
Lesson 2   (Items unconnected with *enough*)
Lesson 3   *enough* + Noun

You may also have to defer the use of the textbook exercises on *enough* until you reach Lesson 4.

So far we have focused on planning for the separation of items which have been juxtaposed in the textbook. This process will often require some addition, omission or substitution in the teaching material. Let us now consider other aspects of the textbook which will affect the planning of lessons.

B Fatigue and the four language skills

Firstly, it is well known that, after a certain period of activity, people get tired and their attention wanders. They then need a rest or a change of activity. Research suggests that, even when university students are listening to a lecture in their own language, they tire after about 20 minutes. The saying 'A change is as good as a rest' is certainly true in the classroom – and the lecture-room.

Secondly, we must remember that, in any group of learners, individual differences and preferences will occur. For example, while a few adults do not rely heavily on the comfort of the written word when doing oral practice, many do – even though the spellings may be misleading. To give a class a chance to hear *and* say *and* see *and* write a piece of language is to cater for all the preferences of individual members. On the basis of these two observations alone we may say that, although in a good lesson the content is fixed, the activities of the class will vary so that several or all of the four skills will be practised.

However, some textbooks tend to highlight one skill or pair of skills and downgrade or omit the others. Grammar/translation textbooks focus primarily on reading and writing, whereas audio-lingual textbooks concentrate on listening and speaking – though by the very fact that a textbook is written, reading cannot be totally excluded. You would do well, therefore, to find out if your textbook provides insufficient practice of one of the skills. In recent years, for example, I have heard teachers say: 'I like the book and so do my class, but there's hardly any writing activity. Can you suggest how to supplement the textbook?' You need to plan ahead, making sure you have the requisite supply of readers, or an additional textbook for writing work, or some cassettes of dialogues, or whatever. Your scheme of work will indicate at what stages this supplementary material will be used. You may consider that the first five units of the textbook (taught in, say, eight weeks) have sufficient material for writing activity, but that from then onwards supplementary writing material is regularly required.

Methodology books (like this one) often treat each of the four language skills separately. It is possible to imagine a learner who needs only one skill; for example, a scholar who needs only to be able to read texts in a foreign language. A case could perhaps be made for confining his instruction to lessons in reading comprehension. However, most of us do not deal with such learners. More usually in language use, a combination of skills occurs. For instance, conversation involves both listening and speaking. So, in addition to ensuring that the four skills are reasonably covered in themselves, we must also check that the integration of the skills occurs in our lessons.

C   Balanced coverage of the language

You may find that it is not only language skills that are out of balance in the textbook. You will also have to adapt the textbook if it spends too much or too little time on particular elements of the language itself.

For example, many courses spend much of the first book practising the Present Progressive tense. They give this tense such prominence that the learner is in danger of over-using it forever after. Some textbooks even attempt to use it for telling stories. This is unsatisfactory because the narrative function normally demands the Past Simple tense, just as authentic descriptions normally demand the Present Simple tense. Thus by dwelling too long on the Present Progressive such courses prevent the learner from meeting the two important functions of describing things and telling stories. Without these the lesson material tends to be unnatural, stereotyped and therefore boring.

So here, right from the beginning of a course, is a situation where you may well feel compelled to adapt the textbook by adding suitable material from elsewhere to practise both the Present Simple and the Past Simple, while omitting some of the textbook material on the Present Progressive.

D   Non-textbook material

Up to now I have made the assumption that for most teachers the textbook is the basis of the course and the year's work. Even the teacher in **EXAMPLE 2** at the beginning of the chapter uses a textbook as a basis, though he adapts it to his own liking, perhaps in some of the ways we have been discussing. As we saw, one way of supplementing a textbook is by adding some material from elsewhere when you think the textbook fails to provide adequate material. However, the textbook itself is not always intended by the writer or the publisher to be the only material of the course. There are now on the market courses which, apart from the student's book, provide some or all of the following:

Student's workbook	Tape or cassette
Reader	Film strip
Teacher's book	

The teacher's book may indicate how the rest can be integrated, so you may be saved the trouble of drawing up a plan. But you may well want to go beyond the ready-made plan. For instance, you may want to encourage your learners to read beyond what the course itself provides. Setting up a class library of supplementary readers should not be too difficult if money and shelving space are available. More difficult is planning the reading activity. There is one school of thought which advocates little or no reading and writing in lessons because, it is argued, the learners need the maximum time for listening and speaking. This seems to me misguided. Apart from the mutual reinforcement provided by practising several skills, our learners may well need help in their silent reading. Of course we want them to read independently of the teacher outside the classroom as much as possible; but we can help them to do this by building into our lesson plans provision for extensive reading. Furthermore, we need to allow for some follow-up activity, such as getting a learner to recount the plot of his book to the rest of the class.

If there is a class reader (that is, if every learner has the same book to read) your plan for covering the book will have to fit in with your plan for the whole course. You will have to decide how much time per week you can afford – perhaps a whole lesson, perhaps only half of one.

Part 3: Planning individual lessons

Four major points about lesson planning are:
(i)   We need a plan of some sort.
(ii)   We cannot be forever referring to it during the lesson.
(iii)   It must therefore be simple enough to remember in broad outline.
(iv)   In any case we will have to be flexible enough to depart from it when necessary.

However, the new and inexperienced teacher would do well to make careful lesson notes. This will help him to find out how much can be done in one lesson, which activities are successful and which are not, and so on. The actual form these notes will take will vary according to the teacher's own preferences, but they will probably include:
(i)   (a) Class, date, etc.
        (b) Objectives – often expressed as the desired terminal behaviour of the learners; e.g. to be able to use the comparative form *more* + Adj + *than*.
        (c) Materials/aids – minimum details needed to remind the teacher what to prepare and bring; e.g. 15 car advertisements from magazines (1 per pair).

(ii) (a) Introduction – may briefly revise some previously taught material which will be needed for this lesson, or otherwise prepare for the main teaching item.
(b) Body – divided into stages to indicate the development of the lesson, giving details of what the learners will do at each stage.
(c) Conclusion – could take various forms; e.g. a recap, a test, a game, a song, issuing of homework, etc.

(iii) Evaluation – some comments written after the lesson to try to answer the questions: what worked? what did not work? what needs further work?

That is one format for planning an individual lesson. Now for the substance. What do we want in our lesson? While avoiding a rag-bag of a lesson, and aiming at continuity, we should vary:

(i) the content – a whole lesson on one tense, for example, can be boring: a few minutes' work on something totally different is needed;

(ii) the language skills – oral work for 50 minutes, for example, usually means exhaustion, restlessness and boredom;

(iii) the learner activity – using group or pair work the whole time, for example, can also be dull and therefore ineffective;

(iv) the aids – an over-used wall picture, for example, will soon lose its appeal;

(v) the pace – a uniform rate of presentation and practice, whether fast or slow, can induce fatigue.

The lesson plan should emphasise the activities of the learners, because it is these activities that will bring about learning. This emphasis will keep in check any temptation on the part of the teacher to give a 'star turn' with the learners as passive spectators. The amount of learning that goes on in a class is often in inverse proportion to the theatricality of the teacher.

Because teachers vary in their personality, in the way they teach, in their treatment of the textbook and other material, their lesson plans differ. What I have offered so far are guidelines or suggestions rather than rigid rules to follow. To conclude this chapter I give two lesson plans to illustrate this diversity of treatment, which will no doubt be reflected by your own reaction (perhaps disagreement) to my plans. You will notice that the first lesson brings in a lot of supplementary material and uses only one item from the textbook, whereas the second lesson uses most of the textbook material as a basis.

Finally, make sure you have enough material, but do not overcrowd your lesson. It is better to complete your plan a little early than to rush through it because it contains too much. If you are afraid of being left with time on your hands, have a short activity in reserve, such as a song or a game.

I

Lesson plan 1

Class: 4th year

Objectives: (i) to practise description, mainly Present Simple sentences: L/S/R/W;

e.g. York is a beautiful city. It stands on the River Ouse. It has an ancient cathedral . . .

(ii) to practise expressing preferences and reasons for preferences, mainly *would like to . . .* and *you can . . .*: L/S/R/W;

e.g. I'd like to visit York.
Why?
Because it has a railway museum, and you can . . .

The class have already been taught the language items involved, and need to gain facility in their use in context.

Materials/aids: Wall map of the UK.

Textbook: pages 103–4: description of York.

Handouts: brochures describing Edinburgh and Bristol.

Prepared BB: The following table – whole BB:

Town	Sport	Industry	Buildings	Food
York				
Edinburgh				
Bristol				
Our town				

Content: There may well be rather too much in the lesson. If so, either omit Steps 5 and 6, or omit Steps 7, 8 and 9.

Section, Skills and Time	Pupil activity	Teacher activity
1 L/S/R/W 5 min	*Introduction* Find the 3 towns on wall map. Learn what we are going to do. Copy table from BB using whole sheet sideways.	Display map. Display table. Explain and direct.

2 R/W 5 min	*Class* Read text about one town – different groups do different towns. Fill in table with brief notes.	Indicate textbook ref. to two groups; hand out brochure to four groups. Circulate.
3 L/S 5–10 min	*Group* Group secretary reads his notes to group. They say if they disagree. Secretary amends his notes if necessary.	Circulate quickly. Stop any MT chat. Check use of Present Simple.
4 L/S 5 min	*Class* Group secretaries report on each town.	Complete BB table from information. Correct major language errors.
5 L/S 5–10 min	*Group* Discuss which of the 3 towns you would most like to visit and why. Secretary notes majority view and reasons.	Circulate quickly. Stop any MT chat. Check use of *would like to . . ./you can . . .*
6 L/S 5 min	*Class* Group secretaries report preferences of groups and reasons.	Correct major errors only.
7 W 5 min	*Class* Fill in table with brief notes about our town.	Circulate. Answer questions, supply vocabulary, spellings, etc.
8 L/S 5 min	*Group* As 3 above, but our town.	As 3 above.
9 L/S 5 min	*Class* As 4 above, but our town.	As 4 above.
10 L/S/R/W 5 min	*Conclusion* Consider how to write a letter to a pen-friend in one of the 3 towns, discussing mutual visits. What to include. What language items to use. Take brief notes from BB.	Note points on BB as they come up: *I would like . . . Our town has . . . You can . . . There are/is . . .* Set homework deadline.

259

The best and the worst (See p. 261)

Joe Sanders has the most beautiful garden in our town. Nearly everybody enters for 'The Nicest Garden Competition' each year, but Joe wins every time. Bill Frith's garden is larger than Joe's. Bill works harder than Joe and grows more flowers and vegetables, but Joe's garden is more interesting. He has made neat paths and has built a wooden bridge over a pool. I like gardens too, but I do not like hard work. Every year I enter for the garden competition too, and I always win a little prize for the worst garden in the town!

Comprehension, Précis and Composition
Answer these questions *in not more than 45 words.*
1   Who has the best garden in town?
2   What does he win each year?
3   Who else has a fine garden?
4   Is Joe's better or not?
5   Is the writer's garden beautiful, or is it terrible?
6   What does he always win a prize for?

Key Structures
The best and the worst.
I want to tell you something about three girls in our class. The girls' names are Mary, Jane and Betty. Read these sentences carefully:
   Mary is tall, but Jane is taller. Jane is taller than Mary. Betty is very tall. She is the tallest girl in the class.
   Jane's handwriting is bad, but Mary's is worse. Betty's handwriting is very bad. It is the worst handwriting I have ever seen.
   The three girls collect photos of film stars. Mary hasn't many photos, but Jane has more. Jane has more photos than Mary. Betty has very many. She has the most.
   Mary's collection of photos is not very good. Jane's is better. Betty's collection is the best.
   Last week the three girls bought expensive dresses. Betty's dress was more expensive than Jane's. Mary's was more expensive than Betty's. Mary's dress was the most expensive.

Exercises
A   How do they compare?
These questions are about Mary, Jane and Betty. Answer each question with a complete sentence:
1   How does Mary's handwriting compare with Jane's?
2   How does Betty's handwriting compare with Mary's and Jane's?
3   How does Betty's dress compare with Jane's?
4   How does Mary's dress compare with Jane's and Betty's?

Lesson plan 2

Class: 2nd year

Objective: To practise comparative and superlative. The class learned these forms in 1st year and now need to revise and develop their use in context.

Materials/aids: Textbook: ALEXANDER, L. *Practice and Progress*. London: Longman, 1967. (Details of the text are given for the reader's convenience – obviously you would not give them in full in your lesson plan.) This is the first of two lessons to be given on Chapter 8 of the textbook, and deals only with the material on p27 (reproduced on p260 of this book). If there is too much in the lesson, omit Step 6 apart from the setting of the homework. The second of the two lessons would include use of supplementary material such as a table from a magazine comparing different makes of car.

Blackboard: Steps 1 and 2: Sketches to be built up during oral work, *not* prepared on BB beforehand.

 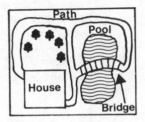

Step 4: substitution table prepared beforehand if enough BB space available, but hidden until needed. Alternatively, write on BB when beginning Step 4.

I think	the	most beautiful film star nicest song worst road best handwriting	in	our class our town the world the top 20	is	

Step 5: table prepared beforehand but hidden until needed. The words in parentheses are not written on the BB until the checking stage. The words not in parentheses are written in from the start.

	Betty	Jane	Mary
Height	(tallest)	(taller)	(tall)
Handwriting	(worst)	(bad)	(worse)

How many photos?	(most)	(more)	not many
Are photos good?	(best)	(better)	not very good
Dresses	(more expensive)	expensive	(most expensive)

Section, Skills and Time	Pupil activity	Teacher activity
1 L/S 5 min	*Introduction* Textbooks closed. Describe actual gardens known to them or examples drawn on BB. Gradual development to the point where individual PP give continuous oral description of about 4 sentences.	Question class, establish key vocabulary, build up BB sketch with help of PP.
2 L/S 5 min	*Comparative* Textbooks closed. Compare 2 gardens sketched on BB.	Question class, establish key grammar: *larger than . . .* *has more . . .* *than . . .*
3 L/S/R/W 10 min	*Comprehension* Textbook page 27 Read silently QQ 1–6, then read Joe Sanders passage to find answers. Write 1-word answers. Offer answers as T goes over exercise orally. Check own work.	Take them through Q1 orally and write answer on BB. Tell them to do the rest silently. Circulate. Call for answers, complete BB table.
4 L/S/R/W 10 min	*Superlative* Textbooks closed. Look at BB substitution table. Suggest orally Column 2 choice and Column 3 completion for 1st example. Write 3 true sentences built from S/Table in same way.	Take them through 1st item orally. Write complete sentence on BB. Circulate. Check that they do not copy table but write sentences from it.

Section, Skills and Time	Pupil activity	Teacher activity
5 L/S/R/W 10 min	*Key structures* Textbooks closed. Copy table from BB. Listen to passage, complete table with comparative or superlative in each space. Correct own work from BB.	Explain exercise. Read out passage up to *'tallest girl in the class.'* Check if PP have completed 1st row. Ask for answers and put on BB. Now continue to end of passage before checking rest.
6 L/S 5 min	*Exercise* at bottom of page 27. Do one or more orally according to time available.	Explain they will do the exercise in writing for homework. Instruct on layout and write 1st one on BB.

Further reading

VAN EK, J. *The threshold level in a European unit/credit system for modern language learning by adults.* Strasbourg: Council of Europe, 1975.

This attempts to outline a syllabus for adults whose needs and objectives can be defined very clearly. An attempt to do the same for the school learner is:

VAN EK, J. *The threshold level for modern language learning in schools.* Longman, 1976.

While the above are mainly concerned with the general learner, the following is a useful collection of articles by writers who are concerned with English for specific purposes (ESP) and in particular with learners needing English for academic or occupational purposes:

HOLDEN, S. (Ed.) *Teaching English for specific purposes.* London: Modern English Publications, 1978.

The following will be found useful both by British 'assistants' working abroad and by teachers of English abroad who have British 'assistants' working with them:

263

JORDAN, R. and MACKAY R. *A handbook for English language assistants.* Collins, 1976.

Next, two series which are useful sources of supplementary grammatical practice material. The British Council series is mainly intended for language laboratory use, but can also be used with a single tape recorder for class work, of course. The very wide range and large number of exercises in each unit, and the comprehensiveness of the series makes it highly likely that you will find material relevant to the particular problem of any class. *Elements of English* is a much smaller but very useful series consisting of small books of grammatical exercises in areas which commonly give difficulty to learners of English.

BRITISH COUNCIL. *English language units.* Longman.
Elements of English series. Longman.

Finally, one of the very few books which deal with lesson-planning for the EFL teacher:

DAVIES, P., ROBERTS, J. and ROSSNER, R. *Situational lesson plans: a handbook for teachers of English.* Macmillan, 1975.

Chapter 11: The teacher and the class

by Gerry Abbott

EXAMPLE 1

> Miss Handel's voice interrupted me. 'Right, have you all finished this?' she said, waving a hand at the blackboard. No-one answered. 'Good. Maria, clean the board, please.' I hadn't finished, but it didn't seem to matter very much. When Maria had finished, Miss Handel stood up and announced that we were going to do another exercise. She started writing on the board. . . .
>
> I noticed that Margarita was busy drawing something, so I stood up and leaned over her shoulder to see what it was: it was a rear view of Miss Handel, and it was really funny, so I snatched it and showed it to Eva. . . .

EXAMPLE 2

> Miss Teak's voice came from somewhere behind me. 'Good! I see you've all finished that . . .' (she looked at my exercise-book as she went past) . . . 'and you've done it very well. We'll do the second exercise and then check them both. Close your exercise-books and look at the board.' She went to the back of the room again.
>
> The blackboard was now clean except for three incomplete sentences. 'Look at the first sentence,' said Miss Teak. 'We'll do that one together, and then you'll do five more . . .'

In factories, operations are carried out in a certain sequence and at certain intervals so as to achieve maximum efficiency. Household kitchens can be laid out so that the user does not waste time and energy. You too might benefit from a 'time-and-motion study' of what goes on in the classroom! While Miss Teak's class was still busy finishing exercise one, for instance, she rubbed that out and wrote the beginnings of exercise two on the board, so as to avoid a delay in the proceedings, during which the girls would have had plenty of time to be distracted while her back was turned.

Two of the main causes of naughtiness among schoolchildren are boredom and fatigue. The main cause of boredom is having to listen to the teacher talking . . . and talking (yawn) . . . and talking; but doing *anything* for too long (more than about twenty minutes) can become

265

boring. If the activity is difficult and exasperating – as oral work can be – then the effect is not boredom so much as fatigue. In either case, the student will often 'switch off' as far as your lesson is concerned; he will find something more stimulating to do. If he only day-dreams, you are lucky. You can no doubt remember what further diversions are possible. . . .

The well-planned lesson might ensure that the class does not get bored or tired. But we do not always have time to prepare all our lessons thoroughly. At such times, with good class management, we can still give a successful lesson. For each of the sections below, I have chosen the five pieces of advice that seem most important to me in teaching forty typical schoolchildren in a typical schoolroom. I do not claim to deal with the maintenance of discipline (which varies from culture to culture); but the first section below offers precautions which, I have found, help to prevent indiscipline from occurring.

Part 1: Beginning the lesson

The inexperienced or nervous teacher tends to start teaching as soon as he enters the classroom. But there are several things to do first, which can 'pay off' in terms of avoiding trouble later on.

A Checking your equipment

Make sure you have got everything you need, and have not left something vital in the staff-room. Having to leave the classroom to get something can be disastrous.

B Checking the 'room equipment'

See that the blackboard is cleaned. See that there is enough chalk and a duster. See that the windows are adjusted to suit the weather or atmosphere in the room. Various pupils can do these chores simultaneously.

C Ensuring access

It is important to make sure that you will have access to every pupil in the class; in a large class, it is vital. Look at this plan, for example, which shows one route a teacher might follow when walking round the class:

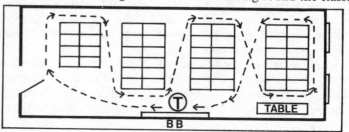

(Incidentally, if your students have their own desks you should make a seating-plan rather like this for each class, with the names of all students shown in their proper places. This helps you to identify faces and memorise names. Where students do not stay in the same seats every lesson, name-cards can be issued.)
This shows a traditional arrangement of desks, but the layout does ensure that you have access to every P in the class. Any neat arrangement that ensures this access is probably satisfactory. Why is this so important? For many reasons, chief among them:
(i) Because during oral work you need to be near a speaker in order to hear him clearly and, if necessary, correct him promptly.
(ii) Because during silent reading and writing you need to be able to answer individuals without disturbing everyone, point out mistakes of spelling, etc. and generally help. The part of the lesson devoted to writing offers the best opportunity for individual teaching.
(iii) Because the least interested pupils tend either (a) to sit farthest away from you or (b) to push movable desks into groups so that they can all be close together.

These are the most likely to cause trouble. A student finds it less easy to play/talk/pass things round, etc. if you are liable to appear by his shoulder at any moment.
So, if necessary, spend a minute or two getting the desks positioned satisfactorily. For a much smaller class, an open square or semi-circular arrangement is suitable.

D Reducing the distance

If there are more desks than students, get the students at the back to fill the desks in front. (Why tax your voice unnecessarily?) Make sure they bring their books, pens, etc. One exception: if you suffer from persistent latecomers, try leaving empty a few desks at the front of the class. Latecomers must always come to you and explain/apologise (in English if possible!) and then sit in one of the empty desks at the front.

E Removing distractions

See to it that pupils have on their desks only those things you want them to have. If you want to start with some purely oral revision, desks should be clear. Do not begin until there is silence, and attention is focused on you – even if you are only going to deal with the class register. The first few minutes of your teaching are usually the crucial ones, when the nature of the lesson is established and its content made clear.

Part 2: During the lesson

A Keeping on the move

For the first five minutes you may find it necessary to stay at the front, e.g. because you are using the BB. But as soon as you can, *move!* Get used to 'teaching on the move'. If you have not yet learnt the names of your class (and learning them helps enormously in class management), you can nominate easily as you go around. *Do not* get into this situation:

T: And what happened next? You. (pointing)
P1: Me, sir?
T: No, the boy in front with the . . .
P2: Me, sir?
T: No! The boy next to you. Yes, you.

A distant student is an uninvolved student.

B Keeping the channels open

A student who is entirely unmotivated is rather like a radio with a flat battery: you can try any channel you like, but you will get little response. Some students are not motivated and you have to charge their batteries; and even the motivated ones need a boost. Three ways of maintaining attention and momentum can be labelled 'interest', 'challenge' and 'enjoyment' – the overlap among them is obvious.

1 Interest. It is well known that one should, whenever possible, choose topics, examples and visual aids which reflect the interests of the class. What many teachers are not so good at is *maintaining* interest during an activity. One simple rule can help: do not put all your cards on the table. That is, whenever it is possible, you should withhold an outcome from the class until the right time comes. A simple example: if you have a set of four pictures (perhaps for a composition, perhaps for grammar work), do not put them all up at once . . . put them up like this:

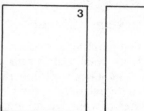

Every time you reveal the next picture, get further practice. Curiosity is maintained. Even if pictures 2, 3 and 4 prove to be most uninteresting in outcome, the students do not know that yet!

Another example: if you are using a handout on which there is (say) a story, cut off the last paragraph and let the class know what you have done. Guessing the ending is both fun and good practice, and again students will be inquisitive. The last part of a taped dialogue can also be withheld for some time.

2 Challenge.   There is no doubt that traditional methods of teaching EFL have been too mechanical and mindless. Give the students' intelligence some work. Challenge them to deduce the meanings of words from their context in a passage; challenge them to formulate their own grammar rules, given a set of examples; challenge them to abstract information from a stretch of rapid speech; challenge them to solve problems written in English, e.g. the one on page 270; and try something that is – as you take care to tell them! – 'a bit difficult, but I'm sure you can do it'. (There is ample research evidence to show that the performance of students is at least partly dependent on the teacher's confidence in their ability.)

3 Enjoyment.   There should be a little fun in every lesson, however simple it is. Performing orally in a foreign language is rather a tense, even embarrassing, business. If you doubt this, observe how easy it is to make a language-learning class laugh. The release of tension is welcome. A little good-natured 'ham' acting by the teacher can pave the way for more successful practice.

The learner's main channels of information and confirmation in the classroom are shown here. It is fairly obvious that the teacher (T) should speak clearly enough and simply enough, so that Channel 1 is 'open'. But do not forget Channel 2. Our pupil needs to be able to hear what other pupils (PP) say in answer to a question, for example. If he does not know the answer but wants to; and if, as is often the case, he is rather shy, he will find the following very frustrating:

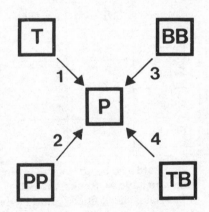

T: What happened?
P: (mumble, mumble)
T: Yes! Very good. Now let's continue . . .

Either make pupils speak up or repeat the answer yourself.

Problem-solving
This is about four men who live near Manchester. One is a policeman; one is a doctor; one is a carpenter and the other is a farmer. Find out the name of each one.

Alan's son broke his leg the other day when Alan was not at home, so the boy's mother had to fetch the doctor. She discovered that the doctor's sister was Brian's wife. On his way to work, Brian often sees the policeman.
The farmer is not married yet, but he is going to get married next week. Colin buys eggs from him.

Use this table to help you.
Put √ for *is*
    X for *isn't*
    ? for *we don't know*

Name	Married	Carpenter	Farmer	Policeman	Doctor
Alan					
Brian					
Colin					
David					

It should also be obvious that those at the back need to be able to read what you have written on the BB. When you are walking round the back of the class, check quickly that legibility is good – and that you have not made any mistakes for transmission on Channel 3!

Lastly, Channel 4 – the textbook (TB). However bad you think it is, do not neglect it if it is a 'set' book (i.e. officially prescribed). Try to refer to it at least once every lesson. The exams may be based on the content of the book rather than on your own handouts, and if so the pupils will know this. When using the textbook (or your handouts, or any visual material that is in the students' hands) never say anything important while they are looking at it. They will probably not take in what you say. Give clear instructions *before* issuing handouts, opening books or starting written work. If you forget some important point, or can see that pupils have misunderstood, stop the whole class, make them look up and then clarify the point carefully. Sight can easily block out sound.

C Putting questions to the class

There are various occasions when you need to get oral feedback from a class, e.g.:
—when checking their comprehension of a reading passage or taped material;
—when eliciting examples from them; and
—when checking their answers to a written exercise.

When we put an oral question to a class of any size, it would be helpful to find out *how many* know the answer. But this cannot be done efficiently if students give oral answers. If you simply stand in front of the class and ask a question, it will be interpreted as an invitation to all. Pupils will normally either shout out their answers or put up their hands; or both may happen. This can be noisy and can become unruly; and in any case, you will not be able to tell how many did not answer, or did not answer correctly.

For this reason many teachers use the 'Hands up!' system when questioning the class. The system is so widely used, in fact, that both students and teachers follow it without thinking whether it is necessary. Think about it. Suppose you are facing a class of 40. You ask a question. 20 hands go up. Quite pleased at the response, you pick one. You get a correct answer. You say 'Good!' and continue the lesson. What have you found out? Simply that one of the 40 students knew the correct answer. No-one ever knows the true state of knowledge in a class, of course. But the situation in your class at that time could, for example, have been like this:

Students who would, if you had asked them, . . .	Was hand up?		Totals
	Yes	No	
have given the right answer.	10	10[(i)]	20
have given a wrong answer (thinking that it was right).	5	5	10
have given no answer (because they didn't know).	5[(ii)]	5	10
Totals	20	20	40

Notes

(i) This situation is not very unusual. Students may have reasons for *not* putting a hand up, including

(a) not wanting to appear to be a 'goody-goody' or swot;

(b) being rather uninterested or bored;

(c) finding the question so easy that they go on to the next one; and so on.

(ii) This too is quite common. I can remember putting my hand up in order not to stand out as one of the few who did not know the answer. There is, of course, a very good chance that you will not be asked. Also, my teachers quite often asked those who did not have their hands up: this was an added incentive for me to raise mine.

The number of raised hands, then, does not indicate the number who know; it indicates the number who *think* they know, plus the number who wish to *appear* to know. Likewise, those whose hands are not raised are not necessarily ignorant of the answer. You should consider how it benefits you or your students when you say 'Put your hands up!' My own practice is to train my students not to raise their hands or call out answers, but to wait until I nominate an answerer. This does have one advantage, as you will see in (ii) below:

(i) I ask a question.

(ii) Short pause as I begin strolling among students.

No-one knows who I am going to nominate, so everyone tries to frame an answer.

(iii) I nominate an answerer.

(Of course, I encourage students to put their hands up when they want to *ask* questions.)

One final point about the questions *you* ask. Please encourage your students to give answers (and not statements) in reply. The so-called 'long answer' or 'full answer' was invented by language-teachers and does not exist outside the language class. When you are checking the understanding of a passage, for instance, an answer is all that is needed:

T:	What did Boxer try to do? . . . Juan?
Juan:	Escape.
T:	Yes. And did he escape, Carmen?
Carmen:	No.
T:	Right. Why not? . . . Carlos?
Carlos:	Because he was weak.
T:	Good . . . etc.

If Carlos says, 'Boxer did not escape, because he was weak', commend him for the accuracy of the information, but get him to give you just the answer.

When you are doing oral practice and you want your students to produce statements, do not ask questions. Just point to the picture, or

272

give the number, or give a cue-word . . . there are many ways of getting statements produced orally. Asking questions is a most inappropriate way.

D Getting PP to read aloud

Unless your students are teacher-trainees (teachers should be trained to read aloud fluently and expressively) avoid asking them to read aloud.

I would recommmend that you read one page (page 177) of the book by Bright and McGregor listed at the end of this chapter, and then look back at what is said about it in Chapter 4 of *this* book. 'Reading aloud round the class' is so popular, however, that you may well have rejected our advice already. 'There's no harm in it', you may say. Perhaps not. Teachers like it because it is so easy: it needs no preparation and fills a lot of time. Students quite like it in many places because it is restful: they can 'switch off' and the chances of being disturbed are small. There is no great harm in it, just as there is no great harm in telling the tide to turn back; it is just pointless.

E Correcting and marking written work

There is much to be said for getting written work corrected (and if necessary, marked) in class, immediately after it has been done. To mention only two advantages;

(i) the student gets immediate feedback about what is correct and what is incorrect; and

(ii) the teacher does not have to stay up so late, marking the work at home!

There are many written exercises in which there is on the whole only one right answer per item; these can certainly be marked in class. When almost everybody seems to have finished (you cannot wait for the very slowest ones), you can get pupils to exchange exercise books. Three simple ways are shown below:

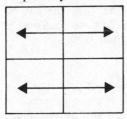 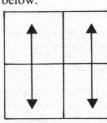 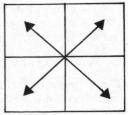

You then indicate the answers clearly on the BB. One policy for marking is that if the sentence is grammatically correct, a mark is awarded. If something is wrongly spelt, it should be corrected but no mark deducted. If marks are not necessary, you may wish not to bother with them but to concentrate simply on correction. On the other hand, if marks are officially required, you might need (at least sometimes) to do the marking yourself; and you should always note where the major difficulties occurred.

Compositions (unless they are totally controlled ones) cannot be marked in such a way, of course. But a lot of correcting could be avoided, and the students' exercise-book or file would look a lot neater, if drafts were done first, in pencil and/or on rough paper. Corrections are made as you go around offering help. If the composition is being done in pairs or groups, each member offers corrections for the draft. What gets written out as a 'fair copy' is a much better version than the original draft; so there are fewer red marks to make on it.

We should remember that the student's exercise book or file is not just a record of his work; it is revision-material, and he should therefore find it a clear and reliable source of information at the end of the year.

Part 3: Ending the lesson

A Finishing 'clearly'

Teacher and student alike find it unsatisfactory to stop in the middle of something (an exercise, a dialogue, a paragraph, etc.). If you see that time is running out and that you are not going to get through everything you planned to do, stop at the 'cleanest' break in activity and do not continue with that material. There may be (say) six minutes left.

To fill that time, you should have at your fingertips a number of brief, enjoyable activities. Get any unnecessary books and equipment put away and start one new activity briefly, whether it is a song, a game, a contest, a poem, a puzzle or whatever. Any of the books of language-teaching games listed at the end of this chapter will give you plenty of ideas. But ensure that the activity you choose is, indeed, brief!

B Observing the bell

Do not go on with the lesson after the bell has gone. It is better to be ready a minute early than to arouse resentment in the class. Learning is just as tiring as teaching, and the students need their break.

C Cleaning the blackboard

This is quite important for the new teacher. It is not just that it is courteous to ensure that nobody else is forced to clean up your mess; it is also a way of ensuring that no other member of staff sees any mistakes you may have made! Get a student to do it while **D** and **E** below are also being seen to.

D Replacing furniture

You may have been working in a room that 'belongs' to someone else; or perhaps all the desks in the school are arranged in a traditional way. If

274

you rearranged them at the beginning of your lesson, get students to put them back where they were.

E   Leaving the classroom

If your students are immediately going to have another lesson in the same room, simply make sure they are sitting (or standing, if that is usual) quietly before you leave. If they are going to leave the room you should ensure that they do so in a reasonably orderly way. Perhaps just standing by the door when you have dismissed the class will be enough to prevent a stampede. If you think not, then dismiss only one group or row at a time. If it is a mid-morning or mid-day break, make sure that all books, pens, etc. have been put away.

A final word. If you are dealing with adult students or small classes, or if you are working in a country where school discipline offers no great problems, you may find some of the above advice superfluous. But if you are in doubt . . . well, it is better to be safe than sorry!

Further reading

JORDAN, R. and MACKAY, R.   *A handbook for English language assistants.*   Collins, 1976.

Mainly for the British teacher beginning to teach in Europe. It concentrates on the teaching of oral English.

MARLAND, M.   *The craft of the classroom.*   Heinemann Educational Books, 1975.

Full of very sensible and practical advice especially for those teaching in European schools. It is not just for language teachers. Nor are the next two:

MCCREE, H.   *Preparations for teaching.*   Ginn, 1969.

As the introduction says, 'mainly for untrained or inexperienced teachers taking up appointments in . . . developing countries.' Similar in aim is:

DODD, W.   *The teacher at work.*   Oxford University Press, 1970.

For games I suggest (in order of preference):

LEE, W.   *Language teaching games and contests.*   Oxford University Press, 2nd edition, 1979.

HILL, L. and FIELDEN, R.   *English language teaching games for adult students.*   Book 1: Elementary, Book 2: Advanced. Evans, 1979.

WRIGHT, A., BUCKBY, M. and BETTERIDGE, D.   *Games for language learning.*   Cambridge University Press, 1980.

You ought to own or have access to at least one of these three.

Finally, do not forget to read page 177 (at least!) of:

BRIGHT, J. and MCGREGOR, G.   *Teaching English as a second language.*   Longman, 1970.

Chapter 12: Putting things in perspective

by Peter Wingard

In this closing chapter I shall not try to summarise the rest of the book or to find some magic formula which will cover it all. What I aim to do is to round the book off in a number of ways.

First, I shall briefly discuss two important trends of recent years, those towards *individualisation* and *authenticity*. Next I shall review the role of two old familiar friends which have made many appearances in this book and will here take their curtain call: *grammar teaching* and *audio-visual aids*. In the final section, I shall suggest where you can obtain further *information and advice* on matters discussed in this book and all other English-teaching concerns; and lastly urge you, above all else, to remain open-minded and to have the courage of your own convictions as an English teacher.

Part 1: Individualisation

In recent years there has been much discussion and experiment concerning the individualisation of instruction in various ways. Obviously students differ in their interests, their rate of learning and their preferred ways or strategies of learning. Can teaching methods and materials take more account of this? One approach which has tried to do so is *programmed learning*. The matter to be learned is divided into very small steps, and set out in such a way that the student can work on his own. Each step includes a self-check to see if the step has been mastered. If it has not, further practice or instruction is followed by a re-check.

A linear programme is the same for all students. They simply vary in the time taken to complete it. A branching programme provides extra 'loops' for those needing more practice or instruction at particular points. A loop is an added step covering the same point as the preceding step but in a different way. Thus the content of a branching programme is still basically the same for all students. It is the method of work rather than the content which is individual in programmed learning.

At one time it was hoped that this approach would greatly reduce the need for skilled foreign language teachers, through reliance on language laboratories, teaching machines and written programmes. This quickly proved to be an illusion. Spoken language is a *social* activity which cannot be fully developed by individuals working in isolation. The novelty of working with a machine or a programme wears off rather soon, and boredom may set in. Also you cannot *really* hold a conversation with a machine. In a normal conversation you often cannot predict for certain the response of your partner. A later generation of machines, now beginning to emerge with micro-chip electronics, may be able to produce a variety of responses according to what is said to it. But this will still be a long way short of real conversation, and will not be a substitute for face-to-face spoken practice, though it will help in preparing students for such practice.

Programmed learning is a behaviouristic approach to individualisation, and has gone into eclipse – too much so, in my view, despite its limitations – with the decline of behaviourist influence on foreign language teaching. There is surely a place for programmed learning in aspects other than conversational exchange – for example, in reading and in pronunciation.

Another approach to individualisation is what we may call a *discovery* approach. This has flourished considerably in recent years in teaching some school subjects in some developed countries, but mostly in subject-matter learning rather than skills learning. It has been particularly common in science and social studies. In this type of learning students are set to work individually or in small co-operative groups. The essential point is that they are expected to discover things for themselves rather than be fed every piece of information by the teacher. This often involves discussion, experiment, measurement and investigation outside the classroom, as well as reference to books and other published sources. A discovery approach has obvious advantages in variety, interest and the training it gives in self-reliance and co-operative work. It has dangers too. In science, for example, it could result in gaps in basic knowledge. It needs enormous resources of learning material, and if these are inadequate it can result in time-wasting and superficiality. These last two can also result if a discovery approach is used with students who are poorly motivated, or lack the basic skills required.

Obviously such an approach does not lend itself so easily to the learning of skills, such as using a foreign language or playing a musical instrument. Thus, where a discovery approach has been widely applied to 'subject-matter' subjects, this has resulted in unpopularity of 'skills' subjects like foreign language. In the general climate of permissiveness in such countries, individualisation has sometimes gone to the extent of declaring that study should be entirely 'learner-centred'. The learner chooses whether he wishes to study a particular subject or not. If he decides to study a subject, he decides what objectives and standards he wishes to set himself. Furthermore, he chooses from a menu of learning activities those most suited to his own preferred strategies for reaching his own goals. The teacher becomes basically a counsellor.

Such a plan might work with well-motivated adults. But it has obvious problems. One is the enormous resources of learning material required to suit everyone's choices. Another is the doubt whether the student is always the best judge of his own needs and capacities, in a field where his experience is slight.

On a more limited scale, however, you might find opportunities of using a discovery approach at times with your intermediate or advanced students. An example would be a small project where groups of students are set to discover information about traffic at several different points on local roads, each group taking a different point. The aims would be to practise conversation, discussion and perhaps also writing, in relation to such a topic. First the whole class discusses a number of matters, such as:

—What different types of vehicle do we need to count?
—At what times of day should we count to get the clearest overall picture?
—Is it important to know which direction each vehicle is going in?

Each group could then be asked to go away and, under its group leader, make a plan for collecting the information in one week with the least possible waste of time and trouble. They might consider such points as:

—Can some of the counting be done on the way to and from school?
—How can the work best be divided among the group to get accurate results? Should we work in pairs?
—What sort of record sheet shall we need?

The groups might then be brought together again, and the secretary of each group, who would have written the group decisions down, could report. After discussion a common plan could be drawn up. The information would be collected during the following days. The groups would meet to draw up their findings. The findings would be presented to the whole class and discussed.

Obviously a project such as that described pre-supposes that the students have had a great deal of previous practice working in this way on much smaller bits of discovery, and will in fact employ English in their discussions.

Another aspect of individualisation is the English for Specific Purposes (ESP) movement. At the heart of this lies the belief that it is more effective to plan an English course on the basis of the predicted needs of an individual or group than to teach everyone the same linguistic matter. The English language needs of a Japanese airline stewardess are obviously not at all the same as those of a Japanese electronics engineer. ESP is a large subject with a large literature, and I cannot attempt to deal with it here. I just want to mention a couple of persistent problems. One is that, whereas a 'learner-centred' approach seems to assume that the learner always knows best, ESP often seems to assume that others – the learner's boss, English teacher or academic supervisor in his subject field – always know best. The student's actual wishes, likes and dislikes are often ignored. Another problem is how far to carry specialisation. If you try to give the Japanese electronics engineer nothing but the English of electronics, you may not find an English teacher who can handle this adequately. Or if the electronics engineer is a near-beginner in English, the language of electronics may not be the most effective medium to start teaching him English.

To many teachers, even in developed countries, much of the above discussion about individualisation may appear to lack contact with the realities of their classrooms. You may feel that such ideas are pure 'pie-in-the-sky' as far as you are concerned. But it would, I think, be unwise to dismiss the whole subject from consideration. The fact remains, as I said earlier, that students do differ in their interests, speed of learning and strategies of learning. Foreign language teaching usually takes too little account of this fact, and anything you can do to take practical account of it you should not neglect. After all, primary school teachers in many countries do so all the time.

Part 2: Authenticity

Another topic that has come to the fore in recent years is the authenticity of learning material. Sometimes English teachers discussing this restrict the term 'authentic' to material actually used in a mother tongue situation; for example, an actual tape recording of a BBC weather forecast, or an actual newspaper advertisement for Ford cars. Many teachers would probably agree, however, that a course-writer would be producing 'authentic' material if he made up a weather forecast or an advertisement, provided his versions were pretty much like the real thing. But as soon as he started simplifying the language, or regularising it in some way, the advocates of authenticity would criticise or reject his material. Extreme followers of this view argue that *all* language teaching material, even for beginners, should be authentic as here defined. One way they justify this is by arguing that the learning of a foreign language is in essence the same as the learning of the mother tongue by a young child. In both cases, they say, the learner constructs a system of rules on the basis of his inborn ideas of how language in general works, plus his experience of the language in question. As he learns more, he keeps on revising this system of rules, gradually getting closer to the full language. Each stage of this process is referred to as an 'inter-language'. The child, so it is argued, learns the MT in this way by exposure to the authentic language, and the foreign learner will likewise learn best from authentic language, even if he does not fully understand it at first.

This argument is a dubious one. The young English child does not experience the same range of English as the English adult. Research has shown, for example, how mothers modify their language when talking to their small children. The process of adaptation is a two-way one. In addition, there are all the differences between learning the mother tongue in a natural situation and learning the foreign language in a classroom situation. These differences are not removed simply by adopting authentic material.

The call for authenticity has a positive value, however, provided it is not carried to extremes. It warns us against teaching language far removed from anything that would occur in a real situation outside the language classroom. For example, the following exchange, apart from the first question and answer, is non-authentic in any situation I can think of:

A	Is this a radio set?	B	Yes, it is.
A	Is it an electric heater?	B	No, it isn't.
A	Is it a radio set or an electric heater?	B	It's a radio set.

Once the answer to the first question is known, the later questions and answers are pointless. Moreover, it is easy to find more authentic ways of using a series of questions and answers similar to these in grammatical structure. Try it. If you are successful, there is no adequate reason for using such a non-authentic sequence as that above in teaching.

For advanced aural practice, authenticity demands that we expose students to unscripted conversation containing such typical features as the use of incomplete grammatical structures, fillers, pauses occurring after structure words, etc, and not restrict a class to hearing idealised scripted conversation. But this does not mean that the idealised forms have no place in teaching. They are easier to grasp, and therefore useful at a less advanced stage, as a basis on which later to recognise departures from them.

The same applies to other types of simplification. For example, a real description of a scientific process in English may contain active and passive, modals, perfect aspect, etc. This is no reason why the *first* descriptions of scientific processes in English which we present to students should not be restricted to Simple Present passive verbs. In this way we lay a foundation for the understanding of more complex descriptions of scientific processes. In so doing we depart from absolute authenticity in the interests of good grading.

This is a familiar situation for the English teacher. Two useful criteria – in this case authenticity and grading – give us conflicting answers, and we have to make up our minds between them on grounds of common sense. This is not to say we can ignore theoretical criteria, but that they do not always give a clear answer to a practical question. We have to weigh them while considering the practical demands of the situation.

Part 3: Grammar teaching

The word 'grammar' has been used in many different ways by various people when talking about language and language teaching. I would like to discuss a few of these ways here.

First, the use of the word 'grammar' in talking about 'grammar-translation' methods. 'Translation' is clear enough, but what does 'grammar' mean here? To a large extent it means the grammar of *words*. The student is presented with tables showing grammatical inflections like *talk, talks, talked* and *cat, cats, cat's, cats'*. Irregular sets are listed such as *eat, eats, ate, eaten*. Words are classified into parts of speech. Certain functional categories such as subject, object, complement are defined. Some rules are given about the use and combination of all these elements into clauses and sentences. The learner then struggles to translate a foreign language text into the mother tongue, slowly and painfully, trying to use bits of this grammatical information when in difficulty. Anyone taught exclusively by such methods is unlikely to acquire much skill or fluency in speaking, listening to or writing the foreign language. Thus it is not surprising that grammar-translation methods are so widely condemned nowadays. Of course this does not mean that we should *never* use translation or present such grammatical information. But as main methods they are unlikely to succeed.

Grammar also plays a leading part in the structural approach. The structure referred to in this phrase is of course grammatical structure. Mostly it is sentence structure or clause structure. Course-makers have listed what they consider the most important grammatical elements. Terminology is unimportant in the teaching, but grammatical patterning is all-important. A thoroughgoing attempt is made to place these grammatical structures in a practical teaching order, and to teach each one by drilling examples of it rather than by describing them. This kind of grammar is still the basis of the majority of course-books in use for teaching English. Its dangers have been mentioned in Chapter 1 and elsewhere. It can lead to mechanical drill which can be boring and easily forgotten. Even if the students remember the drill they may be unable to apply the grammatical point of it in a communicative way.

But it has yet to be shown that a better approach exists for beginners. Despite widespread disillusion with excessive pattern practice, the fact remains that command of the grammatical structure is quite essential to mastery of the language. We do not attain this just by understanding explanations. A clear explanation can provide a flash of understanding and an easy-to-remember term or label can provide a means of jogging the memory later. But practice makes perfect. Advocates of 'notional' teaching mostly agree that plenty of practice is needed for mastery of the grammatical patterns by which notions and functions are realised. The great advantage of the structural approach is that it does try systematically to teach the kinds of sentence we want students to learn to use. It is a caricature of the structural approach to say that it is not at all concerned with communication. Intelligent teachers and course-makers have never limited themselves to conducting mindless mechanical drills but have always tried to include situational practice, and check that students understand the meaning of what they say.

The problem of grading remains, whether you adopt a structural approach or a notional approach. You cannot just sweep it aside by adopting a notional syllabus and introducing an unlimited number of different ways of expressing each notion in that syllabus. A good structural syllabus teaches *one* important use of each structure initially. Later it may come back to the same structure to teach another use of it. A good notional syllabus should likewise be selective. It should normally teach initially only *one* grammatical realisation of each notion for productive purposes. It may also, at the same stage, teach one or two other realisations of the same notion for receptive purposes only. But great care is needed in planning this, if the students are not to finish up in a grand grammatical muddle.

Then there is grammar as it is often taught to students to whom the language is their mother tongue. Here the teaching is both theoretical and practical, both descriptive and prescriptive. The theoretical part gives them a terminology for all the grammatical units and teaches them to analyse sentences using this terminology. The practical part gives them rules to follow on points where there seem to be alternative forms. Often the forms used by the students are denounced as 'uneducated'. Sometimes a more reasonable type of advice is given: 'This form is only suitable for conversation; in formal English you must use that one.' The above kinds of descriptive and prescriptive teaching are also often used in teaching EFL and ESL. It seems necessary when sorting out difficulties which are bound to occur, and when reminding students to use forms appropriate to the different uses of English. But it seems unjustifiable to use more than a very small part of our time on such description and prescription when our students have so little time to practise the actual use of the language. And the practical rules we do use must be based on an appreciation of up-to-date usage, not simply on ancient traditions.

One school of grammar of which much has been heard in recent years is 'transformational-generative' (TG) grammar. This tries to set out rules in a far more rigorous, logical way than previous grammars. The aim is that, if properly constructed, rules will generate a full structural description of any sentence, enabling us to form or decode that sentence correctly. The transformational part describes more precisely than any previous system the relationship between structures which appear different on the surface, and the difference between structures which appear the same on the surface. The above is not even an adequate definition of TG grammar, let alone an account of it. TG grammar is also a theory of how children learn their mother tongue. However, what has been said is enough to enable me to suggest that TG grammar does not claim to support any particular approach to teaching foreign languages. Exercises that we can describe as 'transformational' existed many years before TG was thought of. We find them in many courses based on a structural approach. One common type requires the learner to 'rewrite the sentences in the passive voice'. Such an exercise shares with TG one serious weakness: the failure to emphasise that the active and passive forms are not just two alternative ways of making the same statement, but differ in meaning and use. If the passive is chosen it is often because we are not interested in who did the action, but in the action itself, as in much scientific and technological English: 'The mixture is heated to a temperature of 200°C'. If the passive with *by* is chosen, however, it often means that we *are* particularly interested in who or what did the action: 'The child was knocked down by a motor-cycle'. The beginning of a sentence is most often for known information, the end for new information. So if we already know who has been injured, it is natural to begin our next statement with the child, and finish with the motor-cycle. This we can do by using the passive with *by*. Surely this sort of explanation is not too abstract for our students, and will help them understand and remember the grammatical point; whereas an unexplained transformational exercise will rightly seem to them mere pointless manipulation.

Part 4: Audio-visual aids

While aware of the importance of audio-visual aids, we have thought it best to refer to them wherever they seemed appropriate throughout this book, rather than bring a large number of uses together in a special chapter. We regard them as servants, not masters. We do not favour the approach of starting out with a bag of tricks – cassette recorder, overhead projector, slides, flannel-board, language laboratory, film, video-tape recorder, and so on – and then looking for ways of using them just because we have them. The need has to come first, and the need decides the manner of use. A few general remarks will be made here, however.

Television, film, video-tape and the now rather neglected but useful radio are extremely good for helping motivation, giving practice in understanding the spoken language in interesting situations, taking the students outside the range of classroom experience. Where materials for these media are available, there will usually also be advice for teachers on their use. The most important thing to look out for here is advice on how to integrate the media materials into your total teaching programme. They should not be just a separate treat for the students. There should be ideas on how they can be used to stimulate spoken and written practice, and how they fit into the whole English syllabus. Sometimes programme planners have ignored this point, and made it difficult for teachers to use the programmes without feeling that they are making it impossible to complete an already overcrowded syllabus.

On language laboratories I will confine myself to one point. Before deciding to install one, a college or school should look closely at the question of cost-effectiveness. Will it justify the expense, and the restriction of one room to just this purpose? How many hours a week will it be used? How often will each class be able to use it? Once a week is very little. Anything less seems hardly worth while. Would the money be better spent on tape-recorders and overhead projectors or slide projectors? Who will be in charge of organising the work? What will be the effect on teachers' work-loads? What will be the position regarding maintenance? What has been the experience of other schools or colleges comparable to your own? Very careful thought and planning on such matters are essential if a language laboratory is not to become a white elephant.

With purely visual aids the quality most desirable is flexibility. The printed wall picture lacks this entirely and consequently spends most of its time in the cupboard, or hanging unnoticed on a wall. The overhead projector is very flexible in that you can change a display by adding or taking away parts of it as the students are looking at it. The flannel-board is even more flexible in that you can not only add and take away but also move parts of the display. This makes it particularly good for telling a story or describing a process. The blackboard can also be very flexible but is suitable mainly for displays you can produce swiftly, as they have all to be erased each time. Flash-cards are useful in beginning reading, but have the same inflexibility as wall pictures. Flash-boards (strips of blackboard about 1 metre by 20 centimetres) are better because you can write and erase any word, phrase or sentence.

The cheapness and portability, combined with reasonable quality, of the best cassette tape recorders make them a marvellous boon to the English teacher. We no longer need to lug heavy reel-to-reel recorders about. No more worries about mains supply, adaptors and extension cables. And the price has come down to the point where many schools can afford several machines. No English teacher worth his salt will be satisfied until he has managed to get one. Once you begin to use it, you will find it a constant companion in teaching listening comprehension, pronunciation and oral fluency. It even has uses in teaching reading and writing. For example, to develop fluency in reading, get students to follow a printed text as they listen to a recording of it. In writing, a recorded text is a good way of giving dictation. It should be recorded at normal speaking speed, without special pausing. In this way the students will hear normal speech, pausing, intonation, etc, unlike the artificial effect of sentences broken up for dictation. A little practice with the start, stop and re-wind buttons will enable you to break up the passage and repeat sentences at will.

For the teacher, the most important aids are the syllabus and the course-book. Syllabus design and materials production are complex matters, which should take into account every factor in a teaching situation. Most teachers are not expected to plan their whole course from scratch. You may have a quite detailed syllabus to work to, or a mere sketch. A good detailed syllabus is an enormous help. Clear objectives are the first essential. These lead the course planner on to the detailed listing and ordering of learning items and activities. A too rigid syllabus, however, can be terribly frustrating. Course design and materials production are long-term and co-operative enterprises which we do not attempt to discuss in detail in this book. They cannot be successful if carried out in haste, or imposed by a so-called expert with inadequate consultation, or with inadequate knowledge of local conditions.

The most important aid of all is the textbook. You may find it odd to see it referred to as an aid. In some places it seems rather to be a god, or at least a dictator. Many teachers, probably most, plan all or nearly all their lessons round a basic course-book, whether by choice or by compulsion. This has its dangers, but is basically a sensible thing in most circumstances. It ensures a reasonably well graded progression from year to year, and a rough parity in progression (though not in success of learning) between parallel classes all over the country. It makes life tolerable for the teacher, who would otherwise face an impossible task of collecting and creating all his own material. On the other hand, a rigid lock-step course which accounts for every class hour, every page of which must be worked through in an exactly prescribed manner, is highly undesirable. Teachers should be free, within reasonable limits, to vary the diet supplied by the basic course, adapting, discarding and supplementing. This is what justifies us in calling the textbook an aid, even though the most important aid. In the same way, we hope our own book will be an aid to teachers, in helping them to provide this variation in the basic diet of the students.

Part 5: Information and advice

The teaching of English as an international language is a field in which ideas are developing at a tremendous pace, and materials are being published in a flood. It is difficult for the busy teacher to keep up with developments. As well as matters directly concerned with classroom teaching, which we have concentrated on in this book, there are broader areas and also more specialised areas which you may wish to investigate in the future – areas such as applied linguistics, course design and materials production.

Luckily we have in the profession both nationally and internationally some excellent journals and teachers' associations which can help us to keep up-to-date and develop our knowledge. There are publishers who will provide catalogues and specimen copies on request. There are public examining bodies from whom you may wish to seek information and specimen papers. Rather than give here a long list of these and other organisations, I prefer, in view of teachers' varying needs, to give just two addresses. If you do not find what you are looking for in this book or in any other readily available source, I strongly recommend you to write to one or both of these addresses.

The first, covering all United Kingdom-based activities and also providing world-wide coverage, is:

The English Language Division,
The British Council,
10 Spring Gardens,
London SW1A 2BN.

In conjunction with the Centre for Information on Language Teaching (CILT), this organisation maintains the best language-teaching library in Britain, including unrivalled collections of material relevant to the teaching of English as an international language. Any teacher able to visit London should not fail to spend a few hours, or preferably several days, in this library. The British Council produces a steady stream of useful publications. It can give you up-to-date and expert information about journals, associations, publishers, examining bodies and other matters concerned with EFL and ESL. It can provide by post bibliographies on many aspects of English teaching, and advice in answer to queries.

The other address, covering all USA-based activities and providing a similar range of facilities, is:

The Center for Applied Linguistics,
1611 North Kent Street,
Arlington,
Virginia 22209.

When you have obtained all the information and advice you can from every source, from theorists and practitioners, writers, lecturers and fellow-teachers, not forgetting your students, the question of what you do with it all remains in your own hands. This is a matter of judgement and of having the courage of your convictions. We should not be too ready to jump on the latest band-wagon and condemn all previous schools of thought. On the other hand, inertia and cynicism make too many teachers old and dead before their time. There must be a happy medium somewhere between these extremes.

Further reading

This short list is intended to provide starting points for those who would like to pursue further some of the issues discussed in this book.

PALMER, H. *The principles of language study.* Oxford University Press, 1968.

Palmer's book was first published in 1917. It remains one of the wisest books available on foreign language learning and teaching.

HOWATT, A. *Programmed learning and the language teacher.* Longman, 1969.

Although programmed learning is currently unfashionable in language teaching circles because of its links with behaviourism, it seems likely that developments such as mixed ability teaching, 'self-access' learning and micro-chip technology will revive interest in it. This book provides a clear introduction.

BRUMFIT, C. and JOHNSON, K. (Eds.) *The communicative approach to language teaching.* Oxford University Press, 1979.

A stimulating collection of articles, particularly in regard to the question of authenticity in teaching materials.

ENGLISH-TEACHING INFORMATION CENTRE *ELT documents: projects and syllabus design.* British Council, 1979.

Syllabus design from the viewpoint of attempting to fit English courses to the specific needs of particular groups of learners.

STEVICK, E. *Memory, meaning and method.* Newbury House, 1979.

A balanced and sympathetic account of much recent thinking about foreign language learning and teaching, including some trends which may appear 'way-out' to the conservative-minded, but are here given serious appraisal.